MICHELANGELO
HIS LIFE, WORK AND TIMES

MICHELAGNO BVONAR. PIT.
SCVLTORE ET ARCHITET.

LINDA MURRAY

MICHELANGELO

HIS LIFE, WORK AND TIMES

259 ILLUSTRATIONS
43 IN COLOR

THAMES AND HUDSON

FOR PETER
Tu duca, tu segnore, e tu maestro

New matter, new translations and editorial arrangement
© 1984 Linda Murray

First published in the USA in 1984 by
Thames and Hudson Inc., 500 Fifth Avenue,
New York, New York 10110

Library of Congress Catalog Card Number 83-51411

Printed and bound in Italy by Amilcare Pizzi s.p.a.,
Milan

ACKNOWLEDGEMENTS

It is always a pleasure to pay debts of gratitude. My first,
and deepest, is to E.H. Ramsden, who generously allowed
me to use her splendid translation of Michelangelo's
letters, and whose notes and appendices to those two
volumes have, in their wisdom and the depth of their
research, been of invaluable help. My next debt is to
George Bull, who has allowed me to use his translation of
Vasari's 1568 Life, and whose help with some of the
knottier problems in translating the letters written to
Michelangelo has greatly shortened my labours. I am
indebted to my husband for his generous help with
translations of Giovio, Gilio and Varchi, for the bibliography and index, for his support and advice throughout
the preparation of the text, and also for driving me 2626
miles so that I should see Caprese Michelangelo.

AUTHOR'S NOTE

The name Michelangelo, still quite common in Italy, is
nowadays spelt in the way used here. In the sixteenth century it was usually spelt Michelagnolo or Michelagniolo.

In Florence before the Gregorian calendar reform of 1585
– as in England – the new year started on Lady Day, 25
March. I have given all dates in accordance with the New
Style (N.S.), already then in use in Rome, in which the
year starts on 1 January.

A list of the abbreviations used for sources will be found
in the Bibliography on p. 233.

Marginal references are to illustration pages.

CONTENTS

INTRODUCTION

Michelangelo Buonarroti's very long life of nearly ninety years – he was born on 6 March 1475 and died on 18 February 1564 – saw changes as far-reaching and as fundamental as any which have been witnessed in modern times. He lived through the reigns of thirteen popes and worked for seven of them, and after his death three successors to the papal throne were of vital importance in the completion of his work at St Peter's and to the very survival of the *Last Judgment* in the Sistine Chapel.

He was born into a world which enjoyed relative stability in politics maintained by the flux of petty state rivalries and alliances, reasonable economic conditions, and positive certainty in religion. By the time he died, Italy had been overrun by two separate foreign powers, France and Spain; Medici rule in Florence had changed, from the subtle and sympathetic paternalism exercised first by Cosimo the Elder and then by his grandson Lorenzo il Magnifico, to the iron rule of a determined and heavy-handed tyrant; the city had suffered a long series of disasters – revolution, conquest, interdiction, a destructive siege, a lost war. Political and economic life changed to a more strident struggle, overshadowed by foreign domination. In religion the Reformation had torn Christian Europe in two, and brought in its train war, misery, hatred and intolerance. Rome itself had been sacked in 1527 with incredible barbarity, and the retiring armies of German and Spanish soldiery, feeding themselves by rapine and paying themselves by loot, had left the whole peninsula in a state of despair and ruin.

An account of Michelangelo's life and times has to be derived from a variety of sources. The earliest literary reference to him was in 1504, in a book by Pomponius Gauricus, *De sculptura*, in which he is mentioned merely as an up and coming man. The earliest Life was written by Paolo Giovio, Bishop of Nocera, who wrote brief lives of Leonardo da Vinci, Raphael and Michelangelo (unpublished in his lifetime) between 1523 and 1527. The Life is very short, only 31 lines in Latin:

Both in painting and in sculpture in marble the Tuscan Michelangelo Buonarroti has approached – in his established fame and by common consent – so closely to the position of the ancient artists that able men in both these arts frankly award the palm to him. He was summoned by Julius II to the Sistine Chapel in the Vatican and offered a huge sum of money and there completed in a short time an immense work, a testimony to his mastery of his art. Of necessity he had to paint lying on his back, but he was able to paint certain figures so that they appear far away and almost hidden by the play of light in recession; such as the body of Holofernes in the tent, while others, such as the crucified Haman, are brought forward by the effects of light and shade in such relief that even the most skilled artists are astonished to find themselves perceiving as solid bodies what are no more than painted forms.

Among the most important figures is one of an old man, in the middle of the ceiling, who is represented in the act of flying through the air, delineated with such symmetry that if one looks from different parts of the chapel the eye is deceived into believing the figure has moved and changed its gesture.

He attained also to great fame in the different field of sculpture when he carved a marble figure of Cupid which he buried in the ground for a time and then dug up, so that the small damages and discolorations caused by this treatment allowed him to pass it off as an antique, and he sold it for a high price through an intermediary to Cardinal Riario. Even more felicitous was the way in which he drew from a block of abandoned marble the figure of the Giant [*David*] menacing with his sling, which may be seen at the entrance to the Palazzo della Signoria in Florence. He was commissioned to make a Tomb for Pope Julius II, and, having received many thousand gold pieces, he made for it various very large statues which were so much admired that it was said that no one since the Ancients had carved marble with more skill or speed than he, or painted with more harmony and skill.

But in contradiction to so great a genius his nature was so rough and uncouth that his domestic habits were incredibly squalid, and deprived posterity of any pupils who might have succeeded him. Even though he was besought by princes he would never undertake to teach anyone or even allow them to stand watching him at work. (PB.1.10–11.)

What is interesting about Giovio's view of Michelangelo is his insistence on the money aspect of his work, without any comment at all on the intellectual side, and also his delightful remark – so surprising from one who was, after all, a cleric – that the Sistine Ceiling contained the figure of an old man flying through the air. In the 1540s Giovio was collecting further material for a book on Italian artists, and at this point the artist Giorgio Vasari first becomes involved with what is now his major claim to fame and a masterpiece far excelling anything he ever painted. Vasari writes:

At that time I often went in the evening, at the end of the day's work, to see ... Cardinal [Alessandro] Farnese at supper, where there were always present, to entertain him with beautiful and honourable discourse ... Annibale Caro ... Monsignor Giovio, and many other men of learning and distinction.... One evening ... the conversation turned to Giovio's museum and to the portraits of illustrious men that he had placed therein ... and one thing leading to another, as happens in conversation, Monsignor Giovio said that he always had, and still had, a great desire to add to his museum and his book of *Eulogies* a treatise with an account of the men who had been illustrious in the art of design from Cimabue down to our own times. Enlarging on this, he showed that he had certainly great knowledge and judgment in the matters of our arts; but it is true that, being content to treat the subject in breadth, he did not consider it in detail and often, in speaking to those craftsmen, he either confused their names, surnames, birthplaces and works, or did not relate things exactly as they were, but rather, as I have said, in breadth. When Giovio had finished his discourse, the Cardinal turned to me and said: 'What do you say, Giorgio? Will not that be a fine work and a noble labour?'

'Fine indeed, most illustrious Excellency,' I answered, 'if Giovio be assisted by someone of our arts to put things in their places and relate them as they really are. That I say because, although his discourse has been marvellous, he has confused and mistaken many things one for another.'

'Then,' replied the Cardinal, being besought by ... the others, 'you might give him a summary and an ordered account of all those craftsmen and their works, according to the order of time; and so your arts will receive from you this benefit as well.'

That undertaking, although I knew it to be beyond my powers, I promised most willingly to execute to the best of my ability; and so, having set myself down to search through my records and the notes that I had written on the subject from my earliest youth, as a sort of pastime and because of the affection that I bore to the memory of our craftsmen, every notice of whom was very dear to me, I gathered together everything that seemed to me to touch on the subject and took the whole to Giovio. And he, after he had much praised my labour, said to me: 'Giorgio, I would rather that you should undertake this task of setting everything down in the manner in which I see that you will be excellently well able to do it, because I have not the courage, not knowing the various manners, and being ignorant of many particulars that you are likely to know; besides which, even if I were to do it, I would make at most a little treatise like that of Pliny. Do what I tell you, Vasari, for I see by the specimen that you have given me in this account that it will prove something very fine.'

And then, thinking that I was not very resolute in the matter, he caused Caro ... and others of my dearest friends to speak to me. Whereupon, having finally made up my mind, I set my hand to it, with the intention of giving it, when finished, to one of them, that he might revise and correct it, and then publish it under a name other than mine. (v2.7.681–2.)

It is clear from this account that Vasari must have been preparing just such a work over a long time, and must have been dismayed at the thought that

A self-portrait of Vasari from the 1568 edition of his *Lives*.

Giovio was going to steal a march on him. The modesty indicated in the last line does not ring very true. 'Other name', indeed!

In his autobiography Vasari says that he first met Michelangelo when he was twelve (about 1524), and that he was briefly in his workshop – a total fiction. Vasari was a pupil of Andrea del Sarto, and after working with him for some years he earned a living by travelling all over Italy, from Venice to Naples, painting pictures. Though he saw Michelangelo during visits to Rome, there was at that time no great intimacy between them. The *Lives* were begun during these years and were based on the theme that the revival of the arts had been principally the work of Florentine artists, and that the glory and supremacy of Florentine art was in Michelangelo, whose biography was the only one of a living artist in the first edition of 1550.

Michelangelo received a copy from Vasari, but was not entirely happy about Vasari's account of him. He sent him a sonnet as a thank offering, but it is not without a double edge:

> If with your pen and colours you had made
> Art the complement of Nature
> You would in part have dimmed her lustre
> By rendering her beauties enhanced by your art.
>
> But since with learned hand you set yourself
> In writing, a far worthier task, and take from her
> The glory that still you lacked,
> In giving life to others:
>
> If she strove in any century
> By making lovely works, yet she would concede
> That to their long appointed ends they would succumb.
>
> But you make their extinguishing memories
> Revive, and in spite of her give life,
> Eternally. (MR.277.)

In 1553 Michelangelo's assistant Ascanio Condivi published a Life – the first printed monograph on any artist – which shows clearly that he had been charged with the specific task of putting right what Michelangelo considered to be Vasari's errors, and at the same time publishing Michelangelo's own version of what he himself called the 'Tragedy of the Tomb', the long and unhappy story of the commission to design the tomb of Pope Julius II, which as even Giovio makes clear had harmed Michelangelo's reputation. For all his first-hand information, Condivi's Life contains some glaring errors of fact.

After 1554 Vasari himself got to know Michelangelo better, so that his second edition of 1568, like Condivi's Life, is really – at least in part – a primary documentary source for Michelangelo's life and works, through which Michelangelo himself tells his story.

Among purely documentary sources, letters are by far the most numerous and the most informative, although in very many cases only one side of the correspondence exists. There are about 480 of his own letters, ranging in date from 1494 to 1563, and hundreds of letters from others, often almost equally informative and in many cases hitherto untranslated into English. His correspondents include relatives, friends, fellow artists, popes, tradesmen, and at least two would-be critics (Aretino and Varchi). Then there are the petitions, contracts, statements and other legal documents which punctuate his career. Other scraps of biographical information are to be found in his notebooks (the *Ricordi*) and in letters, poems and memoirs by others (such as

VITA DI MICHELAGNOLO
BVONARROTI.

MICHELAGNOL Buonarroti Pittore e Scultore singulare, hebbe l'origin sua da Conti da Canossa, nobile & illustre famiglia del tenitorio di Reggio, si per virtù propria, & antichità, si per hauer fatto parentado col sangue Imperiale. Percioche Beatrice sorella d'Henrico. II. fu data per moglie al Conte Bonifacio da Canossa, alhora Signor di Mantoua, donde ne nacque la Contessa Mathilda, donna di rara & singular prudenza & religione. Laquale doppo la morte del marito Gotthifredo, tenne in Italia oltre à Mantoua, Lucca, Parma & Reggio, & quella parte di Toscana, che hoggi si chiama il Patrimonio di san Piero. Et hauendo in uita fatte molte cose degne di memoria, morendo fu sepolta nella Badia di san Benedetto fuor di Mantoua, la qual ella haueua fabricata & largamente dotata. Di tal famiglia adunq Nel. M.CC.L. Venendo à Firenze per potestà vn Miser Simone, meritò per sua virtù d' essere fatto Cittadino
A

The first page of Condivi's Life, published in 1553. The claim to be descended from the Counts of Canossa was a pleasing fiction which Michelangelo liked to indulge; the relationship was, however, recognized by Count Alessandro da Canossa, who wrote to Michelangelo on 8 October 1520 a most flattering letter addressing him as 'Honoured relative' (C.2.473).

Benvenuto Cellini's racy autobiography). Finally, there are his own poems, which express poignantly, passionately, his innermost feelings about his art, and the parallel progress of his mind and soul. Difficult even for an Italian, these defy translation.

Michelangelo's letters fall into three distinct types. The 340-odd to his family are concerned mainly with practical matters: the banking of money, the buying of property, the help given to his father and his brothers so as to establish them in satisfactory positions. They are punctuated throughout his long life by his scathing protests about their propensity to regard him as a bottomless pit of money into which they seemed to consider themselves entitled to dip, with or without his permission, and certainly without any thanks. From these sour and disillusioned pages arises the conclusion that, far from recognizing his genius, they regarded him as little better than a super-successful artisan. The praises of other artists, the adulation of admirers, the favour of popes, prelates, princes, kings and governments, the splendour of the works themselves and the value placed on them by patrons and collectors – which stimulated Ariosto, who died in 1533, to make the pun 'Michael, more than human, Angel divine', starting the cult whereby his extraordinary powers were credited to divine inspiration – all this appears to have counted for little against a covert prolongation of the original family objections to his becoming an artist. It was, in their view, an occupation unworthy of a member of their social class, a class of small landowners who lived poorly either on minute revenues from the sale of their produce (but without sullying their hands with any kind of manual labour) or as clerks in the counting houses of contemporaries such as the Strozzi, who sprang from the same social class but who moved, through their wealth, possessions and enterprise, in a world which the Buonarroti could only infiltrate in very subordinate capacities.

Again and again, his anger erupts against them. Yet in his austere solitariness he clung to his unworthy family, and needed their support and understanding. No one can pretend that he was easy to get on with; his rows with a succession of assistants are witnesses not only to his exacting standards, but also to his quick temper, as even his oldest friends found out.

The second category of Michelangelo's letters is, again, purely practical: orders for marble from the quarries, instructions for deliveries and for payments. These, however, provide valuable evidence about his movements and about the progress of his works.

The third category, though small, is far more rewarding. It includes letters to other artists, to patrons and friends, to admirers, his own accounts of the great row over the Julius Tomb, his difficulties over the unfinished work at S. Lorenzo in Florence, his few letters to Vittoria Colonna and Tommaso Cavalieri, his firm, but perhaps too courteous, rebuff to Aretino, his letters to Vasari and to his generous-hearted friend Luigi del Riccio. These letters show a direct and simple public face, just as his private face is deeply caring even if often irritable. The exceptions are his letters to Cavalieri; they have been advanced, very curiously, as evidence of homosexuality, yet the inflated language of the four surviving drafts (the letters themselves do not exist, and two of the drafts are near-duplicates) is quite common in sixteenth-century Italian correspondence and betokens little more than the elaborate courtesy informing letters between people who hardly knew each other. If these drafts surprise at all, it is because it seems strange for a very great artist to address in terms of such elaborate courtesy a much younger man – in 1533, Cavalieri was about twenty-four years old and Michelangelo was fifty-eight – who had no achievements of any kind to give him a claim to such consideration. Cavalieri was a member of an old Roman family; he clearly deeply appreciated Michelangelo's interest in him and was flattered by it (as well he might be). They remained close friends for the remaining thirty-odd years of Michelangelo's life. Cavalieri married, raised a family, served his city, and was one of the devoted group who helped to care for Michelangelo in his last illness and stood at his bedside when he died.

Michelangelo's few close friendships, and many of his poems, stress his solitariness. With one exception, all his friends were men, which is hardly surprising in that Renaissance Rome was essentially a masculine society. He seems – with that one exception – to have shunned the company of women as determinedly as he avoided all but the most essential contacts with society; though it should be remembered that in Renaissance Rome women that did receive men freely were almost all in the ranks of the higher grade of courtesan. Popes and their entourages he had to visit and receive, but he made friends with difficulty, and mostly they came from literary circles, both secular and religious, where his poems were much admired. Some friends he also had among a few artists and architects, including Giuliano da Sangallo until his death in 1516, Sebastiano del Piombo, until they quarrelled in 1536, Vasari, Vignola, who worked under him at the Farnese palace, Ammanati, whom he helped with the staircase at the Laurenziana Library, and the affectionate Daniele da Volterra to whom the beautiful bust of Michelangelo in his old age is due. He also had some friends among the Florentine exiles who rejected the Medici domination of Florence imposed by papal and imperial arms. Other friends, from the fringes of these circles, included the unattractive Febo da Poggio, who caused Michelangelo distress, even anger, and, in the circle of the banker Luigi del Riccio, the beautiful boy Cecchino de' Bracci, whose death in his teens evoked many sonnets written mostly to please and comfort the boy's uncle and guardian at his untimely death.

The only woman to whom he professed any devotion was Vittoria Colonna, the middle-aged widow of a celebrated soldier, Ferrante d'Avalos, Marquis of Pescara. When Michelangelo met her, about 1536, he was sixty-one and she was forty-six, living a retired life with around her a circle of religious reformers at the heart of the movement for church reform in the long drawn-out early period of the Council of Trent. To her he dedicated many of his sonnets and for her he made several of his most memorable drawings.

He was, as he admitted, emotional, quick to passion, stirred by intelligence, excellence, beauty, charm; and when confronted by a man who possessed these qualities he was moved to love and admiration, though at the same time fearful of the passions thus awakened. This was the reverse of his often cruelly biting wit, his brusque manners, his contempt for the public elegance and urbanity of his great contemporary Raphael. Michelangelo's profound faith, fully declared in so many of his finest sonnets and to be inferred from many of his family letters, and his close association with such deeply religious men as those surrounding Vittoria Colonna, rule out any kind of compromise between his emotions and his convictions, if ever such a compromise were required, unless he is to be regarded as utterly two-faced. This conflict certainly lies at the base of his continued devotion to his unprepossessing family, and his increasing pessimism, disillusion and isolation in the last decades of his life.

PART ONE

APPRENTICE AND MASTER

1475–1505

M ICHELANGELO WAS BORN on 6 March 1475 at Caprese, a small town about fifteen miles north of Arezzo, where his father, Lodovico Buonarroti, held the office of *podestà* – a kind of mayor-cum-magistrate who, according to Tuscan usage, was always an outsider to the community so that family loyalties should never sway his acts or judgments. Lodovico's term of office expired on 1 April 1475; he returned with his wife and two sons, the elder aged two and the younger less than a month old, to live in a house in the Sta Croce district of Florence which he shared with several other members of the family, and to manage as best he could on the meagre resources of a small property at Settignano, then a hill village some three miles from Florence.

Michelangelo was put out to wet nurse by Lodovico in that village with the wife of a stonemason, so that talking once with Vasari, he said to him jestingly: 'Giorgio, if I have anything good in my brain, it comes from by being born in the pure air of your country of Arezzo, even as I also sucked in with my nurse's milk the chisels and hammer with which I make my figures.' (V2.7.137.)

He was sent to school; there are the usual allegations of reluctance to study and aversion to anything but drawing, but his beautiful handwriting, his faultless letters, and his superb poetry suggest that this is the familiar 'wayward genius' myth.

Among his friends was Francesco Granacci, a pupil of Domenico del Ghirlandaio, who, seeing the bent and the ardent longing of the boy, decided to help him and continually exhorted him to the study of art by lending him drawings and taking him with him to his master's workshop or wherever there might be some work going on from which he could derive benefit. . . . His father and uncles, who despised art, were angry with him and often beat him severely; because ignorant of the excellence and nobility of art it shamed them that it should appear in their house. . . . But it did not turn him aside and becoming bolder he wished to try his hand at painting.

Having obtained through Granacci, a print in which was the story of St Antony beaten by devils, the work of a Martin of Holland [Martin Schongauer], a famous artist of the time, he painted it on a panel with paints and brushes which Granacci lent him, and he so managed it that it evoked the admiration of all who saw it, and also envy, as some say even in Domenico [Ghirlandaio] (the most famous painter of the day), as was to be seen later in other ways, who, to make the work seem less marvellous, used to say that it came from his workshop, as if he had had a part in it. In making this little picture, which contained besides the image of the saint, many strange forms and monstrosities of demons, Michelangelo . . . would not paint any part of it without first consulting nature. So he went to the fish market to study the shape and colour of fish fins, and the colour of their eyes and other parts, and representing them in his painting . . . as perfectly as he could, he set in train the admiration of the world and, as I have said, some cause for envy in Ghirlandaio. (AC.11–12.)

This is very much in the Leonardo fashion, following the story of Leonardo's little picture which so terrified the countryman who had commissioned it, because of the life-like representation of the monstrous dragon painted from insects and animals combined. Not only does art imitate nature, but artists' lives tend also to certain almost classical repetitions.

And in truth he [Ghirlandaio] had the reputation of being somewhat jealous, not only of Michelangelo, but also of his own brother [Davide]; for, when he saw him getting on and raising great expectation of himself, he sent him to France, not really for his own benefit, as some said, but so that he should remain the foremost in art in Florence. I wanted to mention this because I have been told that Domenico's son [Ridolfo] attributes the excellence and 'divinity' of Michelangelo to a large extent to his father's teaching, whereas he gave him no help at all, although Michelangelo does not complain about this. . . .

Martin Schongauer's print of the *Temptation of St Antony* was probably made in the 1470s. It is an example of the spread of northern art into Italy, paralleled by the arrival of the Hugo van der Goes *Portinari Altar* in Florence soon after 1475.

Now that the boy was drawing one thing and then another at random, having no fixed place or course of study, it happened one day that he was taken by Granacci to the Medici garden near S. Marco, which the Magnifico Lorenzo had adorned with various antique statues and figures. When he saw them and savoured their beauty, he never again went to Domenico's workshop or anywhere else, but stayed there all day . . . as in the best school for such studies. (AC.12–14).

26
33

At this point there is a formidable, and very interesting, conflict of evidence, for here Condivi, prompted by Michelangelo, is flatly contradicting what Vasari had written in the first *Life* of 1550:

Lodovico, therefore, being friendly with Domenico Ghirlandaio, went to his workshop . . . [and] he was willing to leave Michelangelo with him, which in those days was arranged thus: Domenico took the boy for three years and signed a deed, as now appears in a journal by Domenico Ghirlandaio written in his own hand and by the hand of Lodovico Buonarroti with receipts from time to time, which things are now with Ridolfo Ghirlandaio, Domenico's son. (VI.2.949.)

Vasari was so angry at being thus refuted that in his second edition he set the facts out with great clarity and a good deal of indignation:

Lodovico . . . resolved . . . to apprentice him to Domenico Ghirlandaio . . . Michelangelo was then fourteen years old. Now he who wrote his life after 1550, when I wrote these *Lives* for the first time, has said that some persons, through not having associated with him, have related things that never happened . . . and has touched in particular on this circumstance, taxing Domenico with jealousy and saying that he never offered any assistance to Michelangelo, which is clearly false as may be seen from an entry in the hand of Lodovico, Michelangelo's father, written in one of Domenico's books. . . . That entry runs thus: '1488, the last day of April. I, Lodovico de Buonarrote, have placed my son Michelangelo with Domenico and David di Tomaso di Currado [alias Ghirlandaio] for three years next to come. . . .' (v2.7.138.)

There follows a note on how much Michelangelo was to be paid during his apprenticeship, and his father's receipt for the money, after which Vasari continues:

These entries I have copied from the book itself in order to prove that all that was written then, as well as all that is about to be written, is the truth. Nor do I know anyone who had been more associated with him than I have, or has been a more faithful friend and servant to him . . . neither do I believe that there is anyone who can show a greater number of letters written in his own hand with greater affection than he has expressed to me. I make this digression for the sake of truth, and it must suffice for the rest of his *Life*. (v2.7.139.)

The simplest explanation is that towards the end of his life – and in 1553 Michelangelo was seventy-eight – he had come to believe in his own legend: that his art, so dissimilar to that of all his contemporaries, was God-given and owed nothing to any man's teaching. To be suddenly confronted with the evidence of a pupillage to an artist whom he considered no more than a competent practitioner in a bygone style was to be lowered not only in public estimation but also in his own. His 'divinity', so often extolled, was thus revealed to have feet of fairly humble clay.

The important fact, however, is that Domenico Ghirlandaio was the finest Florentine exponent of fresco painting of his day, and even if Michelangelo did not stay long enough in the workshop actually to have participated in the major work then in hand, the choir of Sta Maria Novella – and this also can be doubted – he must from the beginning have been aware of the method of

Portrait of Ghirlandaio in Vasari's 1568 *Lives*, adapted from the self-portrait in the choir frescoes in Sta Maria Novella in Florence, painted in 1485–90, during the time when Michelangelo was apprenticed to him.

13

fresco painting, since presumably it went on all around him. Vasari in his 1568 edition even tells the story of Michelangelo making a drawing of the scene in the chapel when the work was in progress, an account he must have had either from Ridolfo Ghirlandaio or even from Michelangelo himself.

Condivi, still true to his master's line, continues the story of Michelangelo's self-education in Lorenzo il Magnifico's garden of sculpture.

One day, studying the head of a faun, already old in appearance . . . he decided to copy it in marble. And since Lorenzo il Magnifico was having marble or masonry work done there [at S. Marco] to ornament the noble library which he and his forebears had collected . . . Michelangelo got the workmen to give him a block and to provide him with tools. He set himself to copy the faun with such care and study that in a few days he perfected it, supplying from his imagination all that was missing in the ancient work; that is, the open mouth as of a man laughing so that the cavity of the mouth and all the teeth could be seen. In the midst of this the Magnifico coming to see what point his works had reached, found the boy polishing the head and . . . he was amazed, considering first the excellence of the work and then the boy's age, and although he praised the work, he joked with him . . . and said, 'Oh, you have made this faun old and have left him all his teeth. Don't you know that old men of that age are always lacking a few?'

To Michelangelo it seemed a thousand years before the Magnifico went away so that he could correct the mistake . . . and . . . he removed an upper tooth from his old man, drilling out the gum as if it had come out by the root, and the next day he awaited the Magnifico with eager longing. He . . . noted the boy's goodness and simplicity, and laughed at him . . . but then weighed up in his mind the perfection of the thing and the boy's age; he . . . resolved to help him and encourage such great genius and to take him into his household; and learning whose son he was he said: 'Tell your father that I would like to speak to him.'

When Michelangelo returned home and delivered the Magnifico's message, his father, who guessed why he was being summoned, was persuaded by the great efforts of Granacci and others; indeed he complained that Granacci was leading his son astray, standing firm on the point that he would never suffer his son to be a stonemason, and it was to no effect that Granacci explained how great a difference there was between a stonemason and a sculptor. . . . When he arrived in the presence of the Magnifico, and was asked if he would be willing to let him have his son for his own, the father was unable to refuse. . . . After he had dismissed the old man he arranged that Michelangelo should be given a good room in his house . . . and treating him as a son, both in other ways and at his table, at which . . . personages of the highest nobility and of great affairs were seated every day. (AC.14–17.)

Vasari in 1550 tells the story somewhat differently:

In those days the Magnifico Lorenzo had in his garden near the Piazza S. Marco the sculptor Bertoldo, not just as a custodian or keeper of the many beautiful antiquities which he had collected there and brought together at great cost, but because of his ardent desire to create a school of excellent painters and sculptors. He wished that they should have as teacher and head this Bertoldo who was a pupil of Donatello. And though he was so old that he could no longer work he was a very capable master and very highly regarded . . . because of the many casts which he made in bronze of battles and other small things in the skilful execution of which there was no one then in Florence who could surpass him. Now, in the great love he had for painting and sculpture, Lorenzo was grieved that in his time no famous and noble sculptors could be found as were found many painters of great excellence and fame. He resolved, as I have said, to create a school and for this he asked Domenico Ghirlandaio that if in his workshop he had among his young men any inclined in that way he should send them to the garden where he wished them to practise and to create a style which would honour him and his city. (VI.2.950–1.)

In his second edition Vasari tells much the same story, but, despite his declaration that what he records is the truth, he is far off the mark. The 'school of sculpture' in the Medici garden is virtually a myth, which Vasari himself helped to create in order to make Lorenzo into a finer patron than he in fact was, and also, by imputing such noble actions to a Medici forerunner, to ingratiate himself with Duke Cosimo I, the all-powerful ruler of Florence. Such a garden with antique statues in it somewhere near S. Marco must have existed, and Bertoldo di Giovanni, who probably looked after it, was a very competent bronze-caster, and a familiar of the Medici household. The brilliant suggestion has been made that the 'di Giovanni' (son of Giovanni) is a recognition that he was an illegitimate son of Giovanni de' Medici, Lorenzo's uncle. Certainly Michelangelo worked in the garden and lived for a couple of years in the Medici household; that part of the story is true; but that it was a kind of 'school' of however informal a type is not borne out by any other evidence.

What is significant about Condivi's version is that the name of Bertoldo does not appear: is this another instance of Michelangelo's ability to forget that somewhere someone taught him something?

It was at this time that Michelangelo had his famous encounter with Pietro Torrigiano.

Domenico sent excellent young men among whom were Michelangelo and Francesco Granacci. When they went to the garden they found there Torrigiano . . . working in clay on some figures which Bertoldo had given him. Michelangelo seeing this made some in emulation . . . and after a few days began to copy a piece in marble. Lorenzo praised it greatly and ordered that he should receive his food so as to help his father, . . . gave him a purple cloak, and gave his father a post in the customs. In fact, all the young men were given salaries . . . and while he lived they were rewarded by him. Michelangelo always had the key of the place and was much more zealous than the others. . . . He drew for many months in the Carmine after the pictures by Masaccio. It is said that Torrigiano after being a friend mocked him, and, moved by envy to see him more honoured than he was himself, and more capable in art, as a mark of affection, punched him in the nose which broke it and crushed it so badly that he marked him for life. (VI.2.951-2.)

30

In the Torrigiano Life in his 1568 edition, Vasari attributes Torrigiano's hatred to the fact that Michelangelo worked harder and was more successful and favoured by Lorenzo, and he adds that Torrigiano fled from Florence to escape Lorenzo's anger, or even was banished for it. Torrigiano went first to Rome, and then served under Cesare Borgia during his campaigns, about 1500. He then went to the Netherlands, and by 1511 was in London, where he completed his masterpieces, the tomb of Lady Margaret Beaufort and the double tomb of her son Henry VII and Elizabeth of York, in Westminster Abbey. He was then involved in the project – later abandoned – for a huge double tomb for Henry VIII and Catherine of Aragon, and in June 1519 he was in Florence recruiting assistants to help with this. It was then that the young Benvenuto Cellini heard his version of the Michelangelo incident:

This Torrigiano was an extraordinarily handsome man and very hot tempered, and he seemed more like a great soldier than a sculptor. Every day he had stories to tell about his brave deeds when he was among those brutes of Englishmen. Then one day he started to talk about Michelangelo . . . after his eye had fallen on one of my drawings copied from a cartoon by that divine artist . . . holding my drawing in his hand he said: 'This Buonarroti and I used to go along together when we were boys to study in Masaccio's chapel in the church of the Carmine. Buonarroti had the habit of making fun of anyone else who was drawing there, and one day he provoked me so much that I lost my temper more than usual and, clenching my fist, I gave

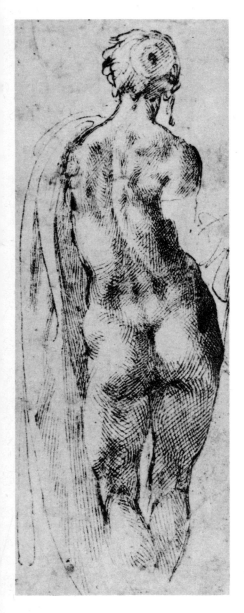

Drawings after the female nude are very rare in Michelangelo's *oeuvre*; he normally used only male models. This drawing, made *c.* 1501–03, may have been inspired by the classical group of the *Three Graces* in Siena (also the source of a famous little painting by Raphael).

him such a punch on the nose that I felt the bone and cartilage crush like a biscuit, so that fellow will carry my signature until he dies.'

This story sowed in me, who used to see Michelangelo's divine masterpieces every day, such a hatred of Torrigiano that far from going to England with him, I could not bear the sight of him. (BC.27–8.)

The injury to his face seems to have affected Michelangelo deeply, and possibly is one of the circumstances which lie at the root of his shyness, his farouche quality, even his misogyny. Portraits show the broken nose clearly, even though tact would have made other artists minimize his disfigurement.

Even if Lorenzo did not actually organize any teaching for young men in his garden of antiquities, the contact with classical sculpture was a kind of seed bed in which talent could grow; as indeed was the environment of the Medici household. Condivi describes the customs of the house:

As it was the custom that those who were present at first should sit down near the Magnifico, each according to his rank, without changing places no matter who arrived later, it quite often happened that Michelangelo was seated above Lorenzo's sons and other distinguished people, the constant company in which the house flourished and abounded.... Michelangelo was between fifteen and sixteen years old when he went to live in the house of the Magnifico, and he stayed there about two years, until the latter's death, which was in 1492....

In the house also lived Poliziano, a most learned and clever man, as everyone knows and his writings fully testify. Recognizing in Michelangelo a superior spirit, he loved him very much and ... continually urged him on in his studies, always explaining things to him and providing him with subjects. Among these, one day he proposed to him the Rape of Deianeira and the Battle of the Centaurs, telling the whole story one part at a time. Michelangelo set out to do it in *mezzo-rilievo*, and he succeeded so well that I recall hearing him say that whenever he sees it again he realizes what a great wrong he committed against nature by not promptly pursuing the art of sculpture, judging by that work how well he could succeed....

Hardly had he finished this work when Lorenzo il Magnifico departed this life. Michelangelo returned to his father's house ... and suffered such anguish over this death that for many days he could do nothing.... But then he recovered and bought a great block of marble which had lain many years exposed to the wind and rain and out of it he carved a Hercules four *braccia* [7 ft 8 in or 2.33 m] high, which was later sent to France.

While he was working on this statue a great quantity of snow fell in Florence, and Piero de' Medici, Lorenzo's eldest son, who had taken his father's place but, being young, lacked the qualities of his father, wanted a snow statue made in the middle of his courtyard. He remembered Michelangelo, sent for him and had him make the statue, and wanted him to stay in his house as in his father's time.... Michelangelo's father, who was by this time more friendly to his son, ... when he saw that he was almost always in the company of distinguished men, clothed him better. Thus he remained with Piero for some months and was much cherished by him.... At this time, Michelangelo, to oblige the prior of Sto Spirito ... made a wooden Crucifix, just under life-size, which today is still to be seen over the main altar of that church. He was very intimate with the prior, from whom he received much kindness and who provided him with a room and with corpses for the study of anatomy.... This was the first time that he applied himself to this study, and he pursued it as long as he had any opportunity....

A certain man nicknamed Cardiere who frequented Piero's house sang and improvised marvellously on the lyre, and used to give pleasure to the Magnifico, who also played and so would practise the art almost every evening after dinner. This man, being a friend of Michelangelo's, confided to him a vision, which was this: that Lorenzo de' Medici had appeared to him in a black robe all in rags over his nakedness, and had commanded him to tell his son that he would shortly be driven from his house, never again to return. Piero de' Medici was so insolent and intemperate that neither the goodness of his brother, Cardinal Giovanni, nor the courtesy and kindness of Giuliano, had as much power to keep him in Florence as those vices had to bring about his expulsion. Michelangelo urged Cardiere to tell Piero of this, and to carry out Lorenzo's command, but Cardiere, fearing Piero's nature, kept it to himself.

One morning when Michelangelo was in the courtyard, Cardiere appeared, terrified and stricken, and once again he told him that Lorenzo appeared to him that night in the same garb as before and that, while he was awake and staring, he struck him a great buffet on the cheek because he had not told Piero what he had seen. Michelangelo scolded him, and he was so persuasive that Cardiere, taking heart, set out to walk to Careggi, a Medici villa about three miles from the city. But when he was almost half-way, he met Piero who was on his way home, and stopping him he disclosed all that he had seen and heard.

Piero laughed at him and calling his attendants made them jeer at him, and his chancellor, who later became Cardinal Bibbiena, said to Cardiere: 'You are crazy. Who do you think Lorenzo loves more, you or his son? If it is his son, would he not appear to him rather than to anyone else, if this were true?'

Thus mocked at, they let him go. When he reached home again and complained to Michelangelo, he spoke so convincingly of the vision that he, taking it for certain, left Florence two days later with two companions and went to Bologna and from there to Venice, fearing that if Cardiere's prediction came true, he would not be safe in Florence. (AC. 17–23.)

Michelangelo's anxieties were not ill founded. The sermons of Girolamo Savonarola, prior of S. Marco and scourge of the Medici, had by now   34–5 assumed an apocalyptic character, with prophecies of doom and catastrophe; Piero's unpopularity, and his totally inept political manoeuvres, fulfilled the dire predictions of Cardiere's vision. Michelangelo left probably in early October; Piero was driven out in November. French invaders under Charles VIII occupied the city and were given a welcome tempered by extreme apprehension. Vasari makes no mention of Cardiere's vision; he simply records that Michelangelo left for Bologna because he feared being attacked for his connection with the Medici.

In Bologna Michelangelo found an influential patron in Giovanni Francesco Aldovrandi, who had served the Bentivoglio family, rulers of Bologna as holders of the papal fief, and who was later to serve Pope Julius II.

Thus Cardiere's vision came true. . . . He stayed on in Bologna with the aforesaid gentleman [Aldovrandi], who treated him with great honour as he was delighted with his intelligence and every morning had him read from Dante or Petrarch and sometimes from Boccaccio until he fell asleep. One day, as he was taking Michelangelo round Bologna, he took him to see the tomb of St Dominic . . . where two marble figures were missing, a St Petronius and a kneeling angel with a candlestick. He asked Michelangelo if he felt equal to making them, and when he said yes, he arranged for the commission to be given to him and had him paid thirty ducats, eighteen for the St Petronius and twelve for the angel. The figures are still to be seen in that place. But then as Michelangelo had suspicions of a Bolognese sculptor [Girolamo Coltellini] who was threatening to cause him trouble, he returned to Florence where things had more or less calmed down by then, and he could live safely at home. He stayed for little more than a year with Messer Gianfrancesco Aldovrandi. (AC. 24–5.)

The interesting thing is that three, not two, statues have always been attributed to Michelangelo on the Arca or Shrine of St Dominic – the *Angel with Candlestick*, the *St Petronius* holding his church, and a *St Patroclus*. The attribution of this last statue – or rather statuette, since all are small, about two feet high – has been doubted partly because of its bad condition. It was smashed when a friar knocked it off the tomb with a ladder at some time before 1572, and it was rather badly repaired. It is so different from the earlier ones by Niccolò dell'Arca, however, that its not being mentioned by Condivi must be one of his mistakes; although the chronicler who recorded its being smashed also says that it was 'almost entirely by Michelangelo', suggesting that it had already been begun by Niccolò.

Angel with Candlestick, for the Shrine of St Dominic in Bologna. One of the rare instances of Michelangelo giving wings to an angel, the figure was made as a counterpart to a stylistically very dissimilar angel by Niccolò dell'Arca.

When Michelangelo was back in his native city he carved an *Eros* in marble. . . . When Lorenzo di Pierfrancesco de' Medici [for whom Michelangelo had in the meanwhile made an *Infant St John the Baptist*] saw this figure he thought it very beautiful and said to him, 'If you would make it look as if it had been buried, I would send it to Rome where it would pass for an ancient work and you would sell it much better.' Upon hearing this Michelangelo reworked it so that it looked as if it had been made many years earlier. Thus it went to Rome, and Cardinal di S. Giorgio bought it as an antique for two hundred ducats. The man who collected this money [Baldassare del Milanese] deceived both Lorenzo di Pierfrancesco and Michelangelo by writing to Florence that Michelangelo was to be paid thirty ducats, as that was the amount he had received for the *Eros*. But . . . it came to the ears of the Cardinal that the *putto* had been made in Florence, and as he was indignant at being cheated he sent one of his gentlemen there. This man . . . was directed to Michelangelo's home. . . and he asked if he would show him something. But as he had nothing to show he picked up a pen and drew a hand for him with such skill that the gentleman was astonished. Then he asked him if he had ever done any . . . sculpture, and when Michelangelo said yes, he had done, amongst other things, an *Eros* . . . the gentleman found out what he wanted to know. . . . He promised Michelangelo that if he would go to Rome with him he would help him to recover the difference and would set everything right with his patron, who he knew would be very pleased. (AC.25–6.)

Lorenzo di Pierfrancesco de' Medici, who is sometimes confused with Lorenzo il Magnifico, was a cousin from a collateral branch of the family, and was the ancestor of the man who eventually ruled the city – Cosimo, the first Grand Duke.

The story of the drawing of the hand, which so surprised the cardinal's envoy, is quite clearly an echo of the famous story of Giotto's 'O', when the painter, asked to provide evidence of his competence for a work, merely took a piece of chalk and drew a circle freehand before his astonished audience. Cardinal di S. Giorgio was Raffaello Riario, builder of the palace in Rome which became the Cancelleria. He was one of the nephews of Sixtus IV, and was celebrated for his love of display and magnificence. He had a famous collection of antiquities, which Michelangelo's *Eros* was originally intended to join.

Michelangelo went to Rome with the cardinal's envoy. He wrote to Lorenzo di Pierfrancesco on 2 July 1496:

This is only to let you know that we arrived safely last Saturday and at once we went to call upon the Cardinal di S. Giorgio, to whom I presented your letter. He seemed pleased to see me and immediately desired me to go and look at certain figures; this took me all day, so I could not deliver your other letters that day. Then on Sunday, having gone to his new house, the cardinal sent for me. I waited upon him, and he asked me what I thought of the things I had seen. In reply to this I told him what I thought; and I certainly think he has many beautiful things. Then the cardinal asked me whether I had courage enough to attempt some work of art of my own. I replied that I could not do anything as fine, but that he should see what I could do. We have bought a piece of marble for a life-sized figure, and on Monday I shall begin work. . . .

Then I gave Baldassare his letter and asked him for the *Cupid*, saying that I would return the money. He replied very sharply that he would sooner smash it into a hundred pieces; that he had bought the *Cupid* and it was his; that he had letters showing that the buyer was satisfied and that he had no expectation of having it to return. He complained bitterly about you, saying that you had maligned him. Some of our Florentines sought to arrange matters between us, but they effected nothing. Now I count upon acting through the cardinal. You shall be informed as to what ensues. That's all this time. I commend me to you. May God keep you from harm. (C.1.1.)

Though the cardinal apparently got his money back, Michelangelo derived little from the transaction except repute; he failed to recover the statue, and

38

Baldassare, the crooked dealer, refused to give him any more money for it, although he sold it to Cesare Borgia, who in turn sold it to the Duke of Urbino, Guidobaldo da Montefeltro. When Cesare Borgia took Urbino by treachery, the Duchess of Mantua, Isabella Gonzaga, wrote to him and asked him for the statue, despite the fact that the dispossessed rulers of Urbino were at that moment refugees in her house; she obtained it and subsequently refused to return it to its rightful owners. Eventually it passed with the rest of the Mantua collections to Charles I of England, and it was probably destroyed in the great Whitehall fire of 1698.

And the fact that the Cardinal di S. Giorgio had little understanding of sculpture is made abundantly clear, because in the whole time that Michelangelo stayed with him, which was about a year, he never worked on any commission for him. (AC.27.)

He must however have lived in the cardinal's palace, for he wrote to his father on 19 August 1497, while his brother Buonarroto was visiting Rome:

This is to let you know that Buonarroto arrived here on Friday.

As soon as I knew of it I went to the inn to see him and he explained to me by word of mouth how things are going with you. He tells me that the haberdasher, Consiglio, is giving you a lot of trouble, that he won't come to any agreement and that he wants to have you arrested. I advise you to see to it that you do come to an agreement and pay him a few ducats on account; send and let me know what you agree to give him and I'll send it to you, if you haven't got it. Although I have very little money, as I've told you, I'll contrive to borrow it, so that you do not have to withdraw it from the Funds, as Buonarroto said. Don't be surprised that I have at times written to you so tetchily, for at times I'm very troubled by reason of the many things that befall those who live away from home.

I undertook to do a figure for Piero de' Medici and bought the marble; and then never began it, because he hasn't done as he promised me. So I'm working on my own and doing a figure for my own pleasure. I bought a piece of marble for five ducats, but it wasn't a good piece and the money was thrown away; then I bought another piece for another five ducats, and this I'm working for my own pleasure. So you must realize that I, too, have expenses and troubles. However, what you ask of me I'll send you, even if I should have to sell myself as a slave.

Buonarroto arrived safely and is lodging at the inn. He's got a room where he's comfortable and will lack for nothing as long as he likes to stay. I have nowhere convenient to have him with me, as I lodge with others, but it suffices that I'll not let him lack for anything. I'm well and hope you are too. (C.1.3.)

At the age of twenty-two, Michelangelo was already caring for his family – as, in spite of their frequent ingratitude, he was to do all his life. This first stay in Rome was to last five years, until 1501. He found other patrons than the unsatisfactory cardinal and the changeable Piero de' Medici, although he kept in touch with the Medici in exile. Two major works emerged from this period: the *Bacchus*, made for Jacopo Galli the banker, and the celebrated *Pietà*, now in St Peter's, which was commissioned for Sta Maria della Febbre by the ambassador of Charles VIII of France, Cardinal Jean Bilhères de Lagraulas, known in Rome as Cardinal di S. Dionisio or S. Dionigi (he was abbot of Saint-Denis near Paris).

The commission was already being discussed in November 1497, since the cardinal then wrote to arrange for Michelangelo to obtain marble from Carrara; when the artist finally went there in March 1498 the cardinal took a great deal of trouble to ensure that the marble should be selected and transported without hitch. The contract was signed on 27 August 1498, but looks as if it superseded some earlier agreement.

This drawing was made in 1560–65 by the architect Giovanantonio Dosio. It shows the road to the left of Old St Peter's, the gaunt structure of Michelangelo's new basilica, with a glimpse of the colonnade of the dome, and the obelisk of Nero which was moved to the centre of the Piazza in front of St Peter's in 1586 by Fontana. Behind the obelisk is the rotunda of the imperial mausoleum of S. Andrea, and behind S. Andrea was the virtually identical chapel of the Madonna della Febbre where Michelangelo's *Pietà* was first placed.

37

Let it be known and manifest to whoever reads this document that the Most Reverend Cardinal of S. Dionisio has agreed with Master Michelangelo, Florentine sculptor, that the said master shall make a marble *Pietà* at his own cost, that is a draped Virgin Mary with a dead Christ in her arms, life size, for the price of 450 gold papal ducats within a year from the day of the beginning of the work. And the said Reverend Cardinal promises to pay him in the following manner, that is: firstly he promises to give him 150 gold papal ducats when he begins the work, and from the beginning of the work he promises every four months to give 100 similar ducats to the said Michelangelo, so that the payment of the said 450 gold papal ducats will be finished in a year, if the said work is finished. And if the work is finished earlier his Reverend Lordship aforementioned will be obliged to pay the whole.

I Jacopo Gallo promise the Reverend Monsignor that the said Michelangelo will do the said work in a year and it will be the most beautiful marble which can be seen in Rome today, and that no other master could make it better today. And *vice versa* I promise the said Michelangelo that the Reverend Cardinal will make the payment according to what is written above. And in faith of it I Jacopo Gallo have made the present by my own hand, year, month, and day as above. Intending by this document to break and annul any other document by my hand and by the hand of the said Michelangelo and that only this one shall have effect.

The Reverend Cardinal has given me Jacopo Gallo some time ago 100 gold papal ducats and today 50 gold papal ducats. (M.613–14.)

The document is signed by both the cardinal and Jacopo Galli. By the time Michelangelo delivered the group, one year late, the cardinal was dead.

The success of the group was immediate and overwhelming.

As a commission from the Cardinal di S. Dionigi . . . he made out of one block of marble that marvellous statue of Our Lady . . . with her dead Son across her lap, of such great and rare beauty that no one who sees it is not moved to pity . . . even though there are some who object to the mother being too young compared to the Son.

When I was discussing this one day with Michelangelo, 'Don't you know,' he said, 'that women who remain chaste remain much fresher than those who are not chaste? How much more so in a virgin in whom there was never the least lascivious desire which could alter her body. Moreover I would say to you that such freshness and flower of youth, besides being preserved in her in so natural a way, has also possibly been helped by divine means in order to prove to the world the virginity and perpetual purity of the Mother . . . Therefore you should not be surprised if, for these reasons, I made the holy Virgin Mother of God much younger, in comparison with her Son, than her age would normally require.'

This thought, which was worthy of a theologian, was perhaps extraordinary, but not in him, whom God and nature had so formed that he worked not only with his hands, but was worthy to receive also divine concepts, as may be seen, not just in this but in many of his thoughts and writings. When he created this work, Michelangelo may have been twenty-five or twenty-six years old. Through these labours he acquired great fame and reputation, so much so that he had already in the opinion of the world not only far surpassed every other artist of his time and those who had preceded him, but rivalled also those of antiquity. (AC.29–30.)

Vasari in his first Life expatiates on the beauties of the group, and on its vividly life-like qualities and marvellous workmanship; he adds that 'in it he did that which in no other work did he again do; he left his name inscribed across a girdle which encircles the breast of Our Lady'. In the second Life, Vasari gives this story an amusing twist:

It happened one day that Michelangelo, entering where it had been placed, found there a large group of Lombards who praised it greatly. One of them asked another who had done it, and he

MICHAEL·AGLVS·BONAROTVS·FLORENT·FACIEBA

replied, 'Our Gobbo, from Milan.' Michelangelo remained silent, and it seemed strange to him that his work should be attributed to another. One night, shutting himself in with a lantern, having brought his tools with him, he carved his name on it. (v2.7.152.)

The *Pietà* transformed Michelangelo from a promising but unknown young man into the foremost sculptor of the age, a force to be reckoned with, a man to be watched. But it produced no further work in Rome.

Then some of his friends wrote to him from Florence, urging him to return, as it seemed very probable that he would be able to obtain the block of marble that was standing in the Opera di Sta Maria del Fiore [the cathedral office of works]. Piero Soderini, who at about that time was elected Gonfalonier for life, had often talked of handing it over to Leonardo da Vinci, but he was then arranging to give it to Andrea Contucci of Monte Sansovino, an accomplished sculptor, very keen to have it.

Now although it seemed impossible to carve a complete figure from the block (and only Michelangelo was bold enough to try without adding fresh pieces), he had felt the desire to work on it many years before, and he tried to obtain it when he came back to Florence. The marble was eighteen feet high, but unfortunately an artist called Simone da Fiesole had started to carve a giant figure and had bungled the work so badly that he had hacked a hole between the legs and left the block completely botched and misshapen. So the Operai [commissioners] of Sta Maria del Fiore . . . threw the block aside, and it stayed abandoned for many years and seemed likely to remain so indefinitely. However, Michelangelo measured it again and calculated whether he could carve a satisfactory figure from the block by accommodating its pose to the shape of the stone. Then he made up his mind to ask for it. Soderini and the Operai decided that they would let him have it, as being something of little value; the stone was of no use to their building, either botched as it was or broken up. . . . So Michelangelo made a model of the young David with a sling in his hand; this was intended as a symbol of liberty for the 46 Palace, signifying that, as David had protected his people and governed them justly, so whoever ruled Florence should vigorously defend the city and govern it with justice. He began work on the statue in the Opera of Sta Maria del Fiore, erecting a partition of planks and trestles around the marble; and working on it continuously he brought it to perfect completion, without letting anyone see it.

As I said, the marble had been flawed and distorted by Simone, and in some places Michelangelo could not work it as he wanted; so he allowed some of the original chisel marks made by Simone to remain on the edges of the marble, and these can still be seen today. . . .

After the statue was finished, its great size provoked endless disputes over the best way to transport it to the Piazza della Signoria. However, Giuliano da Sangallo, with his brother Antonio, constructed a very strong wooden framework and suspended the statue from it with ropes so that when it moved it would sway gently without being broken; then they drew it along by means of winches over planks laid on the ground and put it in place. In the rope which held the figure suspended he tied a slip-knot which tightened as the weight increased; a beautiful and ingenious arrangement. . . .

When he saw the *David* in place, Piero Soderini was delighted, but while Michelangelo was retouching it he remarked that he thought the nose was too thick. Michelangelo, noticing that the Gonfalonier was standing beneath the Giant and that from where he was he could not see the figure properly, to satisfy him climbed on the scaffolding by the shoulders, seized hold of a chisel in his left hand, together with some of the marble dust lying on the planks, and as he tapped lightly with the chisel he let the dust fall little by little, without altering anything. Then he looked down at the Gonfalonier, who had stopped to watch, and said:

'Now look at it.'

'Ah, that's much better,' replied Soderini. 'Now you've really brought it to life.'

And then Michelangelo climbed down, feeling sorry for those critics who talk nonsense in the hope of appearing well informed. When the work was finished, he uncovered it for everyone to see. And without doubt this figure has put in the shade every other statue, ancient or modern, Greek or Roman. . . . The *David* (for which Piero Soderini paid Michelangelo four hundred scudi) was put in position in the year 1504. (v2.7.153–7.)

Piero Soderini (1452–1522) was elected Gonfalonier for life in 1502, in an effort to achieve a stability and continuity similar to that prevailing under the Doges of Venice. Under his rule, until 1512, the city recovered its artistic initiative through his patronage of Leonardo and Michelangelo.

Vasari's account is not quite accurate. The block had originally been acquired as part of a project to place giant figures on the ends of the buttresses of the cathedral (Sta Maria del Fiore); and though various works (including one by Donatello) had been made for the purpose, none remained *in situ*. In 1464, the Operai commissioned Agostino di Duccio to make a giant figure, nine *braccia* high (about 17 ft or 5 m), but either he or his assistant, Bartolommeo di Pietro, made a botch of it and abandoned it, and in 1473 Agostino returned to Perugia. In 1476, Antonio Rossellino was asked to finish it, but he died about 1479 without getting any further. In 1501, fresh steps were taken to find someone capable of doing something with the block, which it had always been intended should represent David, and the contract with Michelangelo was signed on 16 August 1501. Vasari's account, therefore, of the Operai considering the block as a dead loss and giving it to Michelangelo more or less on the off-chance of his contriving to get a figure out of it, seems to derive from Michelangelo's own faulty recollection. This applies also to his statement that it was Simone (Mino) da Fiesole who was responsible for spoiling the block, since it is clear from the records of the Operai that he never had anything to do with it. Michelangelo must also have been Vasari's source for the story that Piero Soderini was the prime mover in the decision to employ the young sculptor; Soderini was an important man in Florence, but he did not become Gonfalonier or head of state until November 1502. Vasari's mention of the *David* excelling even Greek statues may seem odd, in that no antique Greek sculpture was known in Italy at that time; it is clearly a reference to Pliny who describes so many Greek works.

Like Donatello's bronze *Judith with the Head of Holofernes*, which had been placed in front of the Palazzo della Signoria as a warning to tyrants when Piero de' Medici was expelled in 1494, the *David* had taken on a political significance which outweighed its original religious purpose. When it was finished a commission met to decide where it was to stand. This included every artist of note in the city, and also the two state heralds and the trumpeter.

The debate began with an odd statement from the senior herald, who wanted the *Judith* removed because it was ill omened:

The *Judith* is a death-dealing sign, and this is not good because we have as our insignia the Cross and the Lily, and it is not good for a woman to kill a man, and above all because it was placed under a very bad star; since then you have gone from bad to worse and have lost Pisa; and the *David* by Donatello in the courtyard is not perfect because the right leg is feeble. So I would advise that the statue [Michelangelo's *David*] be put in one of these two places, but preferably where the *Judith* is. (G.2.454–63.)

The painter Cosimo Rosselli suggested either inside the Palazzo Vecchio or in front of the cathedral; Botticelli was undecided between the palace balustrade and the adjacent Loggia dei Lanzi, but wanted it visible to passers-by. Giuliano da Sangallo sensibly argued that it should be protected from the weather, since the marble was 'tender' after half a century out in the sun and rain. He suggested putting it under the central arch of the Loggia, or in a niche. The second herald pointed out that in the Loggia it would impede state processions, and Leonardo da Vinci supported the idea of a niche in the back wall; as did Antonio da Sangallo and Piero di Cosimo. Davide Ghirlandaio suggested putting it where the lion, symbol of fortitude, stood in the balustrade; Filippino Lippi actually suggested consulting Michelangelo. The others swithered from one side to another, and not surprisingly no decision was reached. In the end the senior herald had his way. On 28 May 1504 the council decided to remove the *Judith* (it was later put in the Loggia), and the

David was set up in its place, where it remained until 1873; then Giuliano's advice was belatedly taken and it was removed to the Accademia. A figure that had originally formed part of a straightforward religious scheme had become a civic symbol of fortitude and the power of right, an independent, free-standing work embodying secular ideas.

During this period in Florence, between 1501 and 1504, Michelangelo carved the two marble roundels or tondi of the *Madonna and Child* for the Taddei and Pitti families, and painted the circular Holy Family – the *Doni Tondo* – for Angelo Doni. He also planned a series of figures for the Piccolomini Altar in Siena – originally intended as a tomb for the Francesco Piccolomini who died in 1503 as Pope Pius III – and it was probably for this commission that he carved the marble *Madonna and Child* which he later sold to Bruges, and about which he was rather secretive; both Vasari and Condivi gained the impression that it was a bronze. Both also mention a bronze *David*, which they say was commissioned by Soderini, but which was finally cast for the French commander stationed in Florence after the second French invasion of Italy, this time under Louis XII (1499). The work was sent to France, and later lost.

44–5

42–3

46

Vasari's story of the delivery of the *Doni Tondo* shows Michelangelo in a characteristically intransigent mood.

Then Angelo Doni, a Florentine who loved to own beautiful things by ancient or modern artists, decided that he would like his friend to make something for him. So Michelangelo started work on a round painting of the Madonna.... When it was ready he sent it under wrappings to Angelo's house with a note asking for payment of seventy ducats. Now Angelo, who was careful with his money, was disconcerted at being asked to spend so much on a picture, even though he knew that, in fact, it was worth more. So he gave the messenger forty ducats and told him that that was enough. Whereupon Michelangelo returned the money with a message to say that Angelo should send back either a hundred ducats or the picture itself. Then Angelo, who liked the painting, said: 'Well, I'll give him seventy.'

However, Michelangelo was still far from satisfied. Indeed, because of Angelo's breach of faith he demanded double what he had asked first of all, and this meant that to get the picture Angelo had to pay a hundred and forty ducats. (v2.7.158–9.)

And serve him right! One might, however, guess that when Doni came to commission the portraits of himself and his wife, Maddalena Strozzi, from Raphael a couple of years later, he took greater care to safeguard his purse.

Vasari then goes on to describe the commission for the two large frescoes which were to decorate the Sala del Consiglio, the main hall of assembly in the Palazzo della Signoria for citizens entitled to a vote in the affairs of the city.

It happened that while the great painter Leonardo da Vinci was working in the Council Chamber ... Piero Soderini, who was then Gonfalonier, recognizing Michelangelo's abilities, had part of the hall allocated to him; and this was why Michelangelo painted the other wall in competition with Leonardo, taking as his subject an episode in the Pisan War. For this project Michelangelo used a room in the Dyers' Hospital at Sant'Onofrio, where he started work on a vast cartoon which he refused to let anyone see. (v2.7.159–60.)

There follows a long description of the figures in the cartoon, and its reception by Florentine artists, which Vasari must have had from hearsay and from those still working in Florence in his time. It was a composition of struggling nude figures,

...some upright, some kneeling or leaning forward, or halfway between one position and another, all exhibiting the most difficult foreshortenings. There were also many groups of

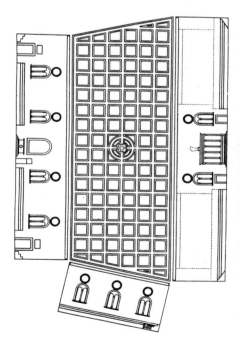

A reconstruction by Johannes Wilde of the great hall in the Palazzo della Signoria, built 1498–1502. The wall on which Leonardo and Michelangelo were to paint was 202 by 40 ft (61.86 × 12.17 m).

47-8 figures drawn in different ways: some outlined in charcoal, others sketched with a few strokes, some shaded gradually and heightened with lead-white. This Michelangelo did to show how much he knew about his craft. When they saw the cartoon, all the other artists were overcome with admiration and astonishment, for it was a revelation of the perfection that the art of painting could reach. People who have seen these inspired figures declare that they have never been surpassed by Michelangelo himself or by anyone else, and that no one can ever again reach such sublime heights. And this may readily be believed, for after the cartoon had been finished and carried to the Sala del Papa, to the honour of art and to the glory of Michelangelo, those who subsequently studied it and made copies of the figures (as was done for many years in Florence by local artists and others) became excellent painters themselves. As we know, those who studied the cartoon included Aristotile da Sangallo (Michelangelo's friend), Ridolfo Ghirlandaio, Raphael Sanzio of Urbino, Francesco Granacci, Baccio Bandinelli, and the Spaniard, Alonso Berruguete. They were followed by Andrea del Sarto, Franciabigio, Jacopo Sansovino, Rosso, Maturino, Lorenzetto and Tribolo when he was a child, and by Jacopo da Pontormo and Pierin del Vaga. All these men were outstanding Florentine masters.

The cartoon having thus become a school for artists, it was taken to the great upper room of the house of the Medici. But this meant that it was unwisely left in the hands of the artists; and when Duke Giuliano fell ill, without warning it was torn into pieces. And it is now dispersed in various places. (v2.7.160-1.)

Vasari's vivid description of Michelangelo 'in competition with Leonardo' evokes the picture of the Old Lion (Leonardo was then fifty-two) confronting the Rising Star in undisguised hostility, each encamped before his adjoining piece of wall. However, this delightful fiction has to fade before the more prosaic fact that they probably never met on site; each worked on his own. Each, of course, failed to complete anything lasting. Michelangelo because he was distracted by Pope Julius II's summons to Rome, Leonardo because his disastrous technique resulted in lengthy working and in the rapid decay of the portions which he did execute. It was Vasari himself who finally destroyed the
46 ravaged remains of Leonardo's famous *Battle of Anghiari* when he reconstructed the Sala in the 1560s, dividing it into several rooms.

The Rocca, or citadel, above the modern village of Caprese Michelangelo. Lodovico Buonarroti was *podestà* in command of this minor Florentine stronghold near Arezzo when his second son Michelangelo was born on 6 March 1475. Through the doorway on the right of the upper picture is the room where Michelangelo was born. Its arched window is on the left in the lower picture.

Humanist Florence

The young Michelangelo came to the notice of the
Florentine ruler, Lorenzo de' Medici (Il Magnifico), and
thus gained access to the Medici circle of humanist
scholars, who furthered his literary and artistic education.
The antique sculptures in the Medici garden near S. Marco
(below right, above the steepled monastery building in the
plan) inspired him to emulation. At the Medici palace (seen
in its fifteenth-century state, below), Cristoforo Landino
applied the revived doctrines of Neo-Platonism to debates
in which Lorenzo de' Medici, Agnolo Poliziano, Pico della
Mirandola and Marsilio Ficino talked of the Highest Good,
or of the Active and Contemplative Life. The woodcut
(right), from Landino's letter-writing manual, *Formulario
di lettere* (1492), shows a humanist lecture; Landino himself
is famous for a patriotic and anti-papal interpretation of
Dante's *Divine Comedy* (1481).

The Latin translator of Plato, Marsilio Ficino (seen below in a medal by Niccolò Fiorentino), taught that life might be an ascent from the bondage of matter through contemplation and through the Platonic transformation of earthly love. Agnolo Poliziano, tutor to the Medici children (drawn by Ghirlandaio, right), suggested the subject for Michelangelo's youthful *Battle of the Centaurs*, his first treatment of the theme of struggling nude figures. The relief was left unfinished when Lorenzo died in 1492 and the Medici circle broke up.

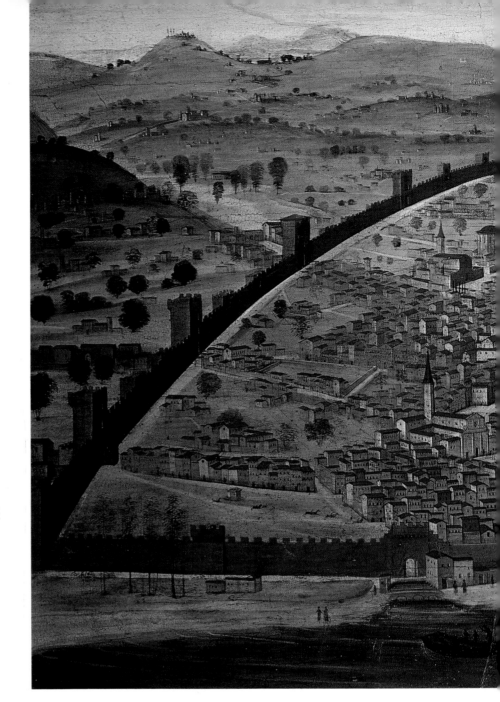

City and parish

Florence as Michelangelo first knew it: a painted copy of a six-sheet woodcut map of *c.* 1500. The complex of the cathedral, the campanile and the baptistery stands out in the centre, and is flanked on the right by the Palazzo della Signoria, with its high tower, and the square bulk of Orsanmichele. The Medici palace, on the left of the cathedral, looms over the surrounding small houses, together with S. Lorenzo, and below, nearer the river, is the spire of Sta Maria Novella. Above these is the group of buildings that includes the Annunziata and Brunelleschi's loggia of the Innocenti (foundling hospital), with the convent of S. Marco nearby. The large Piazza Sta Croce, in the district where the Buonarroti family lived, is at the top right, near the river. The Ponte Vecchio, with houses on it then as now, leads to the huge bulk of Palazzo Pitti, seen as it was before it was enlarged in the sixteenth and seventeenth centuries. S. Spirito lies nearer the Ponte SS. Trinità (later rebuilt). The church just inside the walls, lower right, is the Carmine, and the fortified gateway is the Porta S. Frediano.

The Buonarroti family house (near right) is in the Via Benticordi, a hundred yards or so from the Piazza Sta Croce (the scene of a sixteenth-century tournament, far right). Throughout his life Michelangelo bought property in his own parish. He eventually owned five houses in the neighbouring Via Ghibellina alone.

Artists he studied

At the age of thirteen Michelangelo was apprenticed to Domenico Ghirlandaio, and it was probably around this time that he made drawings (right, above and below) from Giotto's *Scenes from the Life of St John the Evangelist* in the Peruzzi Chapel of his own parish church of Sta Croce (left), and from Masaccio's *Tribute Money* fresco in the Brancacci Chapel of the Carmine (below left).

When Michelangelo returned to Florence from Rome in 1501, already a mature artist, he found that an older and more famous man was the centre of attention. Leonardo da Vinci had been in Florence since the previous year, and had made a cartoon (a full-scale drawing for a painting) of the *Virgin and Child with St Anne*. This work, which was probably a lost later version of the cartoon seen opposite, was shown in public and aroused much enthusiasm. Michelangelo's reaction is shown in the drawing below; clearly, like Raphael, he was impressed by Leonardo's ability to assemble figures in a pyramidal composition in space, and tried his hand at emulating the effect.

The Medici

Ghirlandaio's fresco of the *Confirmation of the Franciscan Rule*, painted in SS. Trinità in 1483–86, contains a gallery of portraits of the Medici and Sassetti families. Lorenzo, Il Magnifico, is seen in the detail on the right; Poliziano appears (left) with one of his pupils, Lorenzo's son Giuliano (1479–1516), who became Duke of Nemours; his is one of the tombs in Michelangelo's Medici Chapel. In the same fresco Ghirlandaio shows Lorenzo's other sons (below), Giovanni (1476–1521) and Piero (1471–1503). It was Piero's folly that precipitated, in 1494, the end of Medici rule in Florence; this was later restored by Giovanni, who, as Pope Leo X, was one of Michelangelo's patrons.

Savonarola

Girolamo Savonarola, 'Prophet, Man and Martyr', as he is described on Giovanni delle Corniole's posthumous gem (far left), was a Dominican from Ferrara whom Lorenzo il Magnifico invited to become Prior of S. Marco (left, below) in 1491. Like all Florence, Michelangelo heard him preach, and he never forgot the power of his eloquence, or his vision of a Florence free, self-governing and honourable.

'The Sword of God over the Land, Swiftly and Soon' was Savonarola's vision of the fall of the Medici, seen in 1492 and recorded, after it came true, in a medal of 1495. His prophecies were collected in the *Compendio di rivelazioni*, with woodcuts showing him in his study and in the pulpit (left and right, above); his sermons provoked near-hysteria. He prophesied the doom attendant on the city's luxury, licence, corruption and general depravity, and denounced the Borgia pope, Alexander VI, whose ban on preaching he defied. Eventually his moral crusade became wearisome. His followers (the so-called Snivellers) made his ideas unpopular by their canting denunciations of even the simplest pleasures, and the republican Florentine government made common cause with the papacy to remove him. In 1498 S. Marco was stormed, he was hanged (with two companions, right), and his ashes were scattered to prevent a posthumous cult.

Christ and the Virgin

The small *Madonna of the Stairs* is
Michelangelo's earliest extant work of
sculpture, preceding the *Battle of the
Centaurs* on which he was working in
1492. It reflects the strong influence of
Donatello, both in the lowness of the relief

and in the close contact between the
Madonna and the infant Christ, who is
suckling and therefore, unusually, shown
from the back. The motive of the stairs is
probably also adapted from Donatello.
The *Pietà*, now in St Peter's, was carved in

Rome in the later 1490s; this was an
unusual subject in itself, more common in
the North than in Italy. It is the only work
that Michelangelo ever signed, and it
established him as the leading sculptor of
the age.

Roman patronage

In 1496 the Cardinal of S. Giorgio, Raffaelle Riario, far from bearing a grudge after he had been duped by Michelangelo's fake antique *Cupid*, sent for the twenty-one-year-old sculptor and received him in his new palace in Rome, the building which became (and is still) the Cancelleria (below). Cardinal Riario himself appears in Raphael's famous fresco of *The Mass of Bolsena*, painted in 1512 (below right). However, in spite of Michelangelo's high expectations – he procured a life-size marble block immediately after his arrival in Rome – Riario commissioned nothing from him. The first of Michelangelo's major sculptures to have survived (an earlier *Hercules*, made in Florence, is lost) is the *Bacchus* (right) carved for the banker Jacopo Galli; Vasari was to call it 'a mixture of marvellous parts . . . with the slenderness of the young male and the softness and roundness of the female'. The circular base and the position of the faun invite the spectator to walk round the group, so that it presents more than one viewpoint – a characteristic uncommon at that date, but which became very important in later years. The figure competed with, rather than imitated, antique sculpture; but in one of the Dutch artist Marten van Heemskerck's precious records of Rome in the 1530s (far right) it is seen in Galli's sculpture garden with one hand severed to make it look more antique. The part survived; it had been replaced by the time Condivi described it in 1553. The marble of hand and figure is identical.

Another Heemskerck view of Rome (right) shows the new St Peter's rising behind the old. The small round church on the south side (old and new St Peter's share a reverse orientation) is Sta Maria della Febbre, where Michelangelo's *Pietà* originally stood.

Carrara

Michelangelo spent years of his life supervising the quarrying of marble; perhaps he enjoyed the life at remote places like Carrara. Marble was quarried here in classical times, and active working resumed in the twelfth century. The marble, of which whole mountains are composed, varies widely in colour and mineral structure. It is quarried (far left, below) in huge stepped terraces, yielding blocks of up to three hundred tons. It was formerly extracted by splitting with wedges and cutting with a saw – laborious, risky and wasteful. The background of Mantegna's *Madonna of the Quarries* (far left, above) is believed to show fifteenth-century quarry workings in the Dolomites. Condivi records that, at Carrara, Michelangelo 'was seized with a wish to carve, out of a mountain overlooking the sea, a colossus which would be visible from afar to seafarers'.

The unfinished *St Matthew* (near left), which Michelangelo worked on between 1503 and 1506, is hacked from his enveloping shell of marble and appears almost like a Lazarus struggling from the tomb. The work exemplifies Michelangelo's method of working a figure back from the front of the block, so that it emerges slowly into the light. Claw chisels of varying sizes are his favourite tools, so that the figure is as much drawn in crosshatching as carved. A detail of the *St Matthew* is shown opposite (above right).

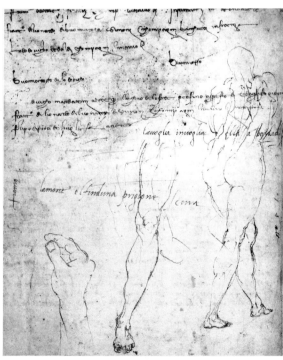

One of Michelangelo's earliest surviving life drawings is dated by a draft of the 1501 Piccolomini contract on the reverse. Most unusually for Michelangelo, it seems to show a female nude model.

The Piccolomini altar

In 1504, for the first of many times, Michelangelo was forced to abandon a work that was already overdue. Fifteen statues for the tomb of Cardinal Francesco Piccolomini in Siena were commissioned in 1501 by the cardinal himself, but Michelangelo worked on the Florence *David* first. In 1503 Piccolomini died, after a reign of twenty-six days as Pope Pius III, and was buried in the Vatican (his tomb effigy is shown far left). The Siena tomb became a commemorative altar. Michelangelo was called to Rome to embark on the tomb of the new pope, Julius II, and he resigned the Siena commission, and the marbles, to Baccio da Montelupo. (He may, however, have begun, if not finished, the *St Paul*, centre left, and the *St Peter*, lower right.) The *Bruges Madonna* (right) was perhaps intended for the tomb, though on Pius' death Michelangelo seems to have neglected to offer the group to the Piccolomini family. It was sold in 1506 to the Mouscheron family, Flemish merchants in whose chapel, in Notre-Dame at Bruges, Dürer saw it in 1521.

This small study for the *Bruges Madonna* was drawn from a male nude model – a common practice at the time, and one which Michelangelo almost invariably followed.

Tondi

During the years when Michelangelo was
carving the *David*, 1501–04, several
smaller works were commissioned by
Florentine admirers. The circular or tondo
form, which was traditional in Florence
for representations of the Virgin and
Child, probably takes its origin from the
desco da parto, a painted circular or
polygonal tray on which gifts were
brought to mothers of newborn children.
The *Holy Family* which Michelangelo
painted for Angelo Doni (far right, above)
is one of his very few easel pictures, and is
remarkable for its treatment of relief,
which is more characteristic of sculpture
than of painting. Doni and his wife
Maddalena were portrayed by Raphael in
1505 (far right, below), the portrait of
Maddalena being clearly influenced by
Leonardo's *Mona Lisa*. The marble tondi
for the Pitti and Taddei families (near
right) were left unfinished when
Michelangelo went to Rome in 1505. The
commissioners were happy to accept
them, the *concetto* or idea being considered
more important than a completed
execution. Both show Michelangelo's
sculptural technique to perfection, from
the sharp punch marks to the use of the
claw chisel in strokes ranging from rough
striations to delicate crosshatching.

The heroic nude

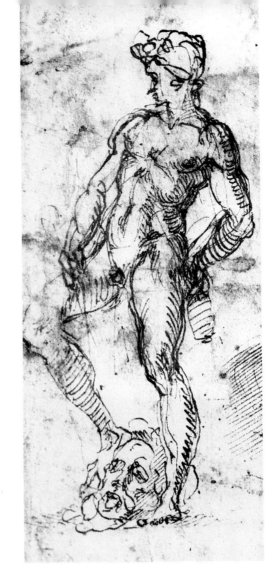

One drawing (near right) is the only record of a bronze *David* begun in 1502 and abandoned when Michelangelo went to Rome in 1505. A professional bronze-caster finished it, and it was taken to France, where it later disappeared. The marble *David* (centre), carved in 1501–04 from a narrow block which earlier sculptors had mutilated, confirmed Michelangelo's position as the premier sculptor of the age. The figure is nearly 14 ft (over 4 m) high.

The Florentine Republic ordered huge mural paintings for the council chamber of the Palazzo della Signoria to commemorate two of its victories. Leonardo's sketch (below) is one of the few records of his *Battle of Anghiari*, which was abandoned in 1506. Michelangelo's cartoon for the *Battle of Cascina* (where Florentine troops were surprised while bathing) survives only in studies (far right, above, and next page) and in a painting of the central part by Aristotile da Sangallo, one of the many artists who came to admire and learn from it (far right, below).

This preparatory drawing, 1504, for the centrally seated figure in the Bathers Scene of the *Battle of Cascina* mural is one of the most highly finished of the numerous studies which survive. The subject gave Michelangelo the opportunity to present a wide variety of complex poses of nude men in action. The partly completed project was abandoned in March 1505, when Julius II summoned Michelangelo to Rome.

PART TWO

JULIUS II

1505–1516

CARDINAL GIULIANO DELLA ROVERE succeeded Pius III (who reigned for only three and a half weeks) in 1503, and took the title of Julius II. He was a nephew of Sixtus IV, and his election was the culmination of a long career in Vatican diplomacy. He was an implacable enemy of the former pope, Alexander VI, and was determined to restore the temporal power of the papacy and to recover the papal estates alienated by Alexander's nepotism, chiefly to his brigand son Cesare Borgia: a project in which he was fairly successful. He also strove to drive the French out of Italy with the warcry of 'Out with the Barbarians!', but his long and bitter campaign was not successful, since he did not scruple to use the Spanish against the French, with the result that though the French were ultimately, after his death, driven out, the Spaniards remained. His patronage of the arts makes him supreme among Renaissance popes: Bramante, Raphael, Michelangelo, the expansion of the Vatican Library and the foundation of the Vatican collection of antiques have given his reign a lustre that has never faded.

Michelangelo was working in Florence when Julius was elected, and it was two years later, in March 1505, that the pope sent for him.

After he arrived in Rome, however, many months were let go by before he was asked to do any work. But eventually the pope chose for his tomb the design made by Michelangelo... for in beauty and magnificence, wealth of ornamentation and richness of statuary it surpassed every ancient or imperial tomb ever made. When he saw it, Pope Julius grew more ambitious and resolved to set about rebuilding the church of St Peter's at Rome, and to raise his tomb inside.

So Michelangelo started work with very high hopes, going first of all with two of his assistants to Carrara to excavate all the marble, on account of which he received a thousand crowns.... He had nothing more by way of money or supplies for the eight months he spent in the mountains.... After he had chosen all the marble that was wanted, he had it loaded on board ship and taken to Rome, where the blocks filled half the square of St Peter's around Sta Caterina and between the church and the corridor leading to Castel Sant'Angelo. In the castle Michelangelo had prepared his room for executing the figures and the rest of the tomb; and so that he could come and see him at work without any bother the pope had ordered a drawbridge to be built from the corridor to the room. This led to a great intimacy between them, although in time the favours he was shown brought Michelangelo considerable annoyance and even persecution, and stirred up much envy among his fellow artists. (v2.7.163.)

Condivi's description of the Julius Tomb project is not only clear; it is also alarming.

There is no doubt that if he had been allowed to finish it, according to his first design, with so large a field in which to show his worth, no other artist, however celebrated (be it said without envy), could have wrested from him the high place he would have held. Those parts which he did finish show what the rest would have been like. The two *Slaves* were done for this work: those who have seen them declare that no more worthy statues were ever carved.

And to give some idea of it, I say briefly that this tomb was to have had four faces, two of eighteen *braccia* that served for the sides, and two of twelve *braccia* for the two ends, so that it was to be a square and a half in plan. All round the outside were niches for statues, and between the niches were term figures; to these were bound other statues, like prisoners, upon certain square plinths, rising from the ground and projecting from the monument. They represented the Liberal Arts, as well as Painting, Sculpture, and Architecture, each with its symbol so that they could be easily recognized: denoting by this that, like Pope Julius, all the virtues were the prisoners of Death, because they would never find such favour and nourishment as he gave them. Above these ran the cornice that tied all the work together. On this platform were four great statues; one of these, the *Moses*, may be seen in S. Pietro in Vincoli. It will be spoken of in its proper place. So the work mounted upward until it ended in a platform on which were two angels who supported a shrine; one appeared to be smiling as though he rejoiced that the soul of the pope had been received amongst the blessed spirits, the other wept, as if sad that the world had been deprived of such a man. At one end was the entrance to the sepulchre in a small chamber, built like a temple; in the middle was a marble sarcophagus, where the body of the pope was to be buried; everything was worked out with marvellous art. Briefly, more than forty statues went into the whole work, not counting the subjects in mezzo-rilievo to be cast in bronze, all appropriate to their stories and proclaiming the acts of this great Pontiff. (AC.36–8.)

In his immense artistic self-confidence, Michelangelo had taken on in one project more than he could perform in a lifetime. The forty figures alone, many of them more than life-size, would have taken him perhaps forty years, doing nothing else. The project expresses an ambition, on the part of patron and artist alike, that verges on megalomania.

As the *braccia* is nearly 23 inches or 58.3 cm, this first project would have been for a tomb 34½ ft or 10.5 m long by 23 ft or 7 m wide. Condivi gives no indication of height, but given that the *Slaves*, which were to be at ground level, and the *Moses*, which was to be above them, would amount to 15 ft or more than 4.5 m without allowing for the bases, the terms, the cornice, or the shrine-bearing angels, it follows that a height equal to the width (23 ft) or even the length (34½ ft) is quite possible.

According to Vasari, the *Slaves* personified the provinces subjugated by Julius in his campaigns, but this cannot refer to the first project since at that time Julius' career as a warrior had not yet begun.

Since the projected monument could never have been fitted into St Peter's in the state it then was in, Michelangelo apparently suggested to the Pope that if the new choir, begun by Rossellino in 1450 and never finished, were completed, it would make a suitable site. It is possible that this suggestion was the germ of the idea of rebuilding the entire church, which, after over a thousand years, was in a ruinous state. However, Julius II's architect for this was a bitter rival of Michelangelo's, Donato Bramante.

Thus the architect Bramante, who was loved by the pope, made him change his plans by quoting what common people say, that it is bad luck for anyone to build his tomb during his lifetime, and other stories. Apart from envy, Bramante was prompted by the fear he had of the judgment of Michelangelo, who kept discovering many of Bramante's blunders. Because Bramante was a great spendthrift and given to every sort of pleasure, so that the funds provided him by the pope, however ample, did not suffice, he tried to gain advantage in his buildings by making the walls of poor materials and inadequately strong and secure for their size and extensiveness. This is obvious for everyone to see in the building of St Peter's in the Vatican, in the Belvedere Corridor, in the monastery of S. Pietro in Vincoli, and in his other buildings, all of which have required new foundations and reinforcements with buttresses and retaining walls, as if they were falling or shortly would have fallen down. Now because he did not doubt that Michelangelo recognized these misdeeds of his, he constantly sought to remove him from Rome, or at least to deprive him of the pope's favour. (AC.35–6.)

Condivi's recital of Michelangelo's grievances against Bramante is based partly on fact, but totally on hindsight. Bramante's project for St Peter's, 218 though magnificent, would never have stood up; and it is also true that the Belvedere and the Tempietto in the courtyard of S. Pietro in Montorio required considerable restoration, some of it during Michelangelo's lifetime. But none of this was apparent in 1506.

Whatever the true explanation, the Tomb was abruptly abandoned. Julius was involved in an expensive war, and committed to rebuilding St Peter's, and could hardly give his own tomb precedence over either commitment.

The marbles which had remained at Carrara were brought to the Ripa Grande port at Rome and then conveyed to St Peter's square to join the rest. As those who had brought them had to be paid, Michelangelo went (as he usually did) to see the pope. But because that day His Holiness was transacting important business concerning Bologna, Michelangelo returned home and paid for the marble himself, thinking that he would straight away be repaid by His Holiness. Then he went back another time to talk to the pope about it, but he found difficulty in getting in, for one of the grooms told him that he would have to be patient and that he had received orders not to admit him. At this a bishop who happened to be there said to the groom: 'You can't know who this man is!'

'I know him only too well,' replied the groom. 'But it's my job to do what I'm told by my superiors and by the pope.'

This attitude incensed Michelangelo, who had never experienced such treatment before, and he angrily told the groom that he should let His Holiness know that if ever he wanted to see him in future he would find that he had gone elsewhere. Then he went back to his workplace, and at the second hour of the night he set out on post-horses, leaving two servants to sell everything in the house to the Jews and then follow him to Florence. After he arrived at Poggibonsi, in Florentine territory, Michelangelo felt safe; but shortly afterwards five couriers arrived with instructions from the pope to bring him back. For all their entreaties, and despite the letter which ordered him to return to Rome under threat of punishment, he refused to listen to a word. Eventually, however, the couriers persuaded him to write a word or two in answer to His Holiness, in which he asked to be forgiven but added that he would never again return to his presence, since he had had him driven off like a criminal, that his faithful service had not deserved such treatment, and that the pope should look for someone else to serve him. (V2.7.167–8.)

He went on to Florence, where, in the three months that he stayed there, three Briefs were sent to the Signoria full of threats, to the effect that they should send him back by fair means or foul. (AC.41.)

The pope seems also to have employed the architect Giuliano da Sangallo as an intermediary; but Michelangelo still refused to come back to Rome. He wrote to Giuliano on 2 May 1506:

I learn from your letter that the pope took my departure amiss, but that His Holiness is ready to place the money at my disposal and to do all that we were agreed upon, and that I am to return and to have no anxieties about anything.

As to my departure, the truth is that at table on Holy Saturday I heard the pope say to a jeweller and to the master of ceremonies, to whom he was talking, that he did not wish to spend one *baiocco* more either on small stones or on large ones. At this I was much taken aback; however, before leaving I asked him for some part of what I needed to continue the work. His Holiness told me to return on Monday, and I returned on Monday, and on Tuesday and on Wednesday and on Thursday, as he was aware. Finally, on Friday morning I was turned out, in other words, I was sent packing, and the fellow who turned me away said that he knew who I was, but that such were his orders. At this, having heard on the said Saturday the said words, and seeing their effect, I was overwhelmed with despair. But this was not the one and only reason for my departure; there was something else besides, which I do not want to write about – it is enough that I had cause to think that if I remained in Rome, my own tomb would be sooner made than the pope's. This, then, was the reason for my sudden departure.

Now you write to me on behalf of the pope. So will you read this letter to the pope and inform His Holiness that I am more than ever ready to continue the work. But if it is indeed his wish to execute the Tomb, he should not trouble himself as to where I do it, provided that at the end of five years, as we agreed, it shall be set up in St Peter's, wherever he chooses, and that it shall be a work of art such as I have promised; for I am certain that if it is carried out, there will be nothing to equal it the world over.

Now, if His Holiness wishes to proceed, let him place the sum agreed at my disposal here in Florence, whence I will write to him. I have quantities of marble on order at Carrara, which I will have sent here, and similarly I will send for the supplies I have in Rome. Even if it were to mean a considerable loss to me, I should not mind, if I could do the work here. And I would forward the pieces one by one, as they are completed, by which arrangement His Holiness

Piero di Cosimo's portrait of Giuliano da Sangallo (c.1443/5–1516). It was probably Giuliano, in Rome between 1505 and 1509, who drew Michelangelo to Julius II's notice.

would derive as much pleasure from them as if I were working in Rome – nay, more, because he would see the finished things, without having any further bother about them. And for the said money and for the said work I will pledge myself as His Holiness directs and will give him here in Florence whatever security he shall demand. Be it what it may, Florence is my full and sufficient security. And I should add that there is no possibility of doing the said work for the same price in Rome, owing to the many facilities which exist here, but do not exist there; again I shall work better here and with greater zeal, as I shall not have so many things to think of. Meanwhile, my dearest Giuliano, I beg you to answer me as soon as possible. That's all. (C.1.8.)

In the end, of course, the pope won.

Piero Soderini . . . sent for Michelangelo and said to him: 'You have tried the pope as a king of France would not have done. However, he is not to be kept begging any longer. We do not want to go to war with him over you and place our state in jeopardy. Therefore, make ready to return.' (AC.41.)

By this time Julius II was in Bologna, a rebellious papal fief which he had just recovered from the Bentivoglio family.

Michelangelo arrived at Bologna one morning and went to S. Petronio to hear Mass and . . . the pope's equerries . . . recognizing him brought him before His Holiness. . . . When he saw Michelangelo in his presence, he said to him with an angry look on his face: 'You were supposed to come to us, and you have waited for us to come to you,' meaning that His Holiness having come to Bologna, a place much closer to Florence than Rome, was as if he had come to him. (AC.43.)

With a courteous gesture and speaking in a firm voice, Michelangelo humbly begged the pope's forgiveness, saying to excuse himself that he had acted as he did in anger, not having been able to bear being dismissed like that, but that if he had done wrong His Holiness should forgive him once more. Then the bishop who had presented Michelangelo to the pope began to make excuses for him, saying to His Holiness that such men were ignorant creatures, worthless except for their art, and that he should freely pardon him. The pope lost his temper at this and struck the bishop with a crozier he was holding, shouting at him: 'It's you who are ignorant, insulting him in a way we wouldn't dream of.'

And when the groom had driven the bishop out with his fists, the pope, having exhausted his anger, gave Michelangelo his blessing. (V2.7.169–70.)

After this scene of high farce – for Michelangelo's swelling indignation at being dismissed as ignorant and worthless, and the pope's furious reaction at the prospect of again losing his irascible artist, may well be imagined – Julius commissioned him to make a bronze statue of himself about 10 ft (3 m) high, seated in full papal panoply, to be placed in the tympanum over the main door of S. Petronio in Bologna. The doorway itself, with the panels carved by Jacopo della Quercia, had not then been completely erected. Only the architrave was in position, and the rest of the doorway was not set up until 1510. The semicircular niche or tympanum was, therefore, empty, since the *Madonna and Child* and the *St Petronius* which Jacopo had made for it were still in the Opera del Duomo.

The command to make a bronze statue must have been unwelcome. Michelangelo was inexperienced in bronze casting, although he had made the *David* which was sent to France. His letters from Bologna over the next two years, most of which are to his brother Buonarroto, record his difficulties. On 19 December 1506:

46

. . . As regards Giovansimone's coming here – I do not advise him to as yet, because I'm living in a mean room for which I have bought only one bed, and there are four of us sleeping in it,

Reconstruction of the portal of S. Petronio as it might have looked with Michelangelo's huge bronze statue of Julius II inserted into the tympanum. The doorway below is some 30 ft high.

The influence of this short-lived work lies behind all the great papal statues thenceforward. A good example is the drawing by Bandinelli for a projected monument to Clement VII.

and I would not have the means to put him up properly. But if he wants to come nevertheless, let him wait until I've cast the figure I'm doing. (C.I.12.)

Giovansimone was his younger brother, and a thorn in his side. Conditions in Bologna must have been very difficult indeed, since the city had to house not only the pope and his entourage, but also the army which had retaken the city. In January, Michelangelo believed he would cast his figure by mid-Lent, and be home by Easter; but then he consistently underestimated the time necessary to complete a work.

Michelangelo finished the statue in clay before the pope left Bologna for Rome, and so His Holiness went to see it. The pope did not know what was to be placed in the statue's left hand, and when he saw the right hand raised in an imperious gesture he asked whether it was meant to be giving a blessing or a curse. Michelangelo replied that the figure was admonishing the people of Bologna to behave sensibly. Then he asked the pope whether he should place a book in the left hand, and to this His Holiness replied:
   'Put a sword there. I know nothing about reading.' (V2.7.171.)

At the end of May, and again in June, he wrote that he had still not cast the figure, the main delay being that probably he was finding it difficult to get expert help, since bronze-casting was a difficult craft, as Cellini's autobiography makes clear. He first employed two Florentines, the sculptor Lapo d'Antonio and the bronzefounder Lodovico Lotti; both served him so ill that he dismissed them summarily, and in their place summoned Bernardino d'Antonio dal Ponte, a Milanese who was the master of artillery to the Florentine Republic. On 6 July 1507 he wrote to Buonarroto:

We have cast my figure, with which I have not been over-lucky, the reason being that Messer Bernardino, either through ignorance or by accident, did not melt the stuff properly.... My figure has come out up to the waist; the rest of the stuff, that is half the metal, remained melted in the furnace, in such a way that I shall now have to have the furnace taken down to extract it.... Messer Bernardino ... has so disgraced himself that he can no longer hold up his head in Bologna. (C.I.31.)

On 10 July 1507:

Messer Bernardino left here yesterday. If he should say anything to you, be nice to him – and leave it at that. (C.I.32.)

The statue was finally hoisted into place above the doorway on 21 February 1508.
   In December 1511, as a result of the maladministration of Cardinal Alidosi, the papal legate, the city revolted against his rule, and the Bentivoglio recovered possession. On 30 December Michelangelo's statue of Julius was pulled down and smashed. Most of the bronze went to Alfonso d'Este of Ferrara in compensation for artillery supplied to the Bolognese. From it he cast a cannon, called *La Giulia*, but he kept the head, which weighed about fifty pounds. One result was that relations between Julius II and the Duchy of Ferrara and the Este family remained embittered.
   Though the statue was totally destroyed (the head has now disappeared too), the memory of it survives in virtually all the grand papal statues for the next century and a half, for the seated figure with arm upraised became the standard for large-scale representations of, above all, the popes of the Baroque age. For all his labour, anxiety, misery and genius, Michelangelo's total reward, after his expenses were paid, amounted to four and a half ducats.

The idea of decorating the vault of the Sistine Chapel seems to have occurred to Julius II at some time in 1506, when Michelangelo was still working on the pope's projected tomb. The subject must have been broached well before the sculptor's furious flight from Rome in May 1506, for on Sunday 10 May 1506 the builder Piero Rosselli wrote to him in Florence:

Saturday evening when the pope was having supper Bramante and I took the risk of showing him some drawings which we had. When he had finished supper I showed them to him, and he sent for Bramante and said: 'Sangallo is to go to Florence tomorrow and bring Michelangelo back here.'

Bramante replied to the pope: 'Holy Father, it won't be any use, because I know Michelangelo well and he said to me many times that he did not want to do the chapel and that you wanted to give him the job, and also that you didn't want to go on with the tomb but only with the painting.' And he said, 'Holy Father, I believe that he hasn't the courage for it, because he hasn't done many figures, particularly as the figures are high up and foreshortened, which is quite another thing from painting on the ground.' . . .

Then I came forward and in front of the pope I abused him and told him what I believed you had said to me; and he didn't know what to answer and realized that he had spoken badly. (C.1.10.)

Meanwhile the Bologna interlude intervened, the pope returned to Rome, and in February 1508, after he had finished working in Bologna, Michelangelo returned to Florence hoping that he was free of Roman entanglements. He immediately resumed work on the series of Apostles for the Duomo, which had been commissioned in 1503, and of which an unfinished *St Matthew* survives. In late March or early April 1508, he was again summoned to Rome, leaving unfinished the Apostles and the bronze *David*. Vasari picks up the story, contributing an alternative version of the conspiracy theory:

40–1

In his absence, Bramante was constantly plotting with Raphael of Urbino to remove from the pope's mind the idea of having Michelangelo finish the tomb. . . . Eventually they persuaded His Holiness to get Michelangelo . . . to paint as a memorial to his uncle Sixtus [IV] the ceiling of the chapel he had built in the Vatican. . . . This, they argued, would make things hopeless for him, since as he had no experience of colouring in fresco he would certainly do less creditable work . . . and he would be compared unfavourably with Raphael, and even if the work were a success, being forced to do it would make him angry with the pope and thus . . . they would succeed in getting rid of him.

74

Michelangelo . . . tried in every way possible to shake the burden off his shoulders. But the more he refused, the more determined he made the pope. . . . Michelangelo resigned himself. . . . Then the pope ordered Bramante to make the ceiling ready for painting, and he did so by piercing the surface and supporting the scaffolding on ropes. When Michelangelo saw this he asked Bramante what he should do, when the painting was finished, to fill up the holes. Bramante said: 'We'll think of it when the time comes.' (V2.7.172–4.)

The idea that Bramante and Raphael conspired against him became an obsession with Michelangelo. Certainly, he did not get on with Bramante, but at this date there can have been no question of Raphael, who did not arrive in Rome until the end of 1508 at the earliest, and was not employed in the Vatican until 1509.

Michelangelo . . . went to the pope and told him that the scaffolding was no good and that Bramante had not known how to make it: the pope replied, in the presence of Bramante, that Michelangelo should do it himself in his own way. So he arranged to have the scaffolding erected on supports which kept clear of the walls, a method for use with vaults . . . which he subsequently taught to various people, including Bramante. In this instance, he enabled a poor carpenter, who rebuilt the scaffolding, to dispense with so many of the ropes that when

Michelangelo gave him what was over he sold them and made enough money for a dowry for his daughter. (v2.7.174.)

This account tallies with Condivi's, but the latter continues:

Michelangelo thus made his own, without ropes, so well knit together and arranged that it became increasingly firm the more weight rested upon it. This opened Bramante's eyes and taught him the way in which a scaffolding should be made; which later in the work on St Peter's was of great benefit to him. (AC.93.)

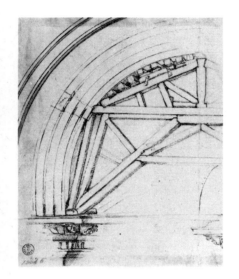

Detail of a drawing done in the St Peter's workshop, and attributed to Bramante, for the scaffolding and centering for the main arches.

No earlier scheme had imposed on the painter the striking features of the Sistine: the involvement of the pendentives with the vault, and the astonishing continuity of Michelangelo's design, where the illusionistic framework binds the various scenes and figures into a whole from one end of the building to the other. This unity of design brought a new problem with it: that of constructing a scaffolding which would serve a larger area than had ever been demanded for earlier schemes of decoration, where a tower system, one bay wide, had sufficed. The Sistine Chapel scaffolding had to be quite different: wider, stronger, heavier, leaving the upper walls, with the 1481 series of Popes, untouched, and allowing the floor of the Chapel to remain in use. Hence Vasari's and Condivi's insistence on the construction of the scaffolding (which in no previous instance had attracted comment). Interestingly, the arguments of modern commentators, which once centred so hotly on the iconography of the Ceiling, tend now to concentrate on the scaffolding and its significance for the chronology of the work.

The peculiar wording of Vasari's description, 'on supports' – *sopra i sorgòzzoni* – is used for structures cantilevered out from a building on struts or brackets, and his further detail, 'kept clear of the walls, a method for use with vaults', suggests that the struts supporting the scaffolding rested on the narrow walk-way beneath the windows and rose obliquely from it to be joined by cross beams which could support a flat floor at the top. There could also have been a stepped arrangement along the sides and at the two ends, from which the pendentive figures and the spandrels could be painted. The objection, that a solid scaffolding would cut off the light from the windows, does not hold good, because the windows would be on the 'working' side of the scaffolding. Also, this is the only form of scaffolding which would not obstruct the floor of the chapel or damage its fine Opus Alexandrinum inlaid decoration; neither would it affect in any way the screen near the centre, nor the *cantoria*, or choir gallery.

A tentative reconstruction of the scaffolding erected for the painting of the Sistine Ceiling.

The Sistine Chapel is a simple rectangular building about 132 ft long by 45 ft wide, and nearly 70 ft high (40.2 m × 13.6 m × 20.7 m). The Ceiling is a shallow barrel vault borne on pendentives which run down between the six high, round-headed windows on either side of the chapel, and the two blind windows on the entrance wall, so that there is a large triangular spandrel over each window and deep lunettes surrounding the windows. Originally, there was a similar arrangement with two windows and a walk-way on the altar wall, but the whole of this area was rebuilt as a flat wall when Michelangelo's own *Last Judgment* was painted there nearly thirty years later. Over the chapel was a guard room, with a sentry walk on the outside.

Both Condivi and Vasari, perhaps the latter echoing the former (but it could well be that both of them had it direct from Michelangelo himself), say that 'he finished the entire work in twenty months, without even the assistance of someone to grind his colours for him'. This raises very difficult problems, for it affects the whole chronology of the work. The first firm record of the contract survives only in a note in Michelangelo's *Ricordi*, or memoranda:

Today, 10 May 1508, I, Michelangelo sculptor, have received from His Holiness our Lord Pope Julius II five hundred [papal] chamber ducats ... on account of the painting of the vault of the chapel of Pope Sixtus for which I began work today under the conditions and agreement which appear in a document written by the Most Reverend Monsignor of Pavia and under my own hand. (R.1.1.)

The Monsignor of Pavia mentioned in the memorandum was Cardinal Alidosi, who had been concerned with the negotiations preceding Michelangelo's submission in Bologna. He was a favourite of Julius II, and was later appointed legate and governor of Bologna, but he ruled the city so badly that he provoked the successful revolt which resulted in the loss of the city and the destruction of the statue of Julius II over the door of S. Petronio. When he met the pope in May 1511 to explain what had happened, he blamed the pope's nephew, Duke Francesco della Rovere of Urbino, for the disaster. The duke, enraged at being blamed for Alidosi's mismanagement and cowardice, stabbbed him mortally in front of the pope.

What happened next is told by Michelangelo himself in an account he wrote in December 1523. The initial plan was for twelve Apostles in the pendentives 110 (Michelangelo says 'lunettes', but the original sketch shows them in pendentives). He wanted a more ambitious scheme, and the pope said he could do as he liked, 'and said he would satisfy me' (C.3.594). Records are sketchy, but it seems that Michelangelo never did receive all that was promised him, and that the last payment, by a piece of deliberate manipulation on the part of Lorenzo Pucci, the papal Datary – a man celebrated for his avarice – was debited to the accounts for the unfinished Julius Tomb. Later, Michelangelo was accused of dishonesty when he objected to the inclusion of this sum in the claim made against him by the heirs of Julius II.

Michelangelo in 1523 implies that it was left to him to decide what should be put in the fresco, over and above the original scheme. Perhaps this is what he preferred to remember fifteen years after the event, when complaining about the poor rewards he received. But the suggestion that it was left to an artist, even a well-educated one, to decide the subject matter represented in the major chapel of the Vatican – and the one in which Conclaves are held – must be dismissed out of hand. Julius' court was particularly rich in Dominican theologians, who would have been able and willing to draw up the programme of so important a work. The rule laid down in the Second Council of Nicaea in AD 787 had never been abrogated: 'The churches are of the fathers who build the churches; the art alone is the artist's.' In other words, Michelangelo might paint whatever design, or in whatever style he pleased, or which pleased his patron; but the content and the iconography would be controlled by theologians.

The new programme for the Ceiling was extremely elaborate: Genesis, 76 from the Creation to the Fall of Man, and Man's degeneration into sin, is accompanied by the Prophets and Sibyls who call for repentance and prophesy 79 Incarnation and Salvation. The scenes and figures are completed by the Ancestors of Christ – those 'who lived in darkness' – and the miraculous salvations of God's people – David and Goliath, the Brazen Serpent, the stories of Judith and Esther. Below Michelangelo's great series are the older sequence of types and antitypes of the Old and New Testaments: the salvation of Israel by Moses, and the salvation of the world by the coming and life of Christ. These are the frescoes planned by Sixtus IV and painted in 1481–83 by Perugino and his associates; they include a clear teaching on the supremacy of the papacy, a teaching also implicit in many of the books of the Prophets in Michelangelo's ceiling.

The enlarged scheme in the ceiling consisted of nine 'panels', four large and five small, portraying ten incidents from Genesis, set within an illusionistic architectural framework. At the corners of each of the five smaller 'histories' are seated the famous *Ignudi* – nude figures of young men in poses of increasing movement and complexity – twenty in all (of which nineteen survive). The original twelve Apostles planned for the pendentives were changed to seven Prophets and five Sibyls.

At that time the chapel was divided into two almost equal halves by the central marble screen (since moved). The part from the entrance to the screen was for laymen; the part from the screen to the altar, the presbytery, was reserved for the clergy. Michelangelo reflected this division in the subject matter of the Ceiling: God Himself appears only in the scenes above the presbytery, ending with the creation of Eve. From the altar the sequence starts with the awesome scene of God creating matter out of chaos, below which the Prophet Jonah twists to look up towards God, while the significance of his gesture, pointing downwards, is now lost because the original fresco of the older series on that half of the wall was the *Nativity of Christ*. The sequence then moves through the Creation of Adam to that of Eve, half-way, and goes on to depict the steady decline of mankind into sin, ending with the Drunkenness of Noah as the depth of human degradation, with the deep pessimism of the Prophet Zacharias over the doorway – a prophet of disaster, murdered between the altar and the sanctuary, but also prophet of the Redemption.

Michelangelo began work above the door, apparently with the Deluge. The Sacrifice of Noah, giving thanks for deliverance, and the Drunkenness of Noah, are placed on either side of it, because a large field was required for the complex scene of the Flood. The figures in the Deluge are quite small, and there are many of them, whereas the two flanking scenes are less complicated in composition and with fewer, larger figures. This simplification of the composition, and the ever increasing size of the Prophets and Sibyls in the pendentives, becomes more striking after the half-way point is passed. This can only mean that Michelangelo was able, at fairly frequent intervals, to see the effect of his work from the ground.

The *Ignudi*, one of the most splendid and original features of this stupendous feat of the imagination, were born of the need to find some way of effecting a transition from the orthogonal perspective of the histories, where the figures are seen straight on, and the illusionistic treatment of the architectural framework surrounding and 'supporting' them. This the *Ignudi* achieve in that the complex poses and the draperies of the figures obscure the perspective of the cornice on which they are seated. All theories of their meaning, ranging from Neoplatonic philosophy, to varying states of the soul, to the physical exuberance of the dance, must remain speculation; but their practical function is quite clear.

On 11 May 1508, the day after Michelangelo's note about his agreement with the pope, the builder Piero Rosselli gave him a receipt for 10 gold ducats for roughening or scoring the ceiling so as to prepare it for a new *arriccio* (the underlying coating of plaster) and to make it ready for the *intonaco* (the layer of wet lime plaster on which frescoes are directly painted), which would be laid in daily sections immediately before the painter began working. Similar receipts, also presumably for scoring, occur on 24 May and 3 and 10 June. On 10 June, Paris de Grassis, the papal chamberlain, wrote in his diary:

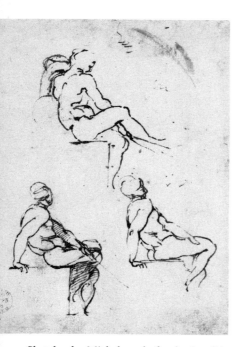

Sketches by Michelangelo for the *Ignudi* in the Sistine Ceiling.

Vespers of the vigil of Pentecost: In the upper part of the chapel the building work was being done with much dust, and the workmen did not stop as I ordered. For which the cardinals complained. Although several times I reproved the workmen they did not stop; I went to the pope who was annoyed with me because I had not admonished them and the work continued without permission, even though the pope sent two successive chamberlains who ordered them to stop, which was done with difficulty. (T.2.219.)

Destroying the existing surface would, in fact, be very dusty 'building work', whereas making a scaffolding (the more usual translation) would be noisy rather than dusty. After 10 June there is a gap in the payments to Rosselli until 17 July, and the last is on 27 July, 30 ducats for scaffolding and *arriccio*. The gap suggests that this is when Bramante's scaffolding was taken down and Michelangelo's new scaffolding was erected. Nothing would have been easier than to use the unsuitable scaffolding for part of the dirty preparatory work.

Michelangelo wrote to his father in Florence on 2 July 1508, and referred to 'my worries'. Vasari's account suggests the reasons:

Then forced reluctantly, by the magnitude of the task, to take on some assistants, Michelangelo sent for help to Florence.... Having started on the work, Michelangelo asked them to produce some samples of what they could do. But when he saw that these were nothing like what he wanted he grew dissatisfied, and then one morning he made up his mind to scrap everything they had done. He shut himself in the Chapel, refused to let them in again, and would never let them see him even when he was at home. So when they thought the joke was wearing thin they accepted their dismissal and went back ashamed to Florence.... Thereupon, having arranged to do all the work by himself, Michelangelo carried it well on the way to completion; working with the utmost solicitude, labour and study, he refused to let anyone see him in case he would have to show what he was painting.... Pope Julius himself was always anxious to see whatever Michelangelo was doing, and so naturally he was more anxious than ever to see what was being hidden from him. (v2.7.17.4–5.)

It is difficult to reconcile Condivi's (and, following him, Vasari's) statement that Michelangelo dismissed his assistants and did everything himself, with the record in the *Ricordi* of payments to Jacopo l'Indaco as his *garzone* or assistant, and various otherwise unknown men, and the evidence of some of the work in the Ceiling itself. There was the need for the daily – and in high summer, twice daily – attendance of a plasterer who was usually the painter's assistant competent to lay in the essential *intonaco*.

Also, the very precise architectural framework repeats on either side of the five small 'panels', and, with the thrones of the Prophets and Sibyls on the pendentives, forms a repeating composition; the thrones of the two Prophets on the pendentives over the altar and the entrance are also identical. The small pairs of caryatid *putti* which decorate the thrones also repeat: each pair is a mirror image of the pair on the other side of the throne, and in the set nearest the door all four pairs are the same mirror repeats. This use and reuse of the same cartoon, reversed and made different by the 'light' falling on the figure, is also obvious in the figures at the head of each spandrel. Under the twelve thrones and in the centre of each lunette are painted plaques bearing the names of those represented, over the spandrels are rams' skulls, and between each pair of *Ignudi* is a fictive gilded bronze medallion depicting an incident from the Old Testament. It is hardly reasonable to suppose that Michelangelo, oppressed with the need to paint the vault itself at top speed, should have been involved, except as the designer, with minor elements; any more than the gilding of the little balusters on the thrones can have been executed except under his general direction.

If what his biographers mean is that the major parts were done by himself alone, there would be full agreement, even though it is reasonable to suppose that the cartoons were transferred by an assistant. There are also the ten *putti* at the bottom of the pendentives on the long walls; they range from graceful and almost mirror image figures under the first four 'plaques' to increasingly freely drawn figures, some of almost grotesque ugliness (though it is fair to say that they owe much of their unpleasantness to gross restoration).

Now when a third of the work was completed (as I [Vasari] found out from Michelangelo himself to clear up any uncertainty), during the winter when the north wind was blowing several spots of mould started to appear on the surface. The reason for this was that the Roman lime, which is white in colour and made of travertine, does not dry very quickly, and when mixed with *pozzolana*, which is a brownish colour, forms a dark mixture which is very watery before it sets; then after the wall has been thoroughly soaked, it often effloresces when it is drying. Thus this salt efflorescence appeared in many places, although in time the air dried it up. When Michelangelo saw what was happening he despaired of the whole undertaking and was reluctant to go on. However, His Holiness sent Giuliano da Sangallo to see him, who explained the reason for the blemishes. Sangallo explained how to remove the mould and encouraged him to continue. (v2.7.176.)

In fact, the *Deluge* was the one part of the Ceiling which did eventually fail, for in 1797 there was an explosion in the Castel Sant'Angelo and part of the Ceiling fell in with the loss of a portion of the *Deluge* and almost all of the *Ignudo* in the adjoining *Sacrifice of Noah*.

The first hint of serious trouble in the progress of the work comes in a letter of 27 January 1509 to his father Lodovico:

I am still in a great quandary, because it is now a year since I had a *grosso* from the pope and I do not ask for anything because my work does not seem to me to go ahead in a way to merit it. This is due to the difficulty of the work and also because it is not my profession. (c.1.62.)

Actually, it was eight months since the payment of 500 ducats, and 'not my profession' was a continual complaint of his. In June 1509 he was still complaining to his father:

I learn from your last that it is said in Florence that I am dead. It is a matter of little importance, because I am still alive. So let them say what they like, and do not mention me to anyone, because there are some malicious people about. I'm bent upon working as hard as I can. I've had no money from the pope for thirteen months now, but I expect to have some at all events within six weeks, as I made very good use of what I had. If he were not to give me any, I should have to borrow money to come home, because I haven't a *quattrino*. However, I can't be robbed. God grant things may go better. . . .

Here I'm living ill-content and not too well, faced with an enormous task, without anyone to manage for me and without money. However, I have good hope that God will help me. (c.1.64.)

He also had grave family troubles. His younger brother Giovansimone was causing their father serious difficulty. Two letters, both of June 1509, tell some of the story:

Most revered father – I learn from your last how things are going at home and how Giovansimone is behaving. I have not had, these ten years, worse news than on the evening I read your letter, because I thought I had arranged things for them in such a way that they were looking forward to setting up a good shop with the help I have promised them, and with this expectation were applying themselves to becoming proficient and to learning their trade, so as to be able to carry it on when the time came. Now I see that they are doing the contrary, and particularly Giovansimone, whence I realize that it is useless to help him. And if, on the day I received your letter, I had been able to, I would have mounted my horse and by this time have settled everything. But not being able to do this, I'm writing him the letter I think he deserves, and if from now on he does not mend his ways, or indeed if he takes so much as the value of a straw out of the house, or does anything else to displease you, I beg you to let me know, because I will try to get leave from the pope and will come home and show him the error of his ways.

I want you to realize that all the toil and sweat I have continually endured has been no less for your sake than for mine and that what I have bought, I have bought so that it might be yours as long as you live; because had it not been for you, I should not have bought it. Therefore, if you would like to let the house and lease the farm, do entirely as you choose; and with that income and with what I will give you, you can live like a gentleman, and if the summer were not approaching, as it is, I would tell you to do so now and to come and stay here with me. But it is not the season, for you would not long survive the summer here. I have thought of taking away the money he has for the shop, and giving it to Gismondo that he and Buonarroto together might do the best they can, and of your letting those houses and the farm at Pazolatica, and of your retiring, with that income and with the help I can give you in addition, to some place where you would be comfortable and could have someone to look after you, either in Florence or just outside, and leaving that ne'er-do-well to nurse his arse. Please think of your own interest and whatever course you pursue let it be of your own choosing, and in all that you do I'm willing to help you as far as I possibly can. Keep me informed. (C.1.66.)

Giovan Simone – It is said that if one treats a good man well, he becomes better, but a ne'er-do-well becomes worse. I have tried for some years now, by deeds and by kind words, to induce you to live virtuously and at peace with your father and with the rest of us; and yet you continually become worse. I do not say that you are a ne'er-do-well, but you behave in a way that no longer pleases me, either me, or the others. I could give you a long lecture on your behaviour, but it would be mere words to you, like the others I've given you. To be brief, I can tell you one thing for certain – that you possess nothing in this world; both your expenses and the roof over your head I provide for you, and have provided for some time now, for the love of God, believing you to be my brother like the others. Now I'm certain you are not my brother, because if you were, you would not threaten my father. On the contrary, you are a brute, and as a brute I shall treat you. For your information, he who thinks fit to threaten or to strike his father is held to hazard his life. But enough – I tell you you possess nothing in this world. And if I hear the least little thing about you, I will ride post to Florence and show you the error of your ways and teach you to destroy your own belongings and to set fire to houses and farms you have [not] earned for yourself. You are not in the position you think. If I do come home, I will give you cause to weep scalding tears, and you will learn what grounds you have for your presumption.

I tell you once again that if you mean to behave and to honour and revere your father, I will help you like the others, and in a little while will arrange for you to set up a good shop. If you do not do so, I will come and arrange your affairs in such a way that you will know what you are better than you have ever known it, and will realize what you do possess in this world, and will be aware of it wherever you go. What I lack in words, I will make up for in deeds.

[PS.] I cannot help but write you another couple of lines to this effect – for twelve years now I have gone about all over Italy, leading a miserable life; I have borne every kind of humiliation, suffered every kind of hardship, worn myself to the bone with every kind of labour, risked my very life in a thousand dangers, solely to help my family; and now, when I begin to raise it up a little, you alone must be the one to confound and destroy in one hour what I have accomplished during so many years and with such pains. By the Body of Christ, to prevent this I am ready to confound, if need be, ten thousand such as you. So behave yourself and do not provoke those who have enough else to bear. (C.1.67.)

Such a letter should have been enough to make any errant brother more circumspect; it worked in the short run but does not seem to have had much effect in the long run. The reference to setting fire to houses and farms should not be taken to mean that he was an arsonist, but that by some imprudence he was burning up the family resources. Lodovico was also worried about a lawsuit brought by his widowed sister-in-law for the recovery of her dowry, which eventually she won. By 15 September 1509 things had looked up somewhat; Michelangelo told his father:

I have given Giovanni Balducci here in Rome 350 broad ducats in gold, payable to you in Florence.... When you receive them take them to the *Spedalingo* and get him to enter them as you remember he entered the others for me....

Make the most of life and let your possessions go rather than fret about them; because I would rather have you alive though poor than you dead and all the gold in the world. (C. I.68.)

Balducci was Michelangelo's banker in Rome, and a close friend. The *Spedalingo* was an official of the Hospital of Sta Maria Nuova in Florence who was responsible for the foundation's property and, as part of the Hospital's charitable functions, served as a banker for the deposit of funds and as an adviser on the purchase of property. As the recipient of numerous bequests, the Hospital was particularly careful about the legal accuracy of the title of properties, and land bought through the *Spedalingo* was a better investment because it was safer.

This was the second payment for the Ceiling. It is only known what Michelangelo transmitted, not what he was actually paid. He wrote to his brother Buonarroto on 17 November 1509:

I am informed by your last that Lorenzo will be passing through Rome and that you want me to entertain him. I don't think you realize how I am living here. However, I must forgive you for that. I will do what I can. As to Gismondo, I learn that he is coming here to expedite his affairs. Tell him from me not to place any reliance on me, not because I do not love him as a brother, but because I cannot help him in any way. I am obliged to care for myself before others, and I cannot supply my own necessities. I am living here in a state of great anxiety and of the greatest physical fatigue; I have no friends of any sort and want none. I haven't even time enough to eat as I should. So you mustn't bother me with anything else, for I could not bear another thing.

As to the shop, I urge you to be diligent. I'm pleased that Giovansimone is beginning to do well. (C. I.70.)

Lorenzo was Lorenzo Strozzi, Buonarroto's employer; Gismondo was his middle brother. Giovansimone appears to have somewhat mended his ways. There is then a long gap, since his next letter is probably of July 1510, also to Buonarroto.

I learn from your last that you are all well and that Lodovico has been offered another appointment. I am pleased about all this and urge him to accept, if it is so arranged that he can afterwards return to his post in Florence. Here I'm working as usual and will have finished my painting by the end of next week, that is to say, the part I began, and when I have uncovered it, I think I shall receive payment and will try to get leave to come home for a month. I do not know what will ensue, but I need it, because I'm not very well. I have no time to write more. I will let you know what ensues. (C. I.74.)

Their father's appointment was as *podestà* at S. Casciano, near Florence. Michelangelo wrote to him.

I had a letter of yours this morning, the fifth day of September, which distressed me and continues to distress me very much, learning as I do that Buonarroto is ill. I beg you, as soon as you get this, to let me know how he is, because if he's really ill I could ride post to Florence this coming week, although it might mean a great loss to me. This is because the five hundred ducats I've earned in accordance with the agreement are due to me, and as much again which the pope has to give me to put the rest of the work in hand. But he has gone away and has left me no instructions, so that I find myself without any money and do not know what I ought to do. I do not want him to be angry if I were to leave, and to lose my due, but to remain is hard. I've written him a letter and await a reply. However, if Buonarroto is in danger, let me know, because I'll leave everything. Make good provision that he may not lack for money to help him. Go to Sta Maria to the *Spedalingo*, and show him my letter, if he doesn't believe you, and get him to give you fifty or a hundred ducats, whichever you want, and have no scruples. Don't worry, for God has not created us in order to abandon us. Reply at once and let me know definitely whether I must come or not. (C.1.75.)

The pope had gone to Bologna, and in order to get his five hundred ducats Michelangelo had to follow. He did so in September 1510, stopping in Florence on the way. This unexpected visit provoked an unhappy row with the father he loved and trusted. In order to provide himself with sufficient money to cut some sort of figure on taking up his appointment at S. Casciano, Lodovico had dipped into Michelangelo's account on the strength of the permission given him in the letter about Buonarroto's illness. Between them he and Buonarroto helped themselves to 250 ducats. Lodovico's letter excusing himself makes painful reading:

... but I took it in the hope of being able to replace it before your return to Florence; I said to myself, seeing your last letter, 'Michelangelo won't return for six or eight months from now and in that time I shall have returned from S. Casciano.'... I will sell everything and will do everything to replace what I took. (C.1.77.)

Characteristically, Michelangelo eventually forgave him all but fifty ducats. He was back in Rome in October 1510, since he wrote to Buonarroto on the 26th with the information that he had received 500 papal ducats and was sending the equivalent of 450 Florentine broad gold ducats to Florence. So he was paid for what he had finished, but no provision had been made for work still to be done. On 23 November he wrote to Buonarroto:

I think in a few days' time I shall have to go back to Bologna, because the papal Datary, with whom I returned from Bologna, promised me when he left here that as soon as he reached Bologna he would make provision for me to continue the work. It is a month since he left, and as yet I have heard nothing. I will wait until the end of next week; then if there is no news, I think I will go to Bologna and will pass through Florence. (C.1.84.)

On 11 January 1511, he wrote to Buonarroto from Rome:

I arrived here safely on Tuesday evening, thank God. I have received the money which was promised by letter when I was in Florence. (C.1.81.)

Presumably the remaining work in the Sistine Chapel could now get under way. If he began any work in January 1511, it was probably on the cartoons for the lunettes (see his letter of December 1523); although many of them seem 110 to have been painted directly, almost freehand, on to the fresh *intonaco*.

The letter containing the words '.... will have finished my painting by the end of next week, that is to say, the part I began, and when I have uncovered it I shall receive payment', is datable to July 1510 only from the mention of Lodovico's impending appointment: these were usually made two months in advance. It has been argued on the strength of these words that Michelangelo had reached the half-way point in the Ceiling, and that the difficulties in the way of his journey to his sick brother's bedside, mentioned in the second letter, refer to the starting of the second half of the Ceiling – the part over the presbytery.

63

On the other hand, Condivi says positively that Michelangelo painted the Ceiling in twenty months, and allowing for the two months of each winter when fresco painting usually stopped, the twenty months (that is, two years) have now elapsed. But Michelangelo, who was his informant on these things, can be seen from his own letter to his father of 27 January 1509 not to have been particularly accurate in matters of timing. In the letter of December 1523, Michelangelo says:

When the vault was nearly finished the pope returned to Bologna; whereupon I went there twice for money that was owed to me, but effected nothing and wasted all that time until he returned to Rome. (C.3.594.)

The pope did not return to Rome until June 1511. In his diary for 14 and 15 August 1511, Paris de Grassis wrote:

The pope on the vigil and day of the Assumption . . . was present at vespers and Mass in the principal Palatine [Sistine] Chapel to celebrate the feast, this chapel being dedicated to the Assumption, and to it the pope came to see the newly uncovered pictures, as well as being led by devotion. (T.2.235.)

Vasari says:

When the work was half finished, the pope who had subsequently gone to inspect it several times (being helped up the ladders by Michelangelo) wanted it to be thrown open to the public. Being hasty and impatient by nature, he simply could not bear to wait until it was perfect and had, so to speak, received the final touch. As soon as it was thrown open, the whole of Rome flocked to see it; and the pope was the first, not having the patience to wait until the dust had settled after the dismantling of the scaffolding. Raphael of Urbino (who had great powers of imitation) changed his style as soon as he had seen Michelangelo's work and straight away, to show his skill, painted the prophets and sibyls of Sta Maria della Pace. (V2.7.176.)

Woodcut of Raphael in Vasari's 1568 *Lives*, after the self-portrait in the *School of Athens* in the Vatican.

It is true that Raphael's style changed after the Sistine Ceiling became visible, and his frescoes in Sta Maria della Pace date from about 1512. They formed one of the ingredients of Michelangelo's sour claim: 'All he knows he learned from me.' Vasari goes on to say that Bramante tried to get the rest of the Chapel for Raphael, but that Michelangelo circumvented this by complaining to the pope, disclosing Bramante's defective workmanship and what he calls 'many faults in his life'. The chain of probabilities which can be deduced is that the central part of the Ceiling, together with the pendentives and the spandrels, was all finished by the time Michelangelo wrote, probably in July 1510, that he would finish 'the part he began' by the end of the week. The inference to be drawn, therefore, from Vasari's statement is that *fino alla metà*, 'half finished' (Michelangelo's 'nearly finished'), means the Ceiling but not the lunettes. This would be confirmed by the story that Bramante tried to get the rest of the Chapel for Raphael: it is highly improbable that anyone would have contemplated changing artists half-way across the Ceiling. The account in Vasari of the pope going up the scaffolding perhaps means that only part of the floor of the scaffolding was taken out, so that the paintings were visible from the floor of the Chapel. There is in any case, evidence that the scaffolding, or a large part of it, was still in place in 1512. The argument that only the half-way point of the Ceiling had been reached in August 1511 would mean that all the rest, with the pendentives and spandrels, and the lunettes, had to be finished by 31 October 1512: surely an impossible assignment.

In June 1511, Michelangelo wrote to his father, who had returned from S. Casciano:

A few days ago I sent you 100 ducats from those I had put aside here for my living and working expenses ... have them put to my account like the rest. This leaves me 80 ducats here, which I think will last me four months, and I still have six months' work to do here before I am due to have any money from the pope, so I am certain to be short ... by 50 ducats. I therefore beg you, out of the 100 ducats you have promised to repay me, that you will pay 50; the balance you may keep on condition that ... you will have them ready within four months as I shall need them here. The hundred I sent you I want to try to save to return to the heirs of the Cardinal of Siena, for you are aware that ... money ... is owed to them. Would you in any case look into the question of buying a farm ... since, when my painting here is finished, I still have 1000 ducats due me from the pope and ... I hope to be paid in full. (C.1.86.)

A footnote to the letter in Lodovico's hand says: 'He gave me the money.' The sum due to the heirs of the Cardinal of Siena is because, when he received the commission for the Piccolomini Chapel in Siena in 1501, he was paid 100 ducats on account, but he hardly executed any of the statues, most of them being done apparently by Baccio da Montelupo.

He sent his father 300 ducats in October 1511 out of 400 he had received, with instructions to remind the *Spedalingo* about buying the farm, and on 10 January 1512 he replied to Buonarroto about a project whereby his brother would accept a loan from a man, together with the man's daughter as a wife. He cautioned his brother with the jaundiced words: 'I do not like your getting involved through avarice with men much more unscrupulous than yourself,' pointing out that the loan might not materialize but that he would certainly be saddled with the wife (C.1.91). More letters followed about the farm project, until in April 1512 he wrote to his father, 'I reckon I shall have finished here within two months and then I will come home.' The farm La Loggia, at Sto Stefano in Pane, near Settignano, was bought on 28 May.

In July 1512 Alfonso d'Este, Duke of Ferrara, came to Rome to make his peace with Julius II (who certainly would not have forgotten the duke's part in the destruction of the statue of himself in Bologna). Alfonso was changing sides in the continually fluid state of papal alliances; also his young nephew Federigo Gonzaga, son of his sister Isabella d'Este, Duchess of Mantua, was then a hostage at the papal court for the political good behaviour of Mantua. The agent of Isabella d'Este in Rome wrote to her in a dispatch sent between 4 and 19 July 1512:

The duke came to the palace with his gentlemen ... and later dined in the papal chamber. His Excellency greatly wished to see the vault of the large chapel which Michelangelo was painting, and Signor Federigo ... arranged for someone to be sent to ask on the pope's behalf, and the duke went up to the vault with several persons who came down one by one, and the duke remained up there with Michelangelo and could not look long enough at those figures, and they pleased him so much that His Excellency desired him to paint a picture for him, and talked to him and offered him money, and he has promised to do it for him ... After the duke had come down I wanted to take him to see the pope's room and those which Raphael is painting, but he didn't want to go. (T.2.243.)

The phrase 'went up to the vault with several persons' can only mean that as late as July 1512 the scaffolding was still in place. Nothing came of the projected commission at the time, but much later, when Michelangelo was in Ferrara in 1529, the idea must have been revived, for a cartoon for a *Leda* was made, which he did not paint himself, but which is known from a copy in the National Gallery, London.

It has always been accepted that the lunettes surrounding the windows were painted after the rest of the Ceiling was finished. They provide a fascinating

77

180–7

transition to what he later achieved in the *Last Judgment* and the Cappella Paolina. On 24 July 1512 he wrote to Buonarroto:

I shall be home in September. . . . I work harder than anyone who ever lived. I am not well and worn out with this stupendous labour and yet I am patient in order to achieve the desired end. (c.1.100.)

But he was always optimistic about the time he needed to finish. In August, Florence was thrown into a turmoil by the terrible Sack of Prato by the Spanish troops, and in September he authorized his father to draw on his account for any money they needed to escape from the Spanish onslaught which was hourly expected.

I warn you that I haven't a *grosso* myself and am, so to speak, barefoot and naked and I cannot have the balance that is owed to me until the work is completed. (c.1.103.)

In October he wrote rather as a Job's comforter that they should

. . . be satisfied that you have bread to eat and can live at peace with Christ and poorly as I do here. For I lead a miserable existence and reck not of life nor honour – that is of this world; I live wearied by stupendous labours and beset by a thousand anxieties. And thus have I lived for some fifteen years now and never an hour's happiness have I had, and all this have I done in order to help you, though you have never either recognized or believed it – God forgive us all. I am prepared always to do the same as long as I live, provided I am able. (c.1.107.)

The final record comes in the diary of Paris de Grassis for the vigil of All Saints, 31 October 1512, with the laconic entry:

Today, for the first time, our chapel is open, the painting being finished, since for three or four years a roof or vault has always been its roof, covering it completely from the rays of the sun. (sk.2.735.)

Nowhere, incidentally, does the dry papal chamberlain ever mention the artist's name. Vasari has a very interesting description of the physical endurance required for the painting:

He executed the frescoes in great discomfort, having to work with his face looking upwards, which impaired his sight so badly that he could not read or look at drawings save with his head turned backwards; and this lasted for several months afterwards. I can talk from personal experience about this, since I painted five rooms in the great apartments of Duke Cosimo's palace; if I had not made a chair where I could rest my head and relax from time to time I would never have finished. Even so, this work so ruined my sight and injured my head that I

Michelangelo wrote in October 1512: 'Dearest father – I learnt from your last letter that you've returned the forty ducats to the *Spedalingo*. You've done rightly, but should you hear that this is risky, please let me know of it. I have finished the chapel I have been painting; the pope is very well satisfied. But other things have not turned out for me as I'd hoped. For this I blame the times, which are very unfavourable to our art. I shall not be home for All Saints, because I have not the means to do what I want to do, but again this is not the time for it. Make the most of life and don't bother yourself about anything else. That's all.' (c.1.104.)

still feel the effects, and I am astonished that Michelangelo bore all that discomfort so well. In fact, every day the work moved him to greater enthusiasm, and he was so spurred on by his own progress that he felt no fatigue and ignored all the discomfort. . . .

When the work was thrown open, the whole world came running to see what Michelangelo had done; and certainly it was such as to make everyone speechless with astonishment. Then the pope, exalted by the results and encouraged to undertake even more grandiose enterprises, generously rewarded Michelangelo with rich gifts and money. (v2.7.178,186.)

Hardly the story the letters tell, particularly about the money. Both biographers tell the strange anecdote about the pope losing his temper with Michelangelo because of the delays in execution, finally striking him because he wanted to go home to Florence for a public holiday, and then pacifying the furious painter, who was at the point of flight, with a sweetener of 500 ducats, brought to him by an envoy who assured him that blows were no more than a mark of the pope's affection.

Perhaps the best of the last words is Michelangelo's, written in verse to an unknown Giovanni in Pistoia, with a comic sketch: 75

> I've got myself a goitre from the strain
> As water gives the cats in Lombardy,
> Or maybe it's in some other country.
> My stomach's pushed by force beneath my chin,
> My beard towards Heaven, and my brain I feel
> Is shoved upon my nape, and my breast is like a Harpy,
> And the brush, ever over my face
> Makes a rich pavement with its droppings.
> My loins have penetrated to my paunch
> And as a counterpoise my bottom is a crupper,
> And with unseeing eyes my steps I take.
> In front of me my skin is stretched
> And to bend it, folds itself behind
> And stretches like a Syrian bow.
> Thus, wrongheaded and strange
> Emerge the judgments that the mind brings forth,
> In that no good shot comes from a crooked gun.
> My painting, when I'm dead, defend it Giovanni,
> And my honour too, since I am not in a good place,
> And am not a painter either. (MR.5.)

When Julius II sat on the papal throne in the Sistine Chapel on All Saints' Day 1512 and looked up at the Ceiling which was to become his only monument completed in his lifetime, he knew that his strength was failing and that he would never live to achieve the liberation of Italy from foreign invaders. In fact, the accomplishment of his vision of an Italy free from foreign occupation took nearly another three and a half centuries.

By Christmas he was ill, tormented by sleepnessness and unable to eat through worry, and in the first days of January 1513 he told Paris de Grassis that he knew he was dying. On the night of 20/21 February he closed his eyes.

When he was approaching death he ordered that the tomb which Michelangelo had begun should be finished for him, giving this charge to the old Cardinal Santiquattro and to his nephew Cardinal Aginense. They, however, had [Michelangelo] make a new design, believing   86 that the first undertaking was too large. Thus Michelangelo once again became involved with the Tragedy of the Tomb, which had no better success than the first time: on the contrary much worse, for it brought him infinite trouble, unhappiness and distress; and what is worse, by the malice of certain men, shame, from which he was hardly able to clear himself for many years. Michelangelo then began work again, bringing a number of masters from Florence, and Bernardo Bini, the treasurer, paid out money as it was required. (AC. 56.)

Cardinal Santiquattro was the man who has already appeared in the history of Michelangelo's tribulations as the Datary, Lorenzo Pucci, raised to the purple by Julius' successor, Leo X, in 1513. Cardinal Aginense, Bishop of Agen, was Julius' cousin (not nephew), Leonardo Grosso della Rovere.

The new contract concluded on 6 May 1513 is the usual very long Latin notarial document, full of 'aforesaids', but there are also two extra documents; one, an Italian translation prepared by the notary and copied by Michelangelo, which suggests that he had no Latin, and the other a statement in which Michelangelo describes, giving measurements, the monument as it was now envisaged. The contract itself names the executors and repeats the gist of Julius' will, which required the execution of his tomb by the 'honourable man Master Michelangelo, Florentine sculptor' and specifies that he is not to take on other important work which would impede the making of the tomb to which he is to give continuous attention, and finish in seven years according to the design and model. The payment is to be 16,500 gold papal ducats, to be paid in instalments, and Michelangelo acknowledges that he has already received 3500 out of the 10,500 ducats which Julius left for the purpose.

The other document is far more interesting.

Be it known to all persons that I, Michelangelo, Florentine sculptor, am charged to make the tomb of Pope Julius in marble by Cardinal Aginense and the Datary who are, after his death, his successors in this work, for 16,500 gold chamber ducats, and the composition of the said sepulchre is to be in this form, that is:

86   A composition to be seen from three sides, the fourth side to be fixed to the wall and not to be seen. The front, that is the head of this composition, is to be 20 palms wide and 14 high, and the other two sides which go towards the wall where this composition is to be fixed are to be 35 palms long and also 14 high, and on each of these three faces are to be two niches which are to rest upon a plinth which will surround the said composition, and with its adornments of pilasters, architrave, frieze and cornice, as is seen from a small wooden model.

In each of the said six niches are to be two figures larger by about a palm than life-size, which makes twelve figures, and in front of each pilaster which is between the niches is to be a figure of similar size; which is twelve pilasters; and therefore twelve figures; and on the upper level of this composition is to be a coffer with four feet, as may be seen from the model, on which is to be the said Pope Julius with his head between two figures who hold him suspended and with his feet between two others; which is five figures on the coffer, all five larger than life-size, almost twice life size. Around the said coffer are six blocks on which are to be six figures of similar size, all six seated; then on the same level as are these six figures, above the side of the sepulchre which is fixed to the wall, is to be raised a *cappelletta* [shrine] which is to be 35 palms high, in which are to be five figures larger than all the others since they are further from the eye. Also there are to be three narratives either in marble or bronze, as shall please the aforementioned successors, in each face of the said sepulchre between one niche and another, as may be seen in the model. And the said sepulchre I undertake to finish all at my own cost with the above mentioned payment, executing it in such fashion as shall appear in the contract in seven years, and if after seven years any part of the said sepulchre remains unfinished, there shall be allowed to me by the said successors as much time as is necessary to do whatever remains, since I cannot do otherwise. (M. 536.)

According to the measurements given in this annexe to the 1513 contract, and taking the Roman palm at its present computation of 0.224 m, that is 8.82 in., the tomb would have been about 10½ ft (3.1m) high to the cornice, 14½ ft (4.5m) wide across the front, and 26 ft (7.8m) deep; and the *cappelletta* rising from the structure would have been a further 26 ft (7.8 m) high. The number of figures remains forty, as in the original project. Only their disposition has changed, and the internal tomb-cell has disappeared. It had also been decided, though this is not in the contract, that the tomb would no longer be sited in St Peter's. Julius did receive the customary burial there, but Michelangelo's monument was eventually placed in S. Pietro in Vincoli, Julius's titular church as a cardinal.

The 1513 project was still vast and impracticable. A drawing exists, copied from a damaged original, which gives some idea of what it was to be like, though it still leaves a lot of questions unanswered; and a drawing by Michelangelo for one of the putti in the Sistine Ceiling has dotted around the rest of the sheet a number of tiny sketches for ideas he had for some of the *Slaves*. Of these *Slaves*, Michelangelo made two (those now in the Louvre) and roughed out a number of the others at a later date. He also carved the *Moses*, which is the only figure from this period which is actually part of the tomb. He worked unremittingly on the commission from 1513 to early in 1516, and transferred his workshop from near St Peter's to new premises in the Macel de' Corvi, a narrow street near the Capitoline Hill, which he occupied until his death.

On 5 November 1512 he wrote to his father:

Also I should be glad if you would see whether there is some lad in Florence, the son of poor but honest people, who is used to roughing it, and would be prepared to come here to serve me and do all the things connected with the house, such as the shopping and running errands when necessary, and who in his spare time would be able to learn. If you find anyone, let me know, because here only rascals are to be found, and I have great need of someone. (C.1.110).

In February 1513 he wrote again:

As to the lad who came here, ... besides all my other worries I've now got this dunghill of a boy. ... I need to be looked after. If he is not disposed to do it, they should not have put me to this expense ... but they are good for nothing. ... Please will you have him removed out of my sight, because I am so disgusted that I can bear no more. ... Although I dismissed him the second day and on several other occasions, he did not credit it. (C.1.115.)

Michelangelo was harassed because his apprentice Silvio Falcone was very ill, and the boy from Florence apparently only wanted to work in the studio and would do nothing in the house. But as a postscript to the same letter of angry complaint he wrote more gently:

If you speak to the boy's father, tell him kindly about the affair; say that he is a good lad but he is too refined and not suited to my service, and that he must send for him. (C.1.115)

It appears also that Buonarroto must have visited him in Rome, and an indiscretion of his resulted in a blistering letter of 30 July 1513. Michelangelo was now employing a stonecutter, probably from Settignano, called Michele, who passed on a bit of gossip which enraged him.

The said Michele tells me that you informed him that you had spent some sixty ducats at Settignano. I remember that at table here you also told me that you had spent many ducats of your own. I pretended not to understand you and was not at all surprised, knowing you. I suppose you wrote them down and kept account of them, so as to be able some day to ask for them back. And I should like to know from Your Ingratitude with what capital you were enabled to earn them. Another thing I should like to know is whether you kept account of those two hundred and twenty-eight ducats of mine you all borrowed from Sta Maria Nuova and of the many other hundreds I spent on the house and on the family, and of the discomforts

Detail from Bufalini's 1551 map of Rome. At the bottom of the Capitoline hill is the Macel de' Corvi (*Macellum Corvorum*, Market of the Crows), where Michelangelo lived and died and had his workshop. It was destroyed in 1885 when the monument to Vittorio Emanuele II was built.

'Signature' of a letter written in 1544 to Luigi del Riccio, one of many in which he endeavours to rally his friend after the death of Cecchino de' Bracci (see p. 174), with a jesting form of his address in the Macel de' Corvi.

and of the miseries I have endured in order to help you. I should like to know if you have kept account of them. If you had the intelligence to realize the true state of affairs, you would not have said 'I have spent so and so of mine,' nor would you have come here to urge me about your affairs, seeing how I have always behaved towards you in the past. Instead, you would have said, 'Michelangelo is aware of what he wrote to us, and if he has not now done as he said, there must be something to hinder him, which we do not know about,' and would have been patient. For it does no good to spur on a horse that is going as fast and faster than it can. But you have never known me and do not know me. God forgive you, for through His grace I have been able to bear what I bear, or rather have borne, that you might be helped. But you will know it, when you haven't got me.

I must tell you that I do not think I shall be able to come home this September, because I'm being pressed in such a way that I haven't time to eat.(C.1.108.)

His state of mind can hardly have been improved by an anonymous letter which he received in November 1513, from someone who knew him well enough to address him with the familiar *tu*, and who began his letter:

My very dear Michelangelo.... Moved by the love I have always had for you as a son, I have decided to write to you these lines of which you will grasp the meaning. During the last while I have often talked to Buonarroto and some of your other brothers, and I have heard from them that with some money of yours you were negotiating to open a shop for them, which they are recommending to you; but since then, by a strange chance, I have heard that the mind and intention of one of your brothers is that they intend, if you open the shop for them, that you will never see either its profits nor the capital; and I am positive that they will succeed, because the means are never lacking to those who intend wrong. ... I do not, because of this, say that you ought not to do good to your brothers and your father, and I know that up to now you have done a great deal for them; but as you know, you have arranged that it is possible to help and enjoy the proceeds but not diminish the capital, and it is now possible, because in houses, property and the *Monte* [loan institute] it is not possible to dip one's fingers. ... I beg you not to show this letter to anyone. ... Understand that I do not do it to create ill will between you and your brothers, but I should have been very upset had you found yourself cheated by your brothers. ... But you can buy property ... for your father and you will have an excuse for your brothers so that they can't complain if you don't open a shop for them, and would be sure that your money, which I know you earn with so much effort, would not be frittered away. (C.1.111.)

Michelangelo did set his brothers Buonarroto and Gismondo up in a business, probably in the wool trade; but it eventually failed.

His next letter to his marble supplier in Carrara is dated in late August, possibly September, 1513, and is angrily to the point:

Baldassare – I am greatly surprised by you, since you wrote to me a long time ago that you had available a number of blocks of marble, and having had so many months of lovely weather suitable for navigation, having had from me 100 gold ducats, and there being nothing more needed, I have no idea why you don't supply me. I beg you immediately to load these marbles which you told me you had ready, and come with them the sooner the better. I will wait for you all this month; after which we will proceed by such paths as we will be advised upon by those who are more in charge of these matters than I am. I merely remind you that you do wrong not to keep faith and to break with those who are useful to you. (C.1.109.)

A letter written from Florence some five years later, in about May 1518, provides an interesting sidelight on one of Michelangelo's small tribulations, as well as giving a date for one of the *Slaves*. It was written to one of the chief magistrates of Cortona, and concerns the painter Luca Signorelli.

Lord Captain – When I was in Rome during the first year of Pope Leo, there arrived there Maestro Luca da Cortona, the painter, whom I met one day near Monte Giordano. He told me that he had come to request something of the pope, I don't remember what, and that he had once nearly had his head cut off in the Medici cause and that this seemed to him, so to speak, not to have received recognition. He told me other things in the same vein, which I don't recall. And to crown these arguments, he asked me for forty julians and indicated to me where I should send them, that is, to the shop of a shoemaker, where I believe he was lodging. And I, not having the money on me, offered to send it to him and this I did. As soon as I got home I sent him the said forty julians by an assistant of mine called, or rather named, Silvio, who is now in Rome, I believe. Then a few days later the said Maestro Luca, who had perhaps not succeeded with his project, came to my house in the Macello de' Corvi, the house which I still have to-day, and found that I was working on a marble figure – upright, four *braccia* in height, which has the arms behind. He grumbled away to me and asked me for another forty julians, because he said he wanted to leave Rome. I went upstairs to my room and fetched the forty julians for him, a Bolognese servant who was in my service being present, and I think the aforesaid assistant who had taken him the others, was also there. He took the said money and went with God. I have never seen him since. But as I was ill at the time, I complained about not being able to work, and he said to me, 'Doubt not but that Angels will come from heaven and take you by the hand and aid you.'

I'm writing to you about this, because if the said things were repeated to the said Maestro Luca, he would remember and not say he had repaid me.

[Only a fragment of the rest of the letter remains, but its substance is as follows:]

Your lordship wrote and told Buonarroto that he says he repaid them and you believe that he did. This is not true. You call me an arrant rascal, and so I should be, if I sought repayment of what I had already had. Your lordship may think what you like. They are owed to me, and this I swear. If you wish to do me justice, you can do so. (C.2.285.)

In 1515, when Michelangelo was still working hard on the monument, the political state of Italy reduced Julius II's heirs, and above all his nephew Francesco della Rovere, Duke of Urbino, from grandeur to penury. The Duke of Urbino sided with Leo X's enemies, the French (for Leo had continued his predecessor's anti-French policy), and as a result of a patched-up treaty between the French and the papacy he was deprived of his territories, which were not his private possession but were a fief held from the papacy, and became a refugee in Mantua. The duchy of Urbino was conferred upon Lorenzo de' Medici, the pope's nephew.

Leo showed no interest in furthering the project of his predecessor's tomb on anything like its original scale. Michelangelo nevertheless continued work on it for quite a while, for, as he wrote to his brother Buonarroto on 3 November 1515:

You ask me for money and say that things are now settling down and that trade is beginning to recover. . . . As to the money I cannot do anything about it, because I have another two years' work to do before I'm square with these people, as I've had so much money. So accommodate yourself to the times. . . . I have had to write to you about these matters, because, understanding them in this way, I feel obliged to do so. I'm well aware you'll make mock of it. (C.1.143.)

He had had about 1000 ducats between May and October 1515 on account, but since he had to pay for marble and for workmen as well as to live, he was disinclined to put his hand in his pocket once again for his brother. Furthermore, once the duke was dispossessed, the fund for the Tomb would eventually dry up.

A new contract was negotiated between Michelangelo and the executors, and signed on 8 July 1516, and it is plain that the proposal for a monument on a reduced scale came from the cardinals and not from him. The document can

84

Reconstruction by Charles de Tolnay of the Julius Tomb 1516 project. The *Moses* is shown on the upper level on the left, the place for which it was originally designed, and two of the *Slaves*, now in Paris, are in front of the herms in the lower range. The dead pope, upheld by angels, was to be surmounted by a group of the *Virgin and Child*. A bronze relief was projected for the space below, and figures were to be placed in the round-headed niches on either side. The design at this stage still incorporated return bays on either side. Compare p.97.

71

be paraphrased as follows: Michelangelo and the cardinals agree that the old contract shall be null and void; except that Michelangelo may not undertake any work of great importance which could prevent the execution of the work, which he promises to prosecute with vigour. He also undertakes to finish the Tomb in nine years, starting from the original date of 6 May 1513, according to a new model and design which he has made. This model (Oh! that it had survived!) is described in insertions in both the Latin and the Italian documents, and is identical in both of them.

Two new clauses appear, however: one, that Michelangelo should enjoy rent free the house in the Macel de' Corvi; and the other, that since he had been, and still was, unwell, he might execute the work wherever he chose – Florence, Pisa or Carrara are specifically mentioned – without prejudice to his possession of the house in Rome (where most of the executed parts of the Tomb were stored). The description reveals that twenty of the forty figures have been abandoned. The tomb was still to stand clear of the wall, though the returns at the sides were to be of one bay only.

After the signing he went to Florence and then on to Carrara, in order to quarry marble for the Tomb. In September he was still in Carrara, for he wrote to his father saying:

As to my affairs here, as yet I have done nothing. I've begun quarrying in many places and I hope, if it remains fine, to have all my marbles ready within two months. Then I shall decide whether to work them here or in Pisa, or I shall go to Rome. I would gladly have stayed here to work them, but I have met with some unpleasantness, so that I should remain with some misgiving. (C.I.159).

The unpleasantness was possibly connected with rumours, which must have been rife in Carrara, that in future marble for work in Florence was going to be extracted from newly developed quarries in the hills above Pietrasanta, instead of coming from Carrara, where it was a monopoly of the Marquis. Up to now, Michelangelo had been on excellent terms with the Marquis, but the opening of new quarries in Florentine territory changed all that, and since, eventually, it was Michelangelo who exploited them, he got the blame. In fact, he was also later accused of undue partiality towards the interests of the Marquis – but these troubles were still in the future.

Michelangelo worked for seven popes; but his greatest patron was the second of them, Julius II, for whom he cast the great bronze statue that the pope's enemies destroyed in Bologna, painted the Ceiling of the Sistine Chapel, and designed the Tomb which haunted him for half his life. The portrait of the warrior pope by Raphael, in the *Mass of Bolsena* fresco in the Stanza d'Eliodoro in the Vatican, was painted in 1511–12, when Julius was wearing the beard which he had sworn not to shave until he had driven the French from Italy. Unhappily, he was still wearing it when he died in 1513.

The Sistine Chapel in the Vatican (below) was built by Pope Sixtus IV in 1473–80 and decorated in 1481–83 with frescoes by Cosimo Rosselli, Perugino, Botticelli and others of scenes from the lives of Christ and Moses. These are intended to link the Old and New Testaments and also to assert the authority of the papacy (as in *Christ Giving the Keys to St Peter*). The drawing (left) shows a reconstruction of the state of the Chapel in 1508, when Pope Julius II ordered Michelangelo to decorate the ceiling. The windows and frescoes on the altar wall were to make way in 1535 for Michelangelo's own *Last Judgment*. The presbytery screen is seen in its original position half-way along.

The Sistine Chapel

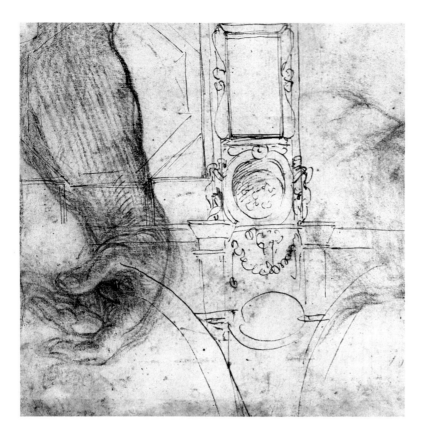

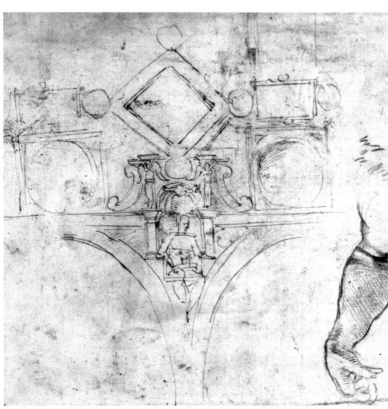

Michelangelo's first sketches for the framework in which the successive subjects are presented (left) are far simpler and more traditional than those he eventually painted. A poem of *c.*1512, which complains bitterly of the discomfort in which he worked, is adorned with a scribble (below) showing him at work on the scaffolding.

The Sistine Ceiling

The subject of the Sistine Ceiling fresco is the creation of the world, the fall, mankind's degradation by sin, the divine wrath of the deluge, and the preservation of Noah and his family. The Ceiling thus forms a thematic antecedent to the series on the walls. The subjects of the nine rectangular panels, flanked by seated nudes (*ignudi*), are as follows, reading from the altar wall (top):

1 God creating matter out of chaos.
2 God creating Sun and Moon; God creating vegetation.
3 God creating animals.
4 God creating Adam.
5 God creating Eve.
6 The temptation and expulsion from Eden.
7 The sacrifice of Noah after the deluge.
8 The deluge.
9 The drunkenness of Noah.

Michelangelo worked in reverse order, probably starting with the Deluge (which is placed out of sequence in order to allow it a full-sized panel). In the spandrels above the windows are Ancestors of Christ (Matthew 1); in the pendentives between them are seven Hebrew Prophets and five pagan Sibyls. There is a steady increase in the size of the ceiling figures, particularly after the half-way point, the Creation of Eve, where the scaffolding will have been partly removed to the second half of the chapel, enabling Michelangelo to see the effect from the ground.

The lunettes round the heads of the windows, showing more Ancestors of Christ, were painted after the rest. They have wonderful patches of shot-colour unexpected in Michelangelo. The lunette with Matthan, seen (right) before and after its recent cleaning, shows that the colours are much brighter than was formerly thought.

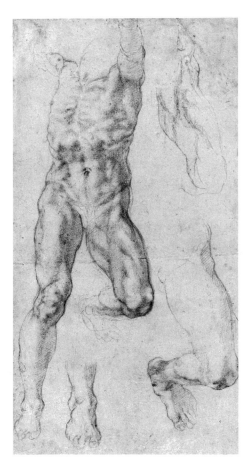

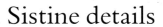

Sistine details

Michelangelo's surviving drawings for the Sistine Ceiling include magnificent male nude studies for the Execution of Haman, in the left-hand double spandrel of the altar wall (left, above), and for the Libyan Sibyl (above and right). The anonymous drawing (left, below) shows the top part of the altar wall, with Jonah in the centre, the Execution of Haman on the left, Moses and the Brazen Serpent on the right, and, below, the two Michelangelo lunettes of Ancestors of Christ which were destroyed when Sebastiano del Piombo first prepared the wall for the *Last Judgment*.

Buried and Risen

The tempera painting of the *Entombment* (left), probably begun about 1500 but never finished, is almost certainly by Michelangelo: the figure of Christ is derived from the *Pietà* in St Peter's, and there exists a drawing for the woman on the left. The *Risen Christ* (below) is believed to have been drawn for the Sistine altarpiece projected in 1512 by Julius II. Its nudity, although founded on scripture ('Then arose Peter, and ran unto the sepulchre; and stooping down, he beheld the linen clothes laid by themselves', Luke 24.12), was bound to give offence in some quarters; as did the nudity of the marble *Risen Christ* which Michelangelo made a decade later. The first version was abandoned because of a flaw in the marble, and the statue which he eventually produced in 1519–20 was 'finished' by his shifty and unreliable assistant Urbano. For many years the work, which stands in Sta Maria sopra Minerva in Rome, wore an unsightly metal loincloth.

The Antique

Michelangelo's debt to antiquity is both clear and subtle. An early *Cupid* was virtually a fake antique; other early works such as the *Battle of the Centaurs* are evident attempts to emulate the work of the ancients. Michelangelo was present when the *Laocoön* was unearthed in 1506; he was

influenced more by its expression of powerful emotion than by its formal elements. On the other hand, the *Medici Madonna* of 1524–33 (far left) adopts in reverse the pose of a classical *Muse* which he probably saw in Venice in 1494 or, more likely, 1529 (near left, below). The crossed legs are unique among his female figures. A woman in the Roboam and Abia lunette, among the Ancestors of Christ in the Sistine Chapel (below), is clearly derived from one of the spandrels of the Arch of Septimius Severus in Rome (near left).

Slaves

On the lower level of the vast tomb for Pope Julius II, on which Michelangelo was working in the three years which followed the pope's death in 1513, there was to stand a row of *Slaves*. As so often with Michelangelo's work, the symbolism is a matter of dispute. It has been suggested that they represent the Arts, over which the pope holds sway. Vasari suggests that they are the rebellious provinces which Julius reduced to obedience in his campaigns; but he had not done so when the Tomb was first projected in 1506. However, the theme of this overweening monument was to have been one of triumph; and no Roman triumph, or triumphal arch, would have been complete without the figures of captives. They were there to reinforce the theme by contrast, however odd all this may sound in a memorial to a man of the Church. Two (below left and centre) were done by 1516, when Michelangelo was called away to start work on Leo X's projects in Florence. They remained in his Roman workshop until 1546, when he gave them to Roberto Strozzi, in whose palace he had stayed during an illness. Strozzi took them to France, and they are now in the Louvre. The other four *Slaves*, very different in conception, remain unfinished. They were begun in Florence in the 1520s, when Michelangelo was working on the Medici Chapel; but when successive contracts for the Julius Tomb changed its philosophical and iconographic themes they were abandoned in the Florentine workshop. After Michelangelo's death they were given to Duke Cosimo I, for whom Buontalenti installed them (right) in the artificial grotto of the Boboli Gardens; there they remained until 1908. They are superb object lessons in Michelangelo's technique in sculpture; but their unfinished aspect is accidental, not deliberate. Like the two early tondi for the Taddei and Pitti families, and also like the four figures on the sarcophagi in the Medici Chapel, they remained unfinished because Michelangelo was prevented from finishing them. Only in recent years has it been argued, thanks to Rodin, that Michelangelo deliberately left works unfinished for aesthetic reasons. The idea is not borne out by those works which, given the opportunity to complete them, he did bring to a high degree of finish.

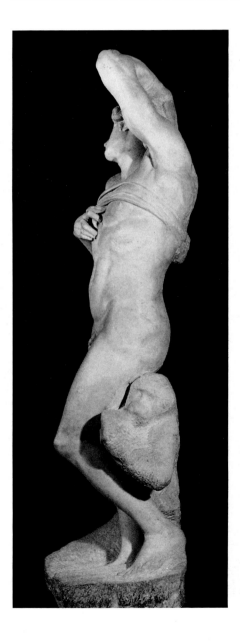

The Tomb of Julius II was commissioned by Julius himself in 1506. The vicissitudes of this project, which was gradually whittled down over the years, blighted Michelangelo's life so that he spoke of the 'Tragedy of the Tomb'. Successive popes, beginning with Julius himself, made it impossible for Michelangelo either to free himself from the project or to find the time necessary to complete it.

86

The Julius Tomb

Rocchetti's drawing of the 1513 project for the Julius Tomb (far left) shows the high *cappelletta* which was to surmount the Tomb, and which was modified into the superstructure of the final monument set up in S. Pietro in Vincoli over thirty years later (near left). The early project was to be as deep from front to back as the *cappelletta* is high (about 25 feet or 8 m). Sketches (far left and left, below) survive for the effigy of the pope upraised by angels, and for the

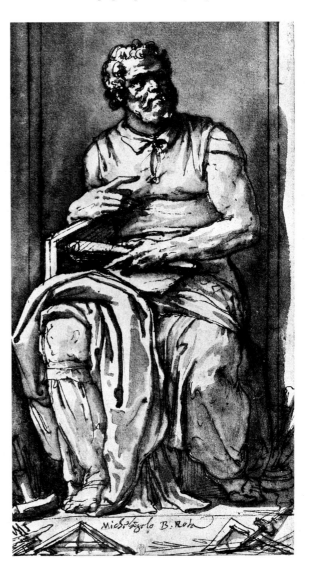

Slaves around the base. The massive seated figures were to be *Prophets*. Only one was carved, the awesome *Moses*, which has become identified with the personality of the artist himself; this was so in his own lifetime, as the contemporary caricature by Federico Zuccaro shows (below).

The *Moses* was originally planned to be seen on the right corner of the platform of the Julius Tomb, and would have been at least twelve feet above ground level. As Michelangelo's immense project dwindled, and as Julius himself receded into history, it came to be seen that the *Moses* itself was monument enough for any man, as well as apposite in its character to the life of the pope.

'And well may the Jews continue to go there (as they do every Sabbath, both men and women, like flocks of starlings), to visit and adore the statue, since they will be adoring something that is divine rather than human.' (Vasari 1568.)

In view of the First Commandment, 'adore' is certainly too strong a word, but the *Moses* may well have provoked amazed veneration.

PART THREE

S. LORENZO

1516–1534

ON 11 MARCH 1513 Cardinal Giovanni de' Medici, second son of Lorenzo il Magnifico, was elected pope in succession to Julius II, and took the name of Leo X. Giovanni de' Medici was the same age as Michelangelo: thirty-eight. He had enjoyed a position of great power under Julius II, who had reinstated Medici rule in Florence in 1512. He was the first Florentine to be elected pope; and the Florentines in Rome, and in their native city when the news arrived there some eleven hours later, went wild with joy. The streets re-echoed with cries of 'Palle, palle!' from the seven balls of the Medici arms.

In December 1515 Leo X held peace negotiations with Francis I of France in Bologna, and on his return journey to Rome he made an official entry into Florence. It is highly probable that the projects of creating a public monument which would mark the ascendancy of the Medici then entered his mind, and he appears to have decided on the completion of S. Lorenzo, the church rebuilt largely with Medici patronage by Brunelleschi from 1419 onwards. The bulk of the church and the monastery was complete, but the west front of the church was merely a crude brick wall which had stood for over fifty years awaiting a decorative façade.

A competition was organized, to which Giuliano da Sangallo (who was to die in 1516), Baccio d'Agnolo, architect to the cathedral, and the sculptor Jacopo Sansovino all submitted designs. It would appear, though the evidence is hazy, that Michelangelo was interested in the project – possibly because, after the rupture between the Duke of Urbino and Leo X, the Julius Tomb project was in doubt. There were few patrons able to provide commissions on the scale to which Michelangelo could work, and some continuity of patronage was essential to him.

On 13 October 1516, Baccio d'Agnolo sent on to him in Carrara a letter from an official in the Cancelleria in Rome, Domenico Buoninsegna, who was the Roman agent appointed by the Pope and his cousin Cardinal Giulio de' Medici for the project in Florence; his Florentine opposite number was the treasurer to the archbishop (at that time Cardinal Giulio), Bernardo Niccolini. Buoninsegna wrote to Baccio from Montefiascone, where the papal court was in residence.

I have spoken to the Cardinal about the façade, and he discussed it with the pope, and he will be happy to agree with you and Michelangelo. . . . it only remains for you and Michelangelo to talk to His Holiness . . . But it would be necessary for you to come to see him before the court returns to Rome, which will be a day or two before All Saints. And this I tell you, so that the friend you know about, and other friends of his, shall not be able to prevent it, because since that friend is not here, it can be more easily concluded. . . . And so far as concerns the money assigned for the matter, know that it will not be lacking, because already there is a large sum put aside which is not being touched and which is saved for this. And I have also said that you could take the marble upon yourself, and this is agreeable; and therefore let Michelangelo know immediately and decide about it and answer quickly. And if you come, find some pretext, so that it shan't look as if you are coming about this undertaking, and so that no one can guess what you are doing.

Tell the Operai that they should inform and certify to our Lord how much of their money they have spent, and then it will be possible to arrange for our Lord to provide his share. (C.I.162.)

The 'friend' about whom Domenico is being so cautious is fairly certainly the architect and sculptor Jacopo Sansovino, who felt that he had rights in the job. The money the Operai – that is the cathedral board of works – should have spent was their contribution to the building of the road from the Pietrasanta quarries to the coast. Michelangelo's dealings with patrons and colleagues were never easy for anyone involved. Buoninsegna wrote to him on 21 November 1516:

I received your letter today, with the other one enclosed, from that friend [Baccio], and I do not know on what day, month or year it was written; but my guess is that it was after the last two, received together, which I read to the cardinal, and I know that everything was referred to the pope, and I replied two days ago, addressing it to Florence, thinking that by the time it arrived you would be there; and I said that they were awaiting your arrival to get a better understanding of the details I notified you about. Then, from this last letter of yours, I see that you have changed your mind, saying that you no longer wish to come. And considering the contents of all your letters, I see that they are so varied that if I am not out of my mind it seems to me that it would not take much more.

For you know that when we were in Florence, you and Baccio spoke to me about the matter of the façade, and the pair of you were taking steps and had it in your minds to take it on; you requested me to take action to see that it happened; and you said to me that I should speak to the cardinal at the earliest opportunity. Therefore, as soon as he arrived at Montefiascone I began to talk to him about it, and he, without more ado, went to the pope and came back to me saying that I should write to you and Baccio, so that you should come and see him to be able to resolve everything in the design and thus draw up other contracts which cannot be done except in the presence of the parties. I therefore wrote to Baccio, and he replied to Bernardo Niccolini that he had told you and was waiting for your reply, and that if you did not want to come he would come when you agreed. And then he made out that you had replied, saying that it was impossible for you to leave there [Carrara], and that he should come himself, and that whatever he did would be all right. And then you wrote the same thing to me, saying that you could hardly leave there, but to leave it to Baccio; and that when they wanted to take marbles from there, it would be acceptable to you since you had plenty which were unsuitable for you and which would serve for the façade. To which I replied that they were keen on the marbles from Pietrasanta, and that if it were possible and could be done they wanted them from there.

Then you replied in those two letters in which you said that you were certain that you would come, and I, as I said, referred everything to the cardinal and he told it to the pope. And now from this last letter of yours I see that you have again decided not to come, and I am equally resolved in my desire not to be bothered any more with such things, since I cannot see what I can get from all this except shame and some embarrassment: I don't know what sort of face I had, going to the cardinal with that last letter of yours. All the same, I might not have shown it to him except that yesterday he went with the pope to Magliana and afterwards to Ostia, and he will have shown it to him. So I await their return, because I don't want him to complain that I never warned him about the things you have written. And as for the suspicion, when they come, that they have been sent on a wild goose chase, I give you no guarantees ... but I well know that so far I'm the one who has been sent on a wild goose chase, and even more by Baccio than by you.

Anyway, I don't say that therefore you should come, neither one of you nor both of you, more than either of you wants to, because I don't want to be the cause of useless expense, nor to be responsible for your getting a fever on account of the change of air, since this year it's such bad weather; but I do say to you that I will not have anything more to do with this affair, nor will I write either to you or to Baccio, unless I am expressly ordered to do so by my superiors, who can command me to do it. And I say again that when either of you laments that useful and honourable works are given to non-Florentines I shall always say that you are the cause of it, with the false and fanciful imaginings you have had about it.

And so that Baccio also shall know the contents of this letter, I am sending it open to Bernardo Niccolini, so that he can read it, seal it, and deliver it to you, so that you shall see the contents and decide what seems apposite; warning you that because of this letter you should not change your minds, because it doesn't matter. So do what you like, bearing in mind that nothing is in writing. And I assure you that I have never sought to cause you any harm or shame whatever, but have acted only in response to all your letters, and to tell you how I have understood it, and made it clear to you to the best of my abilities. That's all. (C.1.173.)

Michelangelo's reply to this outburst is lost (as are most of his letters in this correspondence), but its contents can be inferred from Buoninsegna's next letter from Rome of 11 December 1516. (Both Baccio d'Agnolo and Niccolini had written to Michelangelo disclaiming responsibility for the imbroglio.)

I wrote on the 6th and replied to another of yours in which you tell me that you believed Baccio d'Agnolo and Baccio Bigio were deceiving you, and you based this on things you had heard. . . . About this I can neither see nor say anything, but I must tell you that two days ago Baccio Bigio arrived here, and I heard that he was saying he had been sent for by the pope, because of things at Montefiascone, where I understand they want to build walls in the castle. And since he's been here I talked to him, asking what he'd come for, and he told me it was for a wall Madonna Alfonsina wanted near the customs house. So I told him I had heard that he had come about the walls of Montefiascone. He said that this was in fact what he'd been summoned for, but he didn't want to work or stay in the villa, and it seemed to me that he was rather shamefaced when I said it. I know that, when he was with our cardinal and our Lord, he talked about the façade and said that he wanted to get involved in it; but before he arrived and again afterwards, the cardinal insisted that I should write to you to assure you that the pope was resolved to commission the façade from you and Baccio d'Agnolo, if you wanted to do it, and I was to let you know that you should make up your mind soon . . . because they want to think about beginning the work. . . . And because you may value my advice, although I know it is of little value and that I understand little about these matters, know that I want you to do no more or less than you want, because as I have already told you, I don't wish to involve myself any more, unless I am expressly ordered to do so . . . and this I will continue to do because the contents of this letter are the will of the cardinal. (C.1.182).

Yet he continues by advising Michelangelo to come immediately to Rome and to accept the commission for his own and his city's honour. He admits that Michelangelo cannot agree to any proposal which puts him under Baccio d'Agnolo, but he insists that if he agrees he can chose his own collaborators.

138 Michelangelo finally went to Rome in December 1516, and the matter was settled verbally; it seems that he provided a drawing which the pope accepted and he was to make two models, one of which was to be sent to Rome. Buoninsegna also arranged for 2000 ducats to be provided, and a workshop was to be set up where the marbles could be worked. All seemed now set. The faulty foundations were to be rebuilt; the model was being made. Michelangelo returned to Carrara, where it was difficult to get in touch with him, and where he was, apparently, still quarrying marble, since contracts continued to be signed in Carrara for local marble, despite the express wish of the pope and the cardinal that the new Pietrasanta quarries were to be used. As Michelangelo was responsible for supplying the marble, he probably felt that it was no one's business but his where it came from. The contracts with the quarries continued until 1517, despite the fact that he had received a stiff letter from Cardinal Giulio dated 2 February 1517:

Spectabilis noster charissime: we have received yours and have shown it to our Lord; and seeing that your proceedings are all in favour of the affairs of Carrara, you have surprised in no small measure His Holiness and myself, because they do not conform to your words, as we understood them from Jacopo Salviati, who has been on the site of the quarries and the marble works of Pietrasanta with many intelligent masters, and tells us that there are marbles in very great quantity, very fine and easy to transport; which being so, gives us some suspicion that you wish, for some convenience of your own, to favour the marble of Carrara and take away the reputation of those from Pietrasanta. This you should certainly not do, given the faith we have always had in you. For this, we tell you that, disregarding all other considerations, His Holiness our Lord wishes in every way that in all the works which are to be done, and for St Peter's, and for Sta Reparata [the old name of Florence cathedral], and for the façade of S. Lorenzo, the marbles of Pietrasanta and no others shall be used, for the reasons given above, and principally also because it is understood that they will be less expensive than those of Carrara. But even if they were more so, His Holiness wishes in every case that this shall be done, to set going and to further the works at Pietrasanta for the public good of the city. For this, see to it that you do as we have ordered, and do not fail, because if you were to do otherwise it would be against the will of His Holiness and ourselves, and we would have reason for considerable complaint against you. Our Domenico will write similarly to you. Reply to him about this when you receive it and quickly, removing from your mind all obduracy. *Et bene valete*. (c.1.194.)

On the same day, Domenico Buoninsegna wrote to Michelangelo:

They are ill satisfied with you over the business of the Pietrasanta marbles. ... I got a reprimand from the pope and also from the cardinal, because I had delayed in remitting to Florence those 500 ducats which they ordered me to send some time ago. So I poured the broth over your back, saying that your words had made me delay, although I have sent them since. The pope says that if these are not enough ... he will put in as many more, because he wants the road finished; ... for his works in Florence, and for those at St Peter's here, he wants those from Pietrasanta even if they cost more than double those at Carrara. (c.1.195.)

He continues, endeavouring to persuade Michelangelo to conform to the pope's wishes, with continued assurances of their regard for him. He then lists the figures that are to appear on the façade, with the comment that Michelangelo may clothe them as he pleases, since the cardinal says he knows nothing of tailoring. The row at the bottom was to contain a *St Lawrence*, a *St John the Baptist*, *St Peter* and *St Paul*, and the seated ones above these were to be the *Four Evangelists*. At the top were to be *SS. Cosmas and Damian*, dressed as doctors (*medici*); these early martyrs, said to have practised medicine, were the Medici patron saints. Clearly, in view of the friendly nature of his latest letters, Buoninsegna had come round from his earlier angry frame of mind.

The project was a magnificent and potentially lucrative one, and it continued to be beset by intrigue. Other artists were still angling for a share in the work; on 16 February 1517 Jacopo Sansovino had written to Michelangelo, enquiring solicitously about his health. The supply of marble continued to be a major political issue. Buoninsegna reiterated on 8 March 1517 that the pope and the cardinal wanted only Pietrasanta marble, but he himself had tried to arrange, to save time, that Michelangelo should have some from Carrara. Apparently the Carrarese had retaliated by raising their prices, so that it was 'not worth talking about'. He threw in a revealing incidental comment:

Because there is now no money to spend on marble for St Peter's, the work goes on even more slowly than before. (c.1.207.)

On 20 March Michelangelo wrote back to Buoninsegna:

Messer Domenico – I came to Florence to see the model which Baccio [d'Agnolo] has finished and have found the same thing again, that is to say that it is a mere toy. If you think it should be sent, write me. I'm leaving tomorrow morning and returning to Carrara where I have agreed, with the aid of La Grassa, to make a model in clay, based on the drawing, which I'll send to him. He assures me he will have one made that will be all right. I do not know how it will turn out; I expect in the end I shall have to do it myself. I regret this from the point of view of the cardinal and the pope. I cannot help it.

I must inform you that, for a very good reason, I have terminated the partnership, which I wrote and told you I had formed at Carrara and have commissioned from these same people a hundred cart-loads of marble at the prices of which I wrote you, or a little less. And from another partnership which I have got together, I have commissioned another hundred and they have a year in which to deliver it to me in barge-loads. (C.1.212.)

La Grassa was a carver from Settignano. The 'partnerships' refer to his two companies created for the exploitation of the necessary marbles, which he now disbanded because of the pope's insistence on Pietrasanta; but it is obvious from this letter and from the contract itself, when it came to be signed, that he had for the moment won his argument over the marble. Until the road was finished, the Pietrasanta stone, whatever the pope's wishes, and whatever its quality and quantity, could not be delivered. Letters continued to flow about the need for the model, and about troubles in getting the foundations started. Domenico is worried lest the pope and the cardinal should think they were on another wild goose chase. Sansovino again wrote to Michelangelo on 20 April, courteously, but without providing any information. He was obviously still hoping to be employed. On 2 May 1517, Michelangelo wrote to Buoninsegna, still from Carrara:

Since I last wrote to you, I have been unable to attend to the making of the model, as I wrote and told you I would. It would take a long time to explain the why and the wherefore. I had previously roughed out a little one in clay, for my own use here, which, although it is crinkled like a fritter, I want in any event to send you, so that this thing may not seem to be a figment of the imagination. . . . I feel myself able to execute this project of the façade of S. Lorenzo in such a manner that it will be, both architecturally and sculpturally, the mirror of all Italy, but the pope and the cardinal would have to make up their minds quickly as to whether they wish me to do it or not. And if they wish me to do it, they would have to come to some decision, that is to say, either to commission me to do it on contract and to rely upon me entirely for everything, or on some other basis, of which I am ignorant, which they may decide upon. I will explain why.

I, as I wrote you, and since I wrote you, have given commissions for many blocks of marble and have handed out money on this side and on that, and have begun quarrying in various places. And in one place where I laid out money, the marbles did not afterwards turn out to be any use to me, because things are deceptive, particularly with the big blocks which I need, if they are to be as excellent as I require them to be. And in one block, which I had already had cut, certain defects became apparent on the inner face, which couldn't have been anticipated, so that I did not get out of it the two columns I wanted and half the expense was wasted on it. And thus, with these mishaps, it is inevitable that, among so many, a few blocks run into some hundreds of ducats. But I cannot keep account and shall not be able ultimately to show proof of my expenditure, except for the actual amount of marble I shall deliver. . . . It doesn't seem to me worth while wasting so much time in order to save the pope two or three hundred ducats; and because I'm being pressed about my work in Rome I must come to terms whatever happens.

The terms are these. If I knew that I had the work to do and the cost of it, I should not worry about wasting four hundred ducats, because I should not have to account for them, and I should select three or four of the best men here and should give them a commission for the marbles, which would have to be of the same quality as the marble I have already quarried, which is admirable, though I haven't much of it. For this, and for the money I advanced to them, I should take out a good insurance in Lucca, and should give orders to transport the marbles to Florence, together with those I've got, and should go and work there on the pope's account and on my own. But if I did not come to the above arrangement with the pope, it would be difficult for me, nor should I be able, if I wanted to, to transport the marbles for my work to Florence and then back to Rome afterwards, but should have to come to work in Rome as soon as possible, because I'm being pressed, as I've said.

The cost of the façade in the manner in which I intend to execute it and to put the work in hand, including everything – for the pope would not need to concern himself about anything further – could not be less, according to the estimates I've made, than thirty-five thousand gold ducats, and for this I'll undertake to execute it in six years; on this condition, that within six months I should have at least another thousand ducats in respect of the marble. But if the pope is not disposed to do this, either the expenses which I have begun to incur for the aforesaid work must go towards my profit or loss and I must return the thousand ducats to the pope, or he must engage someone to carry on the enterprise, because for a number of reasons I wish to leave here whatever happens.

As to the said price; should I realize, once the work is begun, that it could be done for less, such is my loyalty towards the pope and cardinal, that I should advise them of it much sooner than if I were to incur a loss. But on the contrary, I propose to execute it on such a scale that the price may not be sufficient.

Messer Domenico, I beg you to let me have a definite answer as to the intention of the pope and the cardinal, which would be the greatest of all the kindnesses you have done me. (C.1.221.)

Buoninsegna replied on 9 May 1517:

I took it immediately to the cardinal who was delighted to read it. He told me to write to you to go on with it and to continue quarrying. And so far as regards the expense incurred by quarrying marble so as to have it ready, all will be made good and you should keep a good account of it. . . . You speak in your letter of the great desire you have to do this work, and everything pleases them. But if I remember rightly it was said that it could be done for 25,000 ducats, and you say that it will cost 35,000 ducats. Let me know if you now have in mind to make a richer work, or whether there has been a mistake in the accounts. (C.1.223.)

He continues about the trouble over the foundations, and Michelangelo's poor relations with Baccio d'Agnolo. Clearly, the work is still full of pitfalls, and Michelangelo still swithering between satisfaction at getting the job, and apprehensions over his assistants, over supplies of marble, and over money. On 30 June 1517 Jacopo Sansovino wrote to Michelangelo, a letter quite different from his previous rather ingratiating ones. He knew by now that there was nothing in the façade for him. He was furious. There is no superscription.

Not having been able to speak to you before you left, I have decided to let you know my feeling about you. You know that between us, from here [?], there was little time. And I spoke with Jacopo Salviati and I heard that Bacino di Michelagniolo [Baccio Bandinelli] was such a worthy man, the best that ever was. But Jacopo Salviati gave you a well-deserved retort, because he knew your nature exactly. And because you praised him, Baccino boasts about getting his share of it like any other. And I also tell you that the pope, the cardinal and Jacopo Salviati are men who when they say Yes it is a charter and a contract, and . . . they are men of honour and not as you say. But you measure them according to your own yardstick, so that with you there are neither contracts nor faith, and every hour you say No and Yes as it suits you. And know that the pope promised me the histories [reliefs], and Jacopo also, and they are men who will keep them for me. And I have done with regard to you all that I could of things which would be useful and honourable for you. And I had not yet perceived that you never do good to anyone; and that, beginning with me, it would be like wishing that water would not drown anyone. And above all you know that we have talked a lot together, and may I be damned for that time when you never had a good word to say for anyone. Now go with God. I now know exactly where I stand; and so will you on your return. Enough. (C.1.231.)

Michelangelo was in Carrara until August; he fell ill when he returned to Florence, and did not arrive in Rome until early January 1518. There a contract was finally signed.

Let it be manifest to all, that today 19 January 1518, His Holiness our Lord Pope Leo X has assigned to Michelangelo di Buonarroto Simoni, Florentine sculptor, who hereby accepts, the construction or making and ornamentation of the façade of S. Lorenzo, Florence, according to the style and agreement which below is stated.

Firstly, the said Michelangelo takes it upon himself to make the said façade all at his own cost, in a time of eight years, beginning this time on the 1st day of February next, and so continuing, for the price of 40,000 broad gold ducats in gold: the said façade must be in fine white marble from Carrara or Pietrasanta, as best shall be judged for the work: and all the cost of quarrying, carriage and working and wastage shall be at the expense of the said Michelangelo. The said work must be composed, arranged and followed according to the example and proportions of the model in wood, composed with figures in wax and made or had made by the said Michelangelo, which he sent from Florence in the month of December last; arranged in the following fashion.

138

From the base of the façade up to the first cornice there are to be eight fluted columns of marble each about eleven *braccia* [6.4 m or 21 ft] high, with their capitals and bases, between which are to be the three doors of the said church, and four free-standing figures, each about five *braccia* [2.9 m or 9½ ft] high, with certain panels in half relief, as in the model.

Item, in this storey as far as the first cornice are to be two return bays, in each of which are to be two columns, and between them a carved figure similar to those on the façade, as may be seen on the model.

Item, above the first cornice in the upper level above each of the columns of the façade, and also of the return bays, is to be a pyramidal form, or rather a pilaster six in seven *braccia* high, between which are to be four figures in front and two at the sides, each carved in the round, and being seated their height is to be four and a half *braccia*, which are to be in bronze.

Item, above the said pilasters is to be a cornice, from which rise eight pilasters in front and on the returns four similar pilasters, that is two in each section, with their socles, capitals and bases between which are, in the front section, four tabernacles and two similar tabernacles in the returns. And in each is to be a marble figure carved in the round of about five and a half *braccia* [3.2 m or 10½ ft] high.

Item, there is to be above each of the said tabernacles a panel, in each of which is to be a seated marble figure, life size, and of more than half-relief as can be seen in the model.

Item, in the divisions of the said model there are in the façade five histories in panels and two in roundels, which are to be in half-reliefs; of the histories in the roundels they are to be six in seven *braccia* each; the histories in low-relief are to be of marble and the figures life size or larger; And because it is possible that the said histories in low-relief will not be as visible as is necessary, the said Michelangelo wishes to be held and obliged to make them or have them made of such relief that they will be adequate and will be properly done and good.

Item, on the top cornice there is to be at the nave in the middle a pediment with its cornices and finials and ornaments of arms and quarterings, the which has to be in a form which can be seen in the model, and also the said ornaments.

Item, since in the said model all the ornaments are not complete, such as the carving of the cornices and doors and other smaller histories, the said Michelangelo wishes to be held to do all these things in the form and place which is suitable, all at his own expense, and also all the walling which is necessary to attach the returns to the old façade of the church.

All these things the said Michelangelo agrees to do for the said price and in the time, all at his expense, making the figures with his own hand and also the histories. And desiring to assign some and to be assisted it is left to him; he is given entire liberty to assign or not assign and to do all in such manner as he thinks our Lord will be best served and satisfied in the said time. And notwithstanding the above agreement, in case of any accident of fortune, such as illness, war, or other which might bring about an impediment to the work, of all this the said Michelangelo resigns himself to the discretion of His Holiness.

And in order to give a start to the work and to pursue it to its perfection, our said Lord wishes that for every year the said Michelangelo shall be paid 5000 broad gold ducats and such amount as he shall ask for up to the said sum, during the time of the said eight years: with the understanding that he shall now be given, so as to begin the quarrying of the marble and for other expenses, 4000 broad gold ducats in gold, the which will be subtracted from and set against the sum of the whole price of the said work.

Item, that the said Michelangelo shall be accommodated without any cost to him, with a room adjacent to the said church of S. Lorenzo, in which it will be possible to work the marbles and the other things for the said façade.

And in all the aforementioned agreement and conditions the said Michelangelo wishes to be held and obliged to accept the judgment of our aforementioned Lord. And in agreement he subscribes in his own hand to be so satisfied.

Placet: I [oannes]

I Michelangelo di Lodovico Simoni above mentioned am satisfied with what is contained in this deed, and in faith of which I subscribe in my own hand in Rome on the abovementioned day. (M.671.)

Michelangelo was back in Florence by the end of January 1518, after closing his Roman workshop and ordering some part-hewn blocks for the Julius Tomb to be sent to Florence. Some parts of the Tomb were left in Rome, and a friend, Lionardo Sellaio, a saddler as his name indicates, undertook to take care of the house and its contents. Michelangelo also left instructions for all his cartoons (presumably those for the Sistine Ceiling) to be burnt. In a letter of 5 February 1518 Sellaio informs him that this has, reluctantly, been done, although he thinks 'not all of them'.

Michelangelo had won the right to get his marble from Carrara; but in the end he went to Pietrasanta after all. He explained in a letter to Domenico Buoninsegna from Florence in early May 1518:

As the [Pietrasanta] marbles have turned out to be excellent for me, and as those that are suitable for the work at St Peter's are easy to quarry and nearer the coast than the others, that is, at a place called Corvara; and from this place no expense for a road is involved, except over the small stretch of marsh land near the coast. But for a choice of the marbles for figures, which I need myself, the existing road will have to be widened for about two miles from Corvara to Seravezza and for about a mile of it or less an entirely new road will have to be made, that is, it must be cut into the mountains with pickaxes to where the said marbles have to be loaded. Therefore, if the pope is only prepared to undertake what is required for his own marbles, that is, the marsh, I haven't the means to undertake the rest and I shouldn't have any marble for my own work. If he does not undertake this, I cannot take any responsibility for the marbles for St Peter's, as I promised the cardinal, but if the pope undertakes the whole of it, I can do all that I promised.

I've told you all about it in other letters. Now, you are experienced and discreet and are, I know, well disposed towards me; so I beg you to arrange the matter in your own way with the cardinal and to reply to me quickly, so that I may reach a decision, and if nothing else eventuates, may return to Rome to what I was doing before. I could not go to Carrara, because in twenty years I shouldn't get the marbles I need, since, owing to this business, I've become an object of great hostility there and I should be compelled, if I return to Rome, to work in bronze, as we agreed.

I must inform you that the commissioners have already made great plans in regard to this business of the marbles since they got my report, and I believe that they have already fixed the prices, the duties and the dues and that the notaries, and arch-notaries, the purveyors and sub-purveyors are already resolved to wax fat on their profits there. So think it over and do whatever you can to prevent this affair falling into their hands, because later on it would be

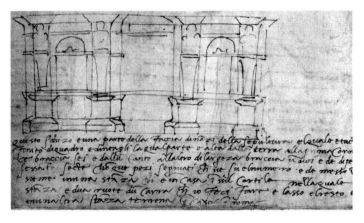

Michelangelo's inscription on this drawing of 1518 for Lionardo Sellaio: 'This sketch is part of the front of the [Julius] Tomb, which part is all finished blocking and cutting . . . and is of seventy-seven pieces indicated by the numbers. And it is all together in a room in the house giving on to the courtyard.' The façade had once been assembled (April 1516), when the Duchess of Urbino came to see the Tomb. After the great Tiber flood of 1530, the workshop floor collapsed, and the marbles were damaged by falling into the cellar.

more difficult to get anything out of them than out of Carrara. I beg you to answer me quickly as to what you think I should do, and to commend me to the cardinal. I am here as his agent, so I will not do anything, except what you tell me, because I assume that to be his wish.

If in writing to you I haven't written as grammatically as one should, or if I've sometimes missed out the main verb, please forgive me, because I'm troubled with a ringing in my ears, which prevents my thinking as clearly as I'd like. (c.2.286.)

He wrote to his brother Buonarroto from Pietrasanta on 2 April 1518:

Would you let me know if Jacopo Salviati has got the consuls of the wool merchants' guild to grant the concession on the basis of the draft, as he promised me, and if he hasn't done so, ask him on my behalf to do so. And if you find that he doesn't want to, let me know, so that I may withdraw from here, as I'm on the highway to ruin and, in addition, I'm not getting on as I'd hoped. Nevertheless, if the promise made to me is kept I'm prepared to carry on with the enterprise, with its enormous expense and trouble, though as yet without any certainty of success.

About the business of the road here, tell Jacopo that I'll do whatever his Magnificence pleases and that he'll never find himself cheated over anything he entrusts to me, because in matters of this kind I do not seek my own advantage, but the advantage of my patrons and of my country. And though I've requested the pope and the cardinal to grant me the supervision of this road, I've done so merely to be in a position to give directions and to have it routed to those places where the best marbles are to be found, which are unknown to anyone. Neither have I made this request in order to profit by it, because I do not take such things into account. On the contrary, I beg his Magnificence Jacopo to have it made by Maestro Donato [Benti], because for this he's invaluable and I'm sure he's to be trusted, and to give me the authority to have it made where and how I think best, because I know where the best marbles are and what kind of road is needed for carting them, and I think I can reduce the cost considerably for whoever does the paying. So acquaint the said Jacopo with what I've written to you, and commend me to his Magnificence and beg him to commend me to his agents in Pisa, so that they may do me the favour of finding barges to transport the marbles from Carrara.

I went to Genoa and got four barges sent to the quayside to load them. The Carrarese bribed the masters of the said barges and are bent on balking me, so that I achieved nothing, and today I'm thinking of going to Pisa to see about others. So commend me to him, as I've said, and write to me. (c.1.268.)

Jacopo Salviati, who has already appeared in the negotiations, was a senior partner in the Salviati bank; he had married Pope Leo X's sister Lucrezia de' Medici, and remained a stalwart friend of Michelangelo's. The concession referred to was a deed by which the Arte della Lana, the wool guild, who were paying for works at the cathedral in Florence, were to grant to Michelangelo for life the inalienable right to quarry marble anywhere in the areas of Seravezza and Pietrasanta and in the quarries pertaining to them, without dues or premiums, and for whatever purpose he should require the marble. He wrote to Buonarroto again on 18 April:

I learn from yours that the concession hasn't yet been granted, which worries me very much. ... If it isn't granted by Thursday evening, as you wrote to me, I shall assume, not that Jacopo Salviati wasn't willing to arrange it, but that he was unable to, and I shall immediately take horse and go in search of Cardinal de' Medici and the pope and shall tell them how I'm placed. And I shall abandon my enterprise here and go back to Carrara, for they implore me to do so as they would implore Christ.

These *scarpellini* [stonecutters] whom I brought from Florence know nothing on earth about quarrying or about marble. They have already cost me more than a hundred and thirty ducats and haven't yet quarried me a chip of marble that's any use, and they go round bamboozling everyone into believing that they have made great discoveries and are seeking to execute work for the Opera and for others, at my expense. I don't know what support they're getting, but the pope shall hear all about it. Since I've been here I've thrown away about three hundred ducats and haven't as yet got anything out of it for myself. In trying to tame these mountains and to introduce the industry into these parts, I've undertaken to raise the dead; for if, over and above the marbles, the guild of wool merchants were to pay me a hundred ducats a month for doing what I'm doing, they wouldn't do badly, without failing me over the concession. So commend me to Jacopo Salviati and write to me by my apprentice as to how the matter goes, so that I may come to an immediate decision, because I'm being worn away here in this state of suspense.

The barges I hired at Pisa have never arrived. I think I've been gulled, and so it is with everything I do. Oh cursed a thousand times be the day I left Carrara! It's the cause of my undoing. But I shall soon return there. Today it is a crime to do right. (c.1.276.)

The concession from the wool guild was signed on 22 April. In September he wrote from Seravezza, where he was now living, to one of the overseers at the Opera or cathedral board of works, Berto da Filicaia:

... Things here are going tolerably well. One may say that the road is finished, since there is little left to do. That is to say, there are a few boulders, or rather outcrops, to be cut away. One outcrop is where the road, which leads from the river, debouches on the old road to Rimagno; another outcrop is a little beyond Rimagno on the way to Seravezza, where a large boulder is lying across the road; and another is near the last houses in Seravezza, going towards Corvara. In addition, there are a few places to be levelled with small pickaxes. And all these being short jobs, could be done in a fortnight, if the *scarpellini* were worth anything. As to the marsh, it is about a week since I was there, when they were still filling in, to the worst of their ability. If they have gone on with it, I reckon they must have finished it by this time.

As to the marbles, I've got the quarried column safely down into the river-bed, fifty *braccia* from the road. It has been a bigger job than I anticipated to sling it down. Some mistake was made in slinging it, and one man had his neck broken and died instantly, and it nearly cost me my life. The other column was almost blocked out; I discovered a flaw in it, which left me short; it was necessary to cut back into the hillside again to the full width to avoid the flaw, and this I've done, and I hope that now it will be all right and I can block it out to the full length.
... The site here is very rough to quarry and the men very inexperienced in an operation of this kind. A great deal of patience will therefore be needed for some months, until the mountains are tamed and the men trained; then we shall get on faster. It is sufficient that what I have promised I shall perform without fail and shall produce the finest work that has ever been produced in Italy – with God's help.

Since I wrote I have had an answer from the men at Pietrasanta who undertook to quarry a specific amount of marble some six months ago; they will neither do the quarrying nor return me the hundred ducats I gave them. It seems to me that they have taken a bold course, which, as I see it, they would not have taken without support. So I intend to come to Florence and to demand damages from them for this dishonesty. I don't know whether this can be done. I hope his Magnificence Jacopo Salviati will help me to get justice. (c.2.343.)

What he means is that he suspects that influence, and possibly bribes, from Carrara, encouraged the men to break their contract. Eventually Michelangelo recovered 90 of his 100 ducats.

An ugly little incident occurred towards the end of December 1518. Domenico Buoninsegna in Rome wrote a pleasant letter to Michelangelo, to the effect that the pope and the cardinal were very satisfied with the way things were going, particularly as the Pietrasanta marbles had turned out so well. He suggests to Michelangelo that, if possible, he should get others to see to the quarrying and the carting of marbles, because these labours seemed to cause him gross overwork and anxiety. He says that he suggests this only because of the affection he has for him. At about the same time, Buoninsegna wrote to Niccolini in Florence.

Find out what Michelangelo is doing, because the boss keeps asking me, and tell Michelangelo that Cardinal Aginense is tormenting himself about the Tomb of Pope Julius, and has shown me letters from the Marquis [of Carrara] that complain bitterly about Michelangelo, and the Marquis claims that he is not withholding the marbles or impeding him in any way, but it is all his fault. Write and tell him, if he's away, about this. (c.2.379.)

Niccolini went in search of Michelangelo, who was in Florence. What then happened is related in a letter from Michelangelo to Buoninsegna, written in January 1519:

I perceive from your letter that Bernardo Niccolini has written and told you that I was indignant with him about a report of yours, which said that the Lord of Carrara was making numerous charges against me, and that the cardinal was complaining about me. The reason I was indignant is this: Because he read it to me in a haberdasher's shop in public, as if it were a formal indictment, so that thereby everyone knew that I was condemned to death; that was the reason why I said to him 'Why doesn't he write to me?' I note that you do write to me. So do write to him, or to me just as it suits you, but after the execution, if it takes place, I beg you for the honour of our country not to disclose the reason.

I understand from your last that I had better place commissions for the marbles for S. Lorenzo. I have already placed three commissions and have been cheated over all three. This is because the *scarpellini* from here have no understanding of marble and as soon as they saw their lack of success, they went with God. . . . For this reason I had to stay there from time to time, to set them to work, and to show them the lines of the marbles and what things to avoid . . . and even how to quarry, because in things of this kind I am skilled. (c.2.386.)

Surely this must have alerted Michelangelo to the true nature of Buoninsegna's friendship? And were Buoninsegna's repeated suggestions to Michelangelo to give up working in the quarries himself, because this would enable him to come to a satisfactory – for him – arrangement over the payments for the supplies? On 21 December 1518 Michelangelo wrote to Lionardo Sellaio from Florence:

You exhort me in your last letter to press on; I appreciate this, because I see that you do it for my good. But I must make it clear to you that such exhortations are, nevertheless, so many knife-thrusts, because I'm dying of vexation through my inability to do what I want to do, owing to my ill-luck. A week ago this evening my assistant Pietro [Urbano] returned from Porto Venere with my assistant Donato [Benti], who is in charge of the transport of the marbles at Carrara, leaving a loaded boat at Pisa, which has never appeared because it hasn't rained and the Arno is completely dried up. Another four boats are commissioned for the marbles in Pisa, which will all come loaded when it rains, and I shall begin work in earnest. On this account I am more disgruntled than any man on earth. I am also being pressed by Messer Metello Vari about his figure, which is likewise there in Pisa and will be in one of the first boats. I have never replied to him, nor do I wish to write to you again, until I have started work: because I'm dying of anguish and seem to have become an impostor against my will.

I have an excellent workshop in preparation here, where I shall be able to erect twenty figures at a time. I cannot roof it because there is no wood here in Florence, nor likely to be any until it rains, and I don't believe it will ever rain again from now on, unless to do me some mischief.

As to the Cardinal [Aginense], I'm not asking you to say anything further to him, because I know he has a bad opinion of my conduct; but he will soon have proof to the contrary. (c.2.382.)

103   The reference to Metello Vari and his figure will be returned to later. In the spring of 1519 Michelangelo, having found his Florentine workmen totally unsatisfactory, brought in men from Carrara who were more used to quarrying than the stonecutters of Settignano, but it did not seem to bring him better luck. He wrote to his assistant Pietro Urbano from Seravezza on 20 April 1519:

Things have gone very badly. . . . On Saturday morning, having made great preparations, I set about having a column lowered . . . but after I had lowered it about 50 *braccia* [about 96 ft or 29 m] one of the rings of the tackle attached to the column broke and the column fell into the river in a hundred pieces. The said ring Donato had had made by a colleague of his, Lazzaro, a smith; . . . had it been properly made, it could have carried four columns. . . . After it broke we saw the utter rascality of it, for it was not solid inside at all, and the iron in it was no thicker than the back of a knife. . . . Those of us who were anywhere near were in imminent danger of our lives, and a splendid block was ruined. I left the superintendence of the ironwork to Donato . . . you see how he's treated me. And the blocks of the pulley he had made for me were likewise all split at the ring in lowering this column and they are also about to give way and they are twice as big as those used by the Opera. . . . But the iron is brittle and poor and could not be worse forged. And this is because Donato keeps in with this colleague of his and sent him to the forge. (C.2.431.)

Donato Benti must have got out of the mess somehow, because he continued to work for Michelangelo until midsummer 1521. However, things now began to go wrong. Condivi, briefed by Michelangelo, lays the blame on the pope and Cardinal Giulio. Vasari does the same in his Life of Michelangelo; but in his Life of Baccio Bandinelli he tells a very different story.

Domenico Buoninsegna . . . attempted to get Michelangelo to make a secret deal with him over the work on the façade of S. Lorenzo, but Michelangelo refused, because he did not want his abilities to be used to defraud the pope. Domenico came to hate him, and continually opposed all his plans, so as to annoy and damage him; though he did it secretly. He arranged, therefore, that the façade should be abandoned, and hindered the Sacristy, which he said were two works which would keep Michelangelo busy for many years; and the marble for the carving of the gigantic group [a *Hercules and Cacus*] he persuaded the pope to give to Baccio [Bandinelli] who then had nothing to do . . . who boasted that he would surpass Michelangelo's *David* and was again aided by Buoninsegna who said that Michelangelo wanted everything for himself. (v2.6.148–9.)

It has also been suggested that Buoninsegna was in collusion with Niccolini, though Vasari never mentions him in the matter. Be this as it may, in 1520 the pope quite suddenly and arbitrarily cancelled the contract for the façade. A long memorandum from Michelangelo, written in Florence in March 1520, but unfortunately without any superscription, rehearses the whole dismal story. Since the memorandum stresses the fact that Michelangelo was to be relieved of all responsibility for supplying the marble, and removed from all control of the quarries, it would seem that this was where the trouble originated. In which case, he may well have been blamed for a peculation of which he was not only innocent, but even entirely unaware. If Buoninsegna was responsible, and had in fact approached Michelangelo with a dishonest proposal, then it is difficult to explain why their subsequent relations remained cordial. The memorandum is as follows:

When I was in Carrara on business of my own, that is to say, obtaining marbles to transport to Rome for the Tomb of Pope Julius, in fifteen hundred and sixteen, Pope Leo sent for me with reference to the façade of S. Lorenzo, which he wished to execute in Florence. I therefore left Carrara on the fifth day of December and went to Rome, and there I did a design for the said façade, on the basis of which the said Pope Leo commissioned me to arrange for the quarrying of the marble at Carrara for the said work. Then, when I had returned to Carrara from Rome on the last day of the aforesaid December, Pope Leo there sent to me, through Jacopo Salviati, for the purpose of quarrying the marbles for the said work, a thousand ducats, which were brought by a servant of Salviati's called Bentivoglio. I received the said money about the eighth of the following month, that is to say, of January, and I accordingly gave a receipt for it.

Then, the following August, having received instructions from the pope aforesaid about the model of the said work, I came to Florence from Carrara to execute it. I accordingly made it to scale in wood, with the figures in wax, and sent it to Rome. As soon as he saw it he ordered me to go there. So I went and undertook the said façade on contract, as appears from the covenant with His Holiness, which I have. And as, in order to serve His Holiness, I had to transport the marbles I needed in Rome for the Tomb of Pope Julius to Florence, as I have done, and then to transport them, when they had been worked, back to Rome, he promised to indemnify me for all the expenses, that is to say, the dues and the freight, which is an outlay of about eight hundred ducats, although the written agreement doesn't say so.

On the sixth day of February, fifteen hundred and seventeen [1518 N.S.], I returned to Florence from Rome, and as I had undertaken the façade of S. Lorenzo aforesaid on contract, defraying all the expenses, and as the said Pope Leo had to pay me four thousand ducats in Florence on account of the said work, as appears in the agreement, I received from Jacopo Salviati on about the twenty-fifth day eight hundred ducats for the same, and gave a receipt and went to Carrara. But as they had not fulfilled the contracts and previous orders for the marbles for the said work, and as the Carrarese were bent upon balking me, I went to have the said marbles quarried at Seravezza, a mountain near Pietra Santa in Florentine territory. And then, when I had already blocked out six columns, each eleven and a half *braccia*, and many other marbles, and had there begun the workings that are to-day established, for no quarrying had ever been done there before, I went to Florence on the twentieth day of March, fifteen hundred and eighteen [1519 N.S.], for money to begin transporting the said marbles, and on the twenty-sixth of March, fifteen hundred and nineteen, the Cardinal de' Medici had paid to me on behalf of Pope Leo for the said work, through the Gaddi of Florence, five hundred ducats, for which I accordingly gave a receipt. Afterwards, in this same year, the cardinal, by order of the pope, told me not to proceed further with the work aforesaid, because they said they wished to relieve me of the trouble of transporting the marbles, and that they wished to supply me with them in Florence themselves, and to make a new contract. And thus the matter stands, from that day to this.

Now at this time, the commissioners of Sta Maria del Fiore, having sent a certain number of *scarpellini* to Pietra Santa, or rather to Seravezza, to take possession of the new workings and to take away from me the marbles I had quarried for the façade of S. Lorenzo, in order to use them for the paving of Sta Maria del Fiore, while the Pope was willing to continue the façade of S. Lorenzo, and the cardinal having allocated the marbles for the said façade to everyone but to me, and having handed over to those who had taken charge of the transport my new workings at Seravezza, without coming to terms with me, I was very upset, because neither the cardinal nor the commissioners were empowered to interfere in my affairs until I had first terminated the agreement with the pope. And the said [façade] of S. Lorenzo having been abandoned in agreement with the pope, and the expenses incurred and the money received having been accounted for, the said workings and the marbles and equipment would of necessity have belonged either to His Holiness or to me; and after this, the one party or the other could have done with it as he chose.

Now concerning this, the cardinal has told me to account for the money received and the expenses incurred and has said that he wishes to release me, so that he may take over, both for the Opera and for himself, those marbles he wants from the aforesaid workings at Seravezza.

I have therefore shown that I received two thousand three hundred ducats, in the manner and at the times herein stated, and have also shown that I spent one thousand eight hundred ducats. That of these, about two hundred and fifty were spent in consideration of the freight up the Arno of marbles for the Tomb of Pope Julius, which I had transported here in order to serve Pope Julius [*sic*] in Rome, which will amount to some five hundred ducats. I am not charging to his account, over and above, the wooden model of the said façade which I sent to him in Rome. I am not charging to his account, over and above, the space of three years I have lost over this; I am not charging to his account the fact that I have been ruined over the said work for S. Lorenzo; I am not charging to his account the enormous insult of having been brought here to execute the said work and then of having it taken away from me; and I still do not know why. I am not charging the loss, amounting to five hundred ducats, on my house in Rome, which I left, including marbles, furniture and completed work. Without charging the aforesaid items to the account, out of two thousand three hundred ducats, I am left with not more than five hundred ducats in hand.

Now we are agreed. Pope Leo takes over the new workings, with the said marbles, that have been quarried, and I the money which remains to me in hand, and I am left free. And I propose to have a Brief drawn up which the pope will sign.

Now you know exactly how the matter stands. Please draw up a draft of the said Brief for me, and set forth the money received for the said work at S. Lorenzo, in such a way that it can never be demanded of me, and also set forth how in exchange for the said money, which I have received, Pope Leo takes over the aforesaid workings, the marbles and the equipment. (C.2.458.)

The reasons for the cancellation of the contract remain obscure. But the four years from 1516, when the project crystallized, to 1520 when it ended, saw immense changes on the political scene, including the emergence of Luther and the effects of the mounting movement towards the Reformation on papal finance. 'The project', says Vasari, 'was so long delayed that the money the pope assigned to it was spent on the war in Lombardy.' Not for nothing did Domenico Buoninsegna remark that there was no money for St Peter's, since the mainstay of the building operations there had been the now reviled traffic in indulgences.

Then there was Medici family history as a factor. Leo X's younger brother Giuliano, Duke of Nemours by virtue of his marriage to a princess of the house of Savoy, had died in 1516 without legitimate issue; the family's dynastic hopes then rested on Leo's nephew Lorenzo, who in 1515 had been created Duke of Urbino in the place of Francesco Maria della Rovere, nephew of Julius II. Lorenzo was the son of the unfortunate Piero de' Medici, who figures early in the life of Michelangelo as the man who had commanded him to build a snowman in the courtyard of the Medici palace, and who had been driven out of Florence in 1494. Lorenzo had married a French princess, Madeleine de la Tour d'Auvergne, but they both died in 1519; he of what was quite clearly syphilis and she in childbirth, leaving a daughter Caterina, who eventually married Henry II of France and became Queen Catherine de Médicis, mother of the last three Valois kings.

With the death of Lorenzo, the hopes that Leo X entertained of founding a new, legitimate ruling family in Florence ended. The façade had been intended as a public sign of Medici glory and dominion; his thoughts now moved to the creation of a fitting memorial to the past greatness of the family of which he and his cousin Cardinal Giulio de' Medici (later Pope Clement VII) were the last descendants in the direct male line. This memorial was to be the Medici Chapel in S. Lorenzo.

The project for the façade thus came to an untimely conclusion, leaving Michelangelo upset at not knowing the true reasons for his rejection, considerably out of pocket financially, yet still tied to patrons of such changeable, fickle mind, for want of any better, and forced to return to the Julius Tomb with a heavy heart and a disillusioned spirit.

On 14 June 1514 in Rome, Michelangelo had signed a contract with a group headed by a Roman gentleman, Metello Vari Porcari, for a *Christ of the Resurrection*; the figure was to be of marble, life-size, nude, standing with a Cross. It was to cost 200 ducats, to be finished in four years, and was to be placed in a niche in S. Maria sopra Minerva in Rome. When Michelangelo left Rome for Florence in 1516, the figure was abandoned in the Roman workshop because of a flaw in the marble – a black streak across the face. Michelangelo undertook to make another figure. On 13 December 1517, Metello Vari wrote to Florence that he needed to know when the figure would arrive; it was now three years and seven months since the commission had been given.

142

143

Michelangelo's *Risen Christ* in Sta Maria sopra Minerva in Rome, in the niche which was designed for it by Federigo Frizzi.

81 It was not until December 1518 that Michelangelo wrote to Leonardo Sellaio that the figure was stuck in Pisa because the Arno was so dry that boat traffic was impossible. In March 1519, Vari wrote again: he needed news of the figure, which, apparently, was a testamentary obligation; it is evident that he stood to lose money. He was willing to accept any other suitable figure, but if Michelangelo said that the figure would be finished by May, this would suffice. It eventually arrived in the port of Rome, the Ripa Grande, by January 1521, and was still there at the end of March.

Michelangelo's assistant, Pietro Urbano, was sent to Rome in June to put it in place and to make the final retouches. He wrote to Michelangelo in June or July that he had got the figure out of the port with great difficulty because

... they wanted Christ to pay duty to get into Rome, and those rogues of friars didn't want to accept it in the church if they weren't paid a second time. They have had one fee, now they want another. (C.2.521.)

Urbano writes quite often, but never commits himself as to what he is doing; yet he says, 'Don't believe my enemies, who lie' (C.2.522), and again in, probably, August 1521, 'whoever says I've gone to Naples or out of Rome, lies in his throat' (C.2.523).

When Michelangelo received a letter from Metello Vari, dated 14 August 1521, the very different story it told must have come as a shock. Pietro had put the figure in place, and Vari had not written earlier because Pietro assured him that he always transmitted his messages to Michelangelo. But now,

Pietro has left without permission and without giving any reasons, and we didn't know why, and all the while time was passing. I enquired about him, and someone came and said, 'Pietro has cleared off with a ring worth 40 ducats,' so I enquired further and found that it was so. (C.2.526.)

Pietro Urbano, *had*, of course, been in Naples – as a local sculptor, Vittorio Ghiberti, would testify in a letter to Michelangelo in October. On 6 September 1521 Michelangelo's friend the painter Sebastiano Luciani (Sebastiano del Piombo, as he later became) wrote to him from Rome:

I'm sure you're fed up hearing the news of your Pietro Urbano, and what didn't concern you I didn't write about because it's not my profession to speak ill of anyone, above all of those who haven't behaved badly to me; but since he has acted shamefully and without consideration towards you, for love of you I am forced to let you know about his behaviour.

Originally you sent him to Rome with the figure, to finish it and set it up. ... But I must tell you that in all he has done he has ruined everything, above all the right foot ... and he has also ruined the fingers of the hands, chiefly the one that holds the cross; ... and they don't look as if they were made of marble, but made by someone who makes pasta ... but it can easily be remedied. Also he shortened a nostril, which had he gone further would have ruined the nose, which then only God could have remedied. ... I have explained to Messer Metello ... that in no way should he leave it in Pietro's hands, who easily could by spite ruin it ... because Pietro shows himself as being very nasty, and more so by being totally rejected by you. ... He has no regard either for you or for anyone alive and thinks himself a great master, but this will make him realize what he is, because I think the poor fellow will never make figures like that, and will forget the art. Because the knees of that figure are worth all Rome. ... Frizzi will take on the job of finishing it and ... will serve you with love because he seems to be a good man. ... Don't be surprised to hear that Pietro cleared off; he wasn't seen for many days because he was in flight from the courts. ... I have heard that he gambles and chases whores and flits about Rome in velvet shoes and has to give them a lot of cash. ... I'm sorry about this, because he's young, but he has done things that would astonish you. (C.2.528.)

In gratitude for the figure, Vari presented Michelangelo with a colt, which he got Pietro to select as knowing his master's tastes. When he travelled outside Rome, Pietro got him to leave the horse with a horse-dealer, and then he tried to sell it, and Vari had to have the horse seized, along with some rings that Pietro had pawned, and he had to redeem the horse for five ducats, which upset him very much. Pietro had also sold some marbles from Michelangelo's workshop, but Lionardo Sellaio's man had prevented them from being removed.

Federigo Frizzi, who was a competent minor sculptor, finished putting the figure in place, and Vari complained that while Pietro was trying to get the figure from the port he could have made the pedestal but did nothing. Vari then asked Michelangelo if he could have the abandoned figure from the workshop, and Michelangelo wrote to Sellaio to deliver it, and also wrote saying that he would do another figure. But Sellaio wrote to him:

You sent Metello a letter, which because of the authority I have from you I opened. To give the roughed-out figure doesn't matter much; but in this letter you pledge yourself to make another out of it, which doesn't seem right to me. You know what Romans are like, and him above all. (C.2.547.)

Even Frizzi said he would not finish the niche unless Vari paid in advance. So he and Sellaio must have known their man. Michelangelo did offer to make another figure, but Vari said he was satisfied with the one he had.

The *Risen Christ* has been taken out of the niche made by Frizzi, and now stands against a pier. It was later given a metal loincloth, though this piece of prudery has since been removed. The rather unsatisfactory quality of the figure may be due to the unfortunate tamperings of Urbano, Frizzi having forborne to touch the figure itself. It may also be due to the fact that it is a repetition of one which made a bad start and had been completed more or less under duress. The roughed-out original, which Vari placed in the courtyard of his house, has disappeared.

Painful family rows added to his anxieties during this period. In September/October 1521 Michelangelo's father, as a result of some kind of misunderstanding, suddenly retreated to the family holding in Settignano. The old man was now seventy-seven years of age, and it had been clear for some time that he no longer grasped very firmly what was going on around him. Michelangelo wrote to him:

Dearest father – I was amazed at your conduct the other day, when I did not find you at home, and now, when I hear that you are complaining about me and saying that I've turned you out, I'm still more amazed; for I'm certain that never to this day, since the day I was born, has it ever occurred to me to do anything, either great or small, opposed to your interest; and all the toils and troubles I've continually endured, I've endured for your sake. And you know that since I returned to Florence from Rome, I've always taken care of you and you know that I have assured you that what I have is yours. After all, it was only a few days ago, when you were ill, that I talked to you and promised you that to the best of my ability I would never fail you as long as I live, and this I reaffirm. I'm now astonished that you should so soon have forgotten everything. You have, besides, made trial of me, you and your sons, these thirty years and you know that I've always considered you and done well by you whenever I could.

How can you go about saying that I've turned you out? Don't you see what a reputation you give me, that it should be said that I've turned you out? This is the last straw, added to the worries I have about other things, all of which I endure for your sake. A fine return you make me!

However, be it as it may, I'll try to imagine that I've always brought shame and trouble upon you and thus, as if I'd done so, I ask your forgiveness. Imagine that you are forgiving a

son of yours who has always led a bad life and has done you every possible wrong on earth. And thus again, I beg you to forgive me, like the reprobate I am, and not to take away my reputation up there by saying that I've turned you out, for it matters more to me than you think. After all, I am your son!

The bearer of this will be Rafaello da Gagliano. I beg you for the love of God, and not for my sake, to come down to Florence, because I have to go away and I have something very important to tell you and I cannot come up there. And because, on his own telling, I've heard several things from my assistant Pietro [Urbano], which displease me, I'm sending him back to Pistoia this morning and he will not return to me any more, as I do not wish him to be the ruin of our family. And you, who all knew what I did not know about his behaviour, should have informed me long ago and so much misunderstanding would not have arisen.

I'm being urged to go away, but I'm not prepared to leave without seeing you and leaving you here at home. I beg you to put aside all rancour and to come. (c.2.494.)

The interesting sidelight which the letter provides on the behaviour of Pietro Urbano is that Michelangelo was the last to discover that his assistant was not the trustworthy man he had always believed. It was, in other words, another nail in the coffin of his trust and faith in others, which is displayed so poignantly in the deep pessimism which informs so many of his personal relationships. A note on the letter itself, in Lodovico's handwriting, refers cryptically to the event: 'when he made me go to Florence, he and Raffaello da Gagliano, and then Michelangelo told me about the beating of his Pie[t]ro in the workshop'.

On 22 April 1521 in Carrara, a formal receipt was given for 100 scudi as earnest money for marble to be newly quarried, and this is first noted in the artist's *Ricordi* for 9–10 April. The contract states specifically:

Maestro Michelangelo is having these marbles made for the Sacristy of S. Lorenzo in Florence, the work which ... Cardinal de' Medici is having made ... as Maestro Michelangelo himself says, but by express agreement it is stipulated between these parties that if the ... cardinal for any reason did not wish that this work should proceed, or because of Master Michelangelo it were not continued with, in that case Michelangelo is obliged to take all the marbles which have been prepared up to the time when the above named shall have had knowledge and notice of the wishes of the cardinal and Michelangelo, and not otherwise. (m.694.)

Obviously, once bitten, twice shy. Between November 1518 and June 1521, Michelangelo wrote to Cardinal Giulio:

Most Reverend Monsignor – They are quarrying hard at Pietra Santa for the work at S. Lorenzo, and as I am finding the Carrarese more submissive than they used to be, I have also placed an order for the quarrying of a large amount of marble there, so that when the weather breaks I expect to have a good part of it in Florence, and I do not think I shall fall short of anything I have promised. May God be gracious to me, for I care for nothing in the world so much as pleasing you. I think that within a month I shall need a thousand ducats. I beg Your Most Reverend Lordship not to let me lack for money. (c.2.366.)

The architecture of the New Sacristy – or Medici Chapel – was completed on Brunelleschi's original fifteenth-century foundations by 1521. Michelangelo, while compelled to accept the given ground plan, departed from the interior design established by Brunelleschi in the Old Sacristy by placing an extra attic storey between the main body of the Chapel and the base of the semicircular dome. The dome itself is based on the dome of the Pantheon in Rome, with coffers diminishing towards the lantern, which, projecting high above the structure, gives the impression inside of a brilliantly lit *oculus* open to the sky.

Section of Brunelleschi's Old Sacristy at S. Lorenzo, looking into the choir.

The original scheme for the Medici Chapel was for four wall tombs. The two most recent deaths, of Giuliano Duke of Nemours in 1516, and Lorenzo Duke of Urbino in 1519, were to be commemorated by a tomb on each side wall; the two brothers, Lorenzo il Magnifico who died in 1492, and Giuliano his younger brother murdered in 1478 in the Pazzi conspiracy, were to be in a double tomb on the wall at the far end of the chapel. A central tomb was at one moment discussed, but rejected by Cardinal Giulio, because there would not have been enough room round the tomb.

The design of the Chapel has several unusual features. The architectural framework of the tombs contains eight doors, of which originally only three were real doors: one from the church into the Chapel, and one into each of the two tiny *lavamani* or sacristies on either side of the altar space. Later, because of the demands of tourism and the Chapel's change of function from a memorial to the dead to a work of art secularized into a museum, another door was opened, matching the one into the church, to provide an independent access. The other four doors were always false, made as part of the symmetry of the design.

The sharing of the work, or rather, Michelangelo's employment of assistant carvers who would work from models prepared by him, is borne out by the survival of a few of these models, notably in the Casa Buonarroti. Vasari, in his Introduction on Sculpture to the 1568 edition of the Lives, describes the making of clay and wax models.

Sculptors are accustomed, when they wish to do a marble figure, to make a model for it . . . for example, a figure half a braccia more or less as it suits him, in clay or wax or plaster . . . To make it [the wax] softer, a little tallow or turpentine and pitch is mixed in, for the tallow will make it more malleable, the turpentine will hold it together, and the pitch will make it black and later give it a certain density so that when it is finished it will harden . . . Because a large clay model has to stand on its own and the clay must not split, one should take shearings or stuffing, as it's called, or horse hair and mix this with the clay which makes it hard and prevents it from cracking. It can have an armature of wood underneath, with tow or hay or hempen string. (v2.1.152–5.)

Vasari goes on to explain how the marble is worked from the model, by fixing a frame round it, and taking the measure of the distances from the frame and carrying these to the marble and cutting away the unwanted stone, so that the figure measured bit by bit can be freed from the block. He describes the method graphically:

. . . as if one were to raise a wax figure from a basin of water, so that first the body and the head and the knees, then being little by little revealed as one drew it upwards one would see the roundness of it appearing beyond the halfway point, and then finally the roundness of the far sides. (v2.1.152–5.)

He continues by criticizing very harshly sculptors who assail the marble by hacking it in front and behind, working without models, and then find that they have made irremediable mistakes. He describes very carefully the process whereby, once the sculptor is sure of what he has to do, he blocks out the figure with powerful chisels, and gradually refines his tools so that he models with more and more delicate chisels before finally using files to finish his forms and remove the evidence of his earlier cutting.

Between 1516, when Michelangelo arrived in Florence, and 1534, when he returned to Rome for good, the Tomb of Julius II hung over him like a thundercloud. While he was working on the Medici projects in Florence, Cardinal Aginense pressed him to continue work on the Tomb, despite the

Section of Michelangelo's New Sacristy (or Medici Chapel). The altar space is on the left.

194

41

Section of Michelangelo's New Sacristy
or Medici Chapel. The altar space is on
the left.

physical impossibility of his doing so, and the circumstances were not
improved by the meddling intrigues of the sculptor Jacopo Sansovino,
disappointed at not receiving the S. Lorenzo commission, who egged the
Cardinal on, possibly because he hoped he might benefit as a result. The four
Slaves, on which Michelangelo did work intermittently, as the blocks
themselves testify, between 1520 and 1534, were in the end not used for the
Tomb and remained in his workshop in Florence (he had premises in what is
now the Via S. Zanobi). By this time, the possibility of other sculptors being
employed on the completion of the Tomb was being discussed.

The death of Leo X, in December 1521, brought further troubles. Cardinal
Giulio de' Medici, the late pope's cousin, who expected to be elected, proved
the rule that 'he who goes in to a Conclave as a pope comes out a cardinal', for
it was the sixty-three-year-old Dutchman Hadrian VI, one-time tutor to the
Emperor Charles V, who was elected (the last instance before modern times of
the election of a non-Italian). As a result of this reversal of papal power,
Francesco Maria della Rovere regained his Urbino duchy (Lorenzo de' Medici,
upon whom Leo had conferred it in 1515, had died in 1519).

The heirs of Julius II now began to make things difficult for Michelangelo.
They demanded, as satisfaction for the non-execution of the Tomb, a refund
of the monies spent by them, together with interest, and Hadrian VI seems to
have supported their case. The artist protested that he could not fulfil both
commitments, and urged upon Cardinal Giulio that if he wanted completion
of the work in Florence, then he would have to get him freed from the Tomb.
It seems pretty clear also that Michelangelo was weary of the whole project.

Michelangelo's affairs in Rome were looked after not only by Lionardo
Sellaio and Jacopo Salviati but by Giovan Francesco Fattucci, a chaplain from
Florence cathedral, who became his representative in the negotiations over the
Julius Tomb. In April 1523 Michelangelo wrote to Fattucci in Rome:

It is now about two years since I returned from placing orders in Carrara for quarrying the
marbles for the cardinal's tombs and when I went to discuss them with him he told me to find
some sound solution for doing the said tombs quickly. I wrote and sent him an account of all
the ways of doing them, as you know, since you read it; that is to say, that I would do them
either on contract, or for a monthly or a daily salary, or without payment, as his lordship
might please, because I was anxious to do them. None of my offers was accepted. It was said
that I had no mind to serve the cardinal.

Then, when the cardinal reopened the matter I offered to make the models in wood to the
full size that the tombs are to be, and to put in all the figures in clay and shearings to the full
size, and finished exactly as they are to be, and I pointed out that this would be a quick and
inexpensive way to do them. ... Then, as soon as I heard that the cardinal was going to
Lombardy I went to see him, because I was anxious to serve him. He told me to expedite the
marbles and to get the men and to do everything I could, so that he might see something
completed without my consulting him further; and that if he survived, he would also do the
façade and that he was leaving orders to Domenico Buoninsegni to arrange about all the
money required.

As soon as the cardinal left I wrote and gave Domenico Buoninsegni an account of all that he
had said to me and I told him that I was ready to do everything the cardinal desired. I kept a
copy of this, which I had witnessed, so that everyone might know that it was not my
responsibility. Domenico immediately came to see me and told me he had no authority
whatever and that if I wanted anything, he would write to the cardinal about it. I told him I did
not want anything. Finally, on the cardinal's return, Figiovanni told me he wanted to see me. I
went at once, supposing he wished to discuss the tombs. He said to me, 'For these tombs we
should require at least one good piece, that is to say, something by your own hand.' He did not
say that he wanted me to execute them. I left, and said that I would return to discuss them with
him when the marbles arrived.

Now you know that in Rome the pope has been informed about this Tomb of Julius and that a *motu proprio* has been drawn up for him to sign, in order that proceedings may be taken against me for the return of the amount I received on account for the said work, and for the indemnity due; and you know that the pope said that this should be done 'if Michelangelo is unwilling to execute the Tomb'. It is therefore essential for me to do it, if I don't want to incur the loss, which you see is decreed. And if, as you tell me, Cardinal de' Medici now once again wishes me to execute the tombs at S. Lorenzo, you see that I cannot do so, unless he releases me from this affair in Rome. And if he releases me, I promise to work for him without any return for the rest of my life. It is not that I do not wish to execute the said Tomb, which I'm doing willingly, that I ask to be released, but in order to serve him. But if he does not wish to release me, but wants something by my hand for the said tombs, I'll do my best, while I'm working on the Tomb of Julius, to find time to execute something to please him. (C.2.571.)

The Figiovanni mentioned in Michelangelo's letter was a canon and sub-Prior of S. Lorenzo; a fussy nuisance of a man and a born trouble-maker, who was, however, eventually of very great use to Michelangelo in the troubles which came upon the city, and upon him, after the siege in 1529.

While the unfinished business of the Julius Tomb thus hung over him, Michelangelo could neither make headway with the Medici commission nor return to Rome. But the wheel of fortune turned again, for Hadrian VI died in September 1523. At the Conclave in November Cardinal Giulio was successful, and became Pope Clement VII. There was much rejoicing, particularly among Florentines, for it was hoped that another Golden Age of Leo was to begin. Events proved otherwise. Clement was temperamentally indecisive, and he was both unwise and unlucky in his alliances. His pontificate proved to be almost wholly disastrous.

On his election Clement VII said of Michelangelo, 'I wish him to attend to *my* affairs.' He was soon projecting further work on S. Lorenzo, even to talking about restarting work on the façade, if he lived long enough. Michelangelo was told to get the Tomb finished by other sculptors. Julius' heirs, however, insisted that, since he had received the fees, he should himself complete the Tomb.

In December 1523 Michelangelo was in Rome, perhaps to discuss both the Tomb and S. Lorenzo. On 23 December Fattucci wrote, reminding him of his good fortune in having Clement as patron, and giving him some good advice.

After you left I went to see Palavisino [Francesco Pallavicini] and we had a long talk, and he told me that the Archbishop of Avignon [Orlando del Caretto] wanted the Tomb to be finished, above all because you had had the greater part of the money. To this I replied that I did not understand him, because for the Tomb you had only had a small part, and that he did not know what had happened and that you had spent more money on the Tomb than you had ever had, and because you never made accounts for Julius, and since the death of Aginense there had been no one who had any standing or voice, and that you had never stopped working, as might be seen from the results. And beginning with the first tomb, you had gone to excavate the marbles, to which you gave a lot of time; and then you were made to paint, and the marbles were neglected. And for the Chapel, the pope always said he would satisfy Michelangelo, and all the money which he had given to you for the extra in the painting was largely put to the cost of the Tomb. Then how he brought you to Bologna, where you were for two years making that work, and never had as much money as you spent in the salaries of assistants and in living; and everything was done on the pope's word. And many other things; 'So that when Michelangelo's accounts for the Tomb are settled he will have in hand much less money than you think.'

And I would think that you should summon up in your mind all the things you have ever done for him right from the beginning, going to Carrara, and about the Chapel and the work in Bologna, because to settle all this with them would amount to such trifles, to tell the truth, that you would have left in hand so little that there would not be anything worth spending.

Clement VII by Sebastiano del Piombo, 1526. A detail of one of his earliest portraits of the Medici pope, who, after the Sack of Rome in the following year, always wore a beard.

But I recall that you told me that for the Chapel there was no contract at all, and he gave you a lot of money as a gift, and they have put it to the cost of the Tomb, so that everything can be referred to judgment and to see how much the work you have done is worth and what you have had, and how much you will have in hand, and if it is possible to make a tomb for that amount of money. And you must remember everything very carefully, and write down in full what you have done and what you have had, so that everything will be clear and we can get out of it as best we can, which is all that is wanted. And send it together with a copy of the contract. Give it to Spina, who will send it promptly.

And now I remind you to think of the great freedom given you by such a pope as this one, to be able to do whatever you think fit; so that every study, every labour and effort will be a joy to make up for the time lost. And I commend myself to you. And write what you are doing, so that I may share in the pleasure.

This letter I have had copied by Lionardo [Sellaio], so that you will read it more easily. I beg you to go and see my mother and tell her that I am well. And be yourself of good heart, because I know what Jacopo [Salviati] has told me. And Spina has instructions to give you whatever money you need. (C.3.592.)

The outcome of Fattucci's sensible and kindly letter was that Michelangelo prepared the statement he wanted; but the matter remained unresolved.

Messer Giovan Francesco – You ask me in one of your letters how my affairs stand regarding Pope Julius. I assure you that if damages could be claimed I should expect rather to be the creditor than the debtor. Because when he sent for me from Florence, which was, I believe, in the second year of his pontificate, I had undertaken to execute half the Sala del Consiglio of Florence, that is to say, to paint it, for which I was getting three thousand ducats; and I had already done the cartoon, as is known to all Florence, so that the money seemed to me half earned. And of the twelve *Apostles* that I also had to execute for Sta Maria del Fiore, one was blocked out, as can still be seen, and I had already transported the greater part of the marble. But when Pope Julius took me away from here I got nothing either for the one or for the other.

Then when I was in Rome with the said Pope, and when he had given me a commission for his Tomb, into which a thousand ducats' worth of marbles were to go, he had the money paid to me and sent me to Carrara to get them. I remained there eight months to have the marbles blocked out and I transported nearly all of them to the Piazza of St Peter, but some of them remained at Ripa. Then, after I had completed the payment for the freight for the said marbles, I had no money left from what I had received for the said work, but I furnished the house I had in the Piazza of St Peter with beds and household goods out of my own money, in anticipation of the Tomb, and I brought assistants from Florence, some of whom are still living, to work on it, and I paid them in advance out of my own money. At this point Pope Julius changed his mind and no longer wanted to go on with it. But I, not knowing this, went to ask him for money and was turned away from the audience chamber. Enraged at this, I immediately left Rome, and what I had in the house went to pieces and the said marbles, that I had transported, remained in the Piazza of St Peter until the election of Pope Leo, and in one way and another they came to grief. Among other things which I can prove, two pieces of four and a half *braccia*, which had cost me over fifty gold ducats, were stolen from me by Agostino Chigi from Ripa; these could be recovered, because there are witnesses. But to return to the marbles, from the time that I went for them and stayed in Carrara, until I was turned away from the Palace, more than a year went by and during that time I never had anything and it cost me several tens of ducats.

Then the first time that Pope Julius went to Bologna I was forced to go there, with a rope round my neck, to ask his pardon, whereupon he gave me his figure to do in bronze, which was about seven *braccia* in height, seated. When he asked me what it would cost, I replied that I believed it could be cast for about a thousand ducats; but that it was not my trade and that I did not want to be obliged to do it. He replied, 'Set to work and cast it over and over again till it succeeds, and we will give you enough to content you.' To be brief, it was cast twice, and at the end of the two years I had stayed there I found myself four and a half ducats to the good. And from that time I never had anything more. But all the expenses I had in the said two years were included in the thousand ducats for which I had said it could be cast, and these were paid me in instalments by Messer Antonio Maria da Legnia[me], a Bolognese.

When I had set up the figure on the façade of S. Petronio and returned to Rome, Pope Julius still did not want me to do the Tomb, and set me to paint the vault of Sixtus and we made a bargain for three thousand ducats. The first design for the said work was for twelve Apostles in the lunettes [*sic*] and the usual ornamentations to fill the remaining area.

After the work was begun it seemed to me that it would turn out a poor affair, and I told the pope that if the Apostles alone were put there it seemed to me that it would turn out a poor affair. He asked me why. I said, 'Because they themselves were poor.' Then he gave me a new commission to do what I liked, and said he would content me and that I should paint down to the Histories below. Meanwhile, when the vault was nearly finished the pope returned to Bologna; whereupon I went there twice for money that was owed me, but effected nothing and wasted all that time until he returned to Rome. When I returned to Rome I began to do the cartoons for the said work, that is for the ends and the sides round the said chapel of Sixtus, in the expectation of having the money to finish the work. I was never able to obtain anything; but one day when I was complaining to Messer Bernardo da Bibbiena and to Attalante that I couldn't remain in Rome any longer but must go with God, Messer Bernardo told Attalante that he would remind him that he intended to have money paid to me in any case. And he had two thousand ducats of the Camera paid to me, which, together with the first thousand for the marbles, they are putting to my account for the Tomb. But I reckoned that I was owed more for the time I had lost and the works I had done. And from the said money, as Messer Bernardo and Attalante had saved my life, I gave the former a hundred ducats and the latter fifty.

Then came the death of Pope Julius and at the beginning of Leo, as Aginense wished to increase the size of his Tomb, that is, to execute a larger work than the one I had first designed, a new contract was drawn up. And when I did not wish them to put to the account the three thousand ducats I had received, and showed that I was owed much more, Aginense called me an impostor. (C.3.594.)

On 7 January 1524, Michelangelo wrote to Giovanni Spina, an excellent and honest man who dealt with the financing of the works at S. Lorenzo; he worked for the Salviati bank in Florence, and himself came of an important banking family.

The bearer of this will be Antonio di Bernardo Mini, my assistant. Will you pay him fifteen ducats in gold in respect of the models of the Tombs for the Sacristy of S. Lorenzo, which I am doing for Pope Clement. (C.3.601.)

The 'models for the tombs' were the wooden models for the architectural framework into which the sculpture was to be inserted. Also in January he wrote to Fattucci:

His Holiness ... wishes the design of the Library to be by my hand. I have no information about it, nor do I know where he wants to build it. ... I will do what I can, although it's not my profession. (C.2.602.)

From 1523 onwards, Clement insisted on Michelangelo's being in control of all the works at S. Lorenzo, and Michelangelo does not seem to have objected to the extra responsibility, after his one protest about architecture not being his profession. He was, however, deeply troubled, once again, over the supply of marble, and this prompted him to write direct to Clement, a couple of months after he became pope. The letter can be dated from the mention of the completion of the lantern of the Chapel, which must have been early in 1524, though it has been dated as late as January or February 1525.

Most Blessed Father – As intermediaries are often the cause of grave misunderstandings, I have, accordingly, made bold to write to Your Holiness without their intervention, about the tombs here at S. Lorenzo. I declare that I know not which is preferable – a disadvantage which

146

proves to be a benefit, or an advantage which proves to be a hindrance. I am certain, idle and unreasonable though I am, that had I been left to carry on as I began, all the marbles for the said work would be in Florence today, blocked out as required, and with less expense than has so far been incurred, and they would be of a quality as admirable as the others I brought here.

Now I see that it is going to be a long business and I do not know how it will proceed. Therefore, should matters turn out to be displeasing to Your Holiness, I desire to be exonerated; since I have no authority here, I do not think I should have the blame either. If Your Holiness wishes me to accomplish anything, I beg You not to have authorities set over me in my own trade, but to have faith in me and give me a free hand. Your Holiness will see what I shall accomplish and the account I shall give of myself.

Stefano [Lunetti] has finished the lantern of the chapel of the said S. Lorenzo here and has uncovered it. It is universally admired by everyone, as I hope it will be by Your Holiness, when You see it. We are having the ball which surmounts it made about a *braccia* in diameter and, in order to vary it from the others, I decided to have it made with facets, and this is being done. (C.3.687.)

It was however, a full year before the difficulties he endured, still through the machinations of Buoninsegna and Niccolini, were finally ended.

The Biblioteca Laurenziana was originally Lorenzo il Magnifico's own collection of manuscripts and books, some inherited from his grandfather Cosimo, and increased by his own large acquisitions. In 1437, Cosimo had bought from the executors of the scholar Niccolò Niccoli, who had died bankrupt, about four hundred rare manuscripts so as to keep the collection from being sold up piecemeal. For the encouragement of learning, he presented them to the monastery of S. Marco to found a public library, and he commissioned Michelozzo, the architect of the Medici palace, to build a new library over a range of monks' cells. This is a long, basilican hall, with a barrel-vaulted nave and cross-vaulted aisles borne on slender Ionic columns, lit from both sides. It once had reading desks, or carrels, of cypress wood on either side. After the expulsion of the Medici in 1494, the Republic confiscated Lorenzo's library and kept it at S. Marco, but Leo X, when still Cardinal Giovanni, recovered it and removed it to Rome in 1508. He continued to add to it, and when he became pope was careful not to merge his private library with the Vatican one. After Cardinal Giulio became pope in 1523 he returned the whole Medici library to Florence, and, following the precedent set by his great-grandfather Cosimo, he gave it to the monastery of S. Lorenzo and arranged for a proper library to be built for it, so that it might be used freely by scholars – as it is to this day.

The siting of a library over a range of monastic buildings was traditional; so was Clement's insistence on its being vaulted above the decorative ceiling and also below the floor, to isolate it from the priests' quarters underneath. More than once in a long correspondence the rueful comment recurs: 'in case some drunkard, as might happen among the priests, should set fire to his room and from his room to the library' (Fattucci to Michelangelo, 3 April 1524, C.3.628).

The structural problems were considerable. In early February Fattucci wrote to Michelangelo:

With this I return to you the tabernacle, the doorway and the sketch of the vault, which greatly pleased His Holiness. . . . Also I should like to know how large are the first frames of the vault, how many there are in each row and how many rows there are. Now, to return to the Library, it appears to our Lord that seven rooms are to be demolished above, and another seven below are to be deprived of light, and this does not please him. (C.3.614.)

The 'tabernacle' was a ciborium proposed for the choir of the church of S. Lorenzo, but not made; the doorway was for the entrance to the Chapel, and again this was not done. The vault refers to the coffered dome of the Chapel, which was an important part of the design, in that it reflects the Pantheon in Rome, which was a place of burial for the illustrious; such an echo in the design of the Medici Chapel was an essential part of its symbolism. The difficulty arising from the provision of an access to the Library, and also the extra thickness of the walls required to support the additional weight, caused a momentary change in the proposed site. The same letter goes on to enquire:

... what you think of the Library on the piazza on the side of the Borgo S. Lorenzo; and see how much the priests or others get in rent from those shops and houses which would have to be taken for the Library, and how many shops would have to go under it, to recompense the priests for their loss. ... And in particular tell me how many rooms would have to be demolished, because in fact, on the other one, half the monastery is being destroyed. (C. 3.614.)

By 10 March 1524, both sites were still being discussed. The pope was insisting on a fine ceiling, not coffered like the Roman ones which he disliked, and the provision of some small rooms for quiet study. Two of these were to be placed at the far end of the library, and another two to flank the entrance. By 3 April, all had changed again and the library was definitely to be built over the range running from the Old Sacristy, where Michelangelo originally wanted it, because of the damage such a two-storey structure would do if it projected into the piazza in front of the church. Michelangelo was obviously thinking ahead to the possibility of the façade project being revived. Even if built from scratch on a new site like the piazza one, the structure would still have to have two storeys, since the contents had to be protected from damp and from flooding (not unknown in Florence well before the great disaster of 1966).

Work on the Library designs, and on the architecture and sculpture in the Chapel, continued in parallel. The seventy-three letters which passed between Fattucci and Michelangelo between 20 December 1523 and 21 December 1526 switch from one job to another, and also discuss the latest state of the negotiations over the Julius Tomb. Unfortunately, the correspondence is very much one-way; only a few of Michelangelo's letters to Fattucci have survived – sometimes only because he made drafts of the more important ones. Their disappearance must be another of the losses resulting from the Sack of Rome in 1527, when even the inlaid marquetry wainscotting in the pope's Vatican Stanze was torn out and burnt, and documents also were no more than handy fuel.

By 13 May 1524 Michelangelo had solved the problem of the large increase in wall thickness required to support the building above, which Clement felt impinged too far on the cloister. He proposed a system of pilasters – or rather strip buttresses – inside and out, which would enable the wall areas between them to remain quite thin.

Into this already huge undertaking of the New Sacristy with its tombs, and the Library, Jacopo Salviati in mid-May dropped the proposal for even more work. Fattucci's letter of 23 May 1524 says:

Last Sunday, being in the Belvedere, when our Lord was discussing the tombs with Jacopo Salviati, and one subject leading to another, Messer Jacopo said to the pope: 'Holy Father, Your Holiness ought to make a tomb for Leo in S. Lorenzo, and if Your Holiness were of my mind, you would make one for yourself also.'

It seemed to me that His Holiness lent a willing ear to this and said, 'How so?'

And Messer Jacopo answered: 'If there were space, I would make two tombs with two chests as are to be made for Lorenzo and Giuliano the Elder, and another with two chests for the two dukes, and another pair opposite, one for Leo and the other for Clement.'

It seemed to me that this pleased him and he said, 'And it would be necessary to put two chests in the Chapel, if I understand you.'

So I am letting you know so that you can think about it for a bit. . . . Don't let it be seen that I have written you anything, so that it appears that you think night and day about our Lord's affairs. And if you see something which can be done, don't consider the expense. (C.3.640.)

On 29 May, Fattucci, when acknowledging a drawing of the pilaster-buttresses, says that Clement wants to know more about the woodwork for inside the library. Fattucci also urges him to think whether the present design for the tombs in the Chapel can be altered:

Think about the tomb for the two popes, that is one each and the other two for the dukes, two tomb chests on each wall and the other wall with the two tomb chests for the Magnifico Lorenzo and the Magnifico Giuliano, as was at first designed; and with the most honourable position for the popes, the other for the two dukes and the least honourable for the two Magnifici . . . and make a little sketch and send it to me, because I am certain it would be very welcome. (C.3.641.)

He ends on a more personal note:

Pray to God for me, because there is much sickness here. Don't say anything to my mother. I am as careful as I can be. (C.3.641.)

On 7 June 1524, Fattucci acknowledges a drawing for a tomb to be placed in one of the *lavamani* flanking the altar; 'But it is too small for a pope.' On 25 June he says:

About the house that cuts off the light from the *lavamano*: our Lord says that you should agree and give what it's worth, so as to buy it and pull it down. (C.3.646.)

The north side of S. Lorenzo had a number of houses attached to it, and those surrounding the New Sacristy, which belonged to the Nelli family, were not finally demolished until 1939–42. Up to then, it was impossible to see the foundations of the New Sacristy, so that the existence of the crypt under the altar remained unsuspected.

On 28 January 1525 the same troubles which had plagued Michelangelo during the work on the façade came to a head once more. Fattucci begins by complaining somewhat that Michelangelo's slowness in answering letters is leaving him, Fattucci, ill-informed:

You never told me why the doors weren't done, nor if the marble had come from Pisa after I had written for it. Nor what Stefano [Lunetti] the miniaturist did, which let you down, so that I couldn't convince Jacopo Salviati, who believed that others were the cause, and I have shown him how Domenico [Buoninsegna] and Niccolini are those who had been prolonging the business and that the marbles didn't come so as to make you angry, and Messer Jacopo tells me that you should tell everything, so that one can arrange for it. Please do this. (C.3.686.)

Another letter from Fattucci on 16 March 1525 must have brought the most welcome news:

I have today heard from Spina, who tells me that you have been told a false lie, and lies are much more serious when they are visible or heard. I said so at once to Messer Jacopo, who laughed and said that Domenico could do you neither good nor ill, and you should laugh at it, and he believes that these are Domenico's partisans or adherents, to cause you anguish. So please don't listen to anyone, because His Holiness, when talking about Sansovino, said that he wanted you to do as you pleased, and that he wished to be able to blame or praise you and no other, and he left everything to you. So go on working and think of nothing else.

Also I have to tell you that Bernardo Niccolini will not annoy you any longer, and will no longer have the tabernacles carried into the sacristy, as you saw, because Messer Jacopo wrote to him yesterday that since he had to go and take office in Arezzo he was to surrender the accounts to Spina concerning what he has done with the marbles, and you will no longer have to struggle with either him or with Domenico, but with Spina. I don't think Spina knows this. Tell him about it. (C.3.693.)

The only possible explanation of the bit about Sansovino is that Buoninsegna must have put it about that Michelangelo was either to be replaced by Sansovino, or ordered by Clement to employ him. Sansovino had since come round from his fury at not being employed on the façade, and had written several times to Michelangelo offering to serve him. The offers had not been taken up. Maybe Buoninsegna had thought Sansovino would be a useful tool.

The negotiations over the Julius Tomb still dragged on. In April 1525 Lionardo Sellaio wrote to tell Michelangelo that Julius' executors were going to take legal action against him. He asked for a power of attorney for Fattucci. Michelangelo replied to Giovanni Spina on 19 April 1525:

Giovanni – I don't think there is any necessity to send a power of attorney in respect of the Tomb of Pope Julius, because I don't want to go to law. They can't go to law if I admit that I'm in the wrong. I'll assume that I've been to law and have lost and must pay up. This I'm prepared to do, if I can. Therefore, if the pope will help me in this matter, which would be a great favour, seeing that, whether through old age or ill-health, I cannot finish the said Tomb, he, as an intermediary, can make it known that he wishes me to return what I've received for its execution, so that I can be quit of this burden; and the relatives of the said pope, having obtained restitution, can have it done to their satisfaction by someone else. In this way His Holiness, our Lord, can assist me greatly. And also in this, that I may have to return as little as possible, by having some of my arguments taken into consideration, though without departing from the principle, such as the time I wasted without remuneration when the pope [Julius] was at Bologna and on other occasions, as Ser Giovan Francesco [Fattucci], who is fully informed, is aware.

As soon as I'm clear as to how much I have to return, I'll review my resources. I'll sell out and so arrange things that I'll make restitution and be able to give my mind to the pope's [Clement's] concerns and get on with the work, since as it is I do not live life at all, much less do I work. There is no course that could be taken that would be safer for me, nor more acceptable to me, nor a greater relief to my mind, and it could be done amicably and without going to law. And I pray God that the pope may be willing to settle it in this way; since I don't think it will be an imposition on anyone. So would you please write to Messer Jacopo [Salviati] and put it in the best way you can, so that the matter may proceed and I may be able to work. (C.3.697.)

His gloomy state of mind at this time can be glimpsed in a note he wrote to Sebastiano Luciani (del Piombo) in Rome in May 1525:

Yesterday evening our friend Captain Cuio and several other gentlemen kindly invited me to go and have supper with them, which gave me the greatest pleasure, as I emerged a little from my depression, or rather from my obsession. I not only enjoyed the supper, which was extremely pleasant, but also, and even more than this, the discussions which took place. But later on my pleasure in the discussions increased on hearing the said Captain mention your name. Nor was this all; still later I was infinitely delighted when, on the subject of art, I heard the said Captain say that you were altogether unique and were held to be so in Rome. So that, had it been possible to be more cheerful, I should have been. Seeing, then, that my opinion is

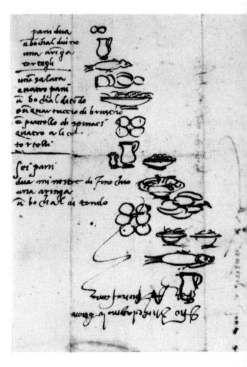

On a letter from Bernardo Niccolini (18 March 1518) Michelangelo has listed the food for three meals, with drawings probably for an illiterate housekeeper. It is very clearly Lenten fare: bread, herrings, tortelli (pasta stuffed with cheese and spinach), salad, spinach, four anchovies, fennel soup, and two sorts of wine, tondo (medium dry) and bruscho (very dry). It is to be hoped that his dinner with Captain Cuio provided more generous fare, for this list confirms the reports of Michelangelo's frugal living, Lent or no Lent.

Vestibule and stairs of Michelangelo's house in the Macel de' Corvi.

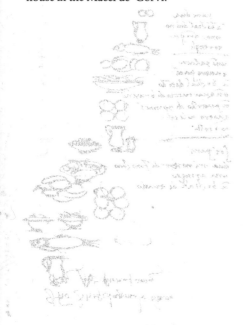

justified, don't say, henceforth, that you are not unique, when I write and tell you that you are, because there are too many witnesses and there is a picture here, thank God, which proves, to anyone who has eyes to see, that I'm right. (C.3.704.)

Cuio Dini was killed in the Sack of Rome on 7 May 1527. The picture by Sebastiano is possibly the portrait of Antonfrancesco degli Albizzi (Houston, Museum, Kress Collection) which arrived in Florence at about this date.

On 14 June 1525 Michelangelo signed a power of attorney for Fattucci to act for him in Rome in the negotiations over the Julius Tomb with Cardinal Santiquattro (Cardinal Aginense had died in 1520), and eventually they arrived at the compromise that Michelangelo should receive a further 8000 ducats (making 16,500 in all) and that he should receive the house in the Macel de' Corvi as his property. He was also allowed to employ other masters on the work, but he must do the group of the *Madonna and Child* in the *cappelletta* himself. Michelangelo did not want to agree. He was now so sick of the whole business that he declared himself willing to refund what he had received, and the heirs could get the Tomb done by other sculptors. His next letter to Fattucci was on 4 September 1525:

I've written to Rome several times saying that as I am obliged to serve Pope Clement in the execution of things which will take a long time to complete, and as I am an old man, I have no hope of being able to execute anything else and that for this reason, being unable to execute the Tomb of Julius, I desire to give satisfaction – if I am obliged to give satisfaction for what I have received – in money rather than in work, because I should not have time to do otherwise. I don't know what else to say to you in reply, because I'm not acquainted with the position nor do I understand the details as you do.

As to executing the said Tomb of Julius as a wall tomb, like those of Pius, I am agreeable to the method, which is quicker than any other.

I think that's all, except for saying this to you – abandon my affairs and your own and come home, because I hear the plague is again raging and I would rather have you alive than my affairs settled. So come home. If I die before the pope there will be no need for me to settle anything further; if I live, I'm sure the pope will settle the matter – if not now, some other time. So come home. I spent yesterday evening with your mother and in the presence of Granaccio and Giovanni the turner, I advised her to get you to come home. (C.3.713.)

When the heirs saw the drawing of the proposed design, they rejected it out of hand. It was based on the tomb of the second Piccolomini pope, Pius III, then in St Peter's, a design similar to the one of Pius II, Aeneas Silvius Piccolomini. These, both of which were removed to S. Andrea della Valle in 1614, were wall tombs of an old-fashioned type. The heirs now reverted to their demand for the return of all the money and the interest on it.

Meanwhile, Clement VII was as demanding as ever. Fattucci reported on 14 October 1525:

He said, 'I want him to think about my things, because I want to make a tomb for Leo and for me.' . . . He also wants to have a colossus made as high as the cornice of his house [the Medici palace]; he wants to put it on the space opposite Messer Luigi della Stufa next to the barber's, and because it is so large he wants it made in pieces. And I tell you, as from myself, that you will have to think about it and have the marble brought in without telling anyone anything. Then he gave me the job of finding four porphyry columns, and I answered that there were two of oriental granite, very fine, at Tre Fontane. He said that this was so, and that I should go and measure them and I could then tell him about them. . . . Think about that colossus, which according to what the pope says will be at least 25 *braccia* high [nearly 48 ft or 14.6 m], and therefore must be made in pieces. Don't tell anyone. . . . Tell me how the work goes and whether you have put a hand to anything other than those four figures, and when you will begin the *Rivers*. (c.3.717.)

Tre Fontane was an ancient abbey on the way to Ostia, south of Rome, in what is now the EUR Zone. The *Rivers* are the four figures of *River Gods* which were to have been placed below the sarcophagi of the dukes' tombs, two for each tomb. Models for at least two of these survive, though in damaged state. Michelangelo replied to Fattucci on 24 October:

194

In reply to your last letter the four figures begun are not yet finished, and there is still a considerable amount to do. The four others, representing Rivers, are not yet started, because we've got no marbles, although they've arrived here. I'm not saying why, because it's none of my business.

As to the affairs of Julius, I'm agreeable to doing a tomb like that of Pius in St Peter's, as I wrote you. I'll have it done here little by little, sometimes one piece and sometimes another, and I'll pay for it myself, if I have my salary and if I retain the house, as you wrote me; that is to say, the house in which I was living there in Rome, together with the marbles and other things in it. That is to say, if, in order to discharge my obligations as to the Tomb, I haven't got to give them, I mean the heirs of Pope Julius, anything other than I had to give them up till now – that is the said Tomb like that of Pius in St Peter's, and if I'm allowed a reasonable time, I'll do the figures myself. And as I've said, if I'm given my salary, I'll always go on working for Pope Clement with such powers as I have, which are slight, as I'm an old man – with this proviso, that the taunts, to which I see I am being subjected, cease, because they very much upset me and have prevented me from doing the work I want to do for several months now. For one cannot work at one thing with the hands and at another with the head, particularly in the case of marble. Here it is said that they are meant to spur me on, but I assure you they are poor spurs which drive one back. I haven't drawn my salary for a year now, and I'm struggling against poverty. I have to face most of the worries alone, and there are so many of them that they keep me more occupied than my work, since I cannot employ anyone to act for me, as I haven't the means. (c.3.719.)

Michelangelo felt so strongly about the stresses caused by the continued struggle over the Julius Tomb, and also about the long battle with Buoninsegna and Niccolini, that he had a copy made of this letter by his assistant Antonio Mini, and it seems clear that he intended Fattucci to show the letter to the pope. He is being very unfair about his salary. Fattucci had been urging him for months to draw it, or to arrange for it to be paid to a bank, but he had done nothing about it. Fattucci's reply came swiftly. It is dated 30 October.

Our Lord is very surprised that you have not replied about the colossus, nor about the tombs nor the ciborium on the altar of S. Lorenzo. Now, about your salary, I tell you that if you haven't had it it's your own fault, because you wouldn't have it. And at this moment I believe Spina has had instructions to pay you the lot, for the past and for the future. And if you wish for more, let me know and leave it to me. And so far as concerns spurring you on by these means, I say that whoever says so wishes you ill, and perhaps worse to your patrons. . . .

For the love of God, if you have any regard for me don't listen to these things, nor entertain these ideas, because they are inventions and fantasies thought up by people who wish you ill. They contrive to put them into your head, knowing your nature, and in this way prevent you from working, because if you don't work you lose favour and thus justify what they have said of you, which I know that you should know better than I do. And for this reason I don't want to write any more about it, because it upsets me very much. . . .

PS. I was in the room of our Lord and he passed through on his way to the Loggia and seeing me he called me over and said, after talking about you for a bit, that just to see your things he had decided to come to Florence in a year or eighteen months. Think how displeased he would be if you were not working like this. So I said that by then all would be in such a state that His Holiness would be satisfied . . . So give up these ideas and get on with the work, leaving who will to repeat stories and tales after their own fashion. (C.3.721.)

This crisis of nerve on Michelangelo's part was taken so seriously in Rome that on the same date Salviati wrote to him, upbraiding him for the fantasies he had got into his head. The letter, like Fattucci's, is one long protest by a man exasperated by wilful incomprehension and distrustfulness.

On 10 November 1525 Fattucci wrote to Michelangelo about the additional 146 small room (never built) for rare books. The pope was still talking about the colossus, the double tomb for Leo and himself, and the ciborium, and by 29 November was worrying about the skylights in the *ricetto*, or entrance hall, to the library.

Now about the windows in the roof with the glass *oculi* [circular skylights] in the ceiling. Our Lord says that they seem a fine and novel thing; even then he will not decide on it, but says it would be necessary to pay two brothers of the Gesuati to do nothing but clear off the dust. Nevertheless, if you agree, I will speak again with His Holiness. Let me know what you want me to do, because I'm pretty certain that since the idea pleased him, by talking to him again about it he will perhaps be satisfied. (C.3.728.)

The difficulty over the windows was that the interior architecture of the *ricetto*, which Clement had insisted should be fine and impressive, could not be matched to the exterior architecture. The window system of the library had been carried across the outside of the *ricetto* for reasons of visual harmony, but the three blind windows could not be reconciled with the blind windows of the interior system since they occurred at quite different levels. Michelangelo's first solution was to light the *ricetto* by means of skylights, and when the pope would have none of this, he proposed to raise the walls of the *ricetto* by two *braccia* and to insert circular windows into the space thus gained. Unfortunately, this meant raising the already completed roof. In the end, for reasons beyond the control of either Michelangelo or Clement, no solution was arrived at, and the upper part of the vestibule remained unfinished until 1900, when the present incorrect solution was imposed.

Meanwhile, discussions concerning the staircase had been going on. A double stair was projected by 13 April 1524. Between then and 12 April 1525 Clement changed his mind, and a single stair over the whole width of the vestibule was wanted. This single flight was modified into a triple flight culminating in a landing which led up to the entrance doorway, with the two side flights having steps of a different height from the central one, and also 147 with a different profile. It was not until the mid-to-late 1550s that the staircase was eventually completed in its present form, by Bartolomeo Ammanati, with the help of its original designer striving across a gap of thirty-odd years to remember what he had originally intended.

In December 1525 Michelangelo replied to Fattucci's letter about the colossus:

If I had as much strength as I have had amusement from your last letter I should believe I could complete, and quickly too, all the things about which you write to me, but as I haven't, I'll do what I can.

As to the colossus of forty *braccia* [*sic*] which you inform me is to go, or rather to be put at the corner of the loggia of the Medici garden, opposite Messer Luigi della Stufa's corner, I've considered it not a little in that position, as you instructed me. It seems to me that at the said corner it would not be well placed, because it would take up too much of the roadway; but at the other corner where the barber's shop is, it would in my opinion, look much better, because it has the piazza in front and would not be such a nuisance to the street. And since there might be some objections to doing away with the said shop, owing to the income it provides, I thought that the said figure might be made to sit down and the said work being hollow beneath – which can be conveniently done with blocks – its seat could come at such a height that the barber's shop could go underneath and the rent would not be lost. And as at present the said shop has an outlet for the smoke, I thought of putting a cornucopia, which would be hollow inside, into the hand of the said statue to serve as a chimney. Then, as I would have the head of such a figure hollow like the other members, I believe it, too, could be put to some use, for there is a huckster here in the piazza, a great friend of mine, who suggested to me in confidence that a handsome dovecote could be made inside. Another idea also occurred to me, which would be even better, but the figure would have to be considerably larger – which it could be since a tower is made up of blocks – and that is that the head might serve as a much-needed campanile for S. Lorenzo. And with the bells clanging inside and the sound issuing from the mouth the said colossus would seem to be crying aloud for mercy, especially on feast days when there is more ringing and with larger bells.

As to bringing in the marbles for the said statue unbeknown to anyone, I thought of bringing them in by night, well covered up, so as not to be seen. There would be a little risk at the gate, but for this too we'll find a way; at the worst the S. Gallo gate won't fail us, because the postern is kept open all night.

As to doing or not doing the things which are being done, which you tell me are to be held over, they had better be left to whomsoever will have to do them, because I shall have so much to do that I'm not bothering with them any more. For me this will suffice – that the thing should be imposing.

I'm not replying to you about everything, because Spina is shortly coming to Rome and will do better by word of mouth than I by writing, and in more detail. (C.3.730.)

The reference to the huckster and the dovecote is a snide allusion to Figiovanni, who had complained to the pope at one point that in rebuilding the monastery of S. Lorenzo for the Library, Michelangelo had turned it into a dovecote. The reply to this letter came from Clement himself, on 23 December 1525; his secretary wrote that the pope had received the drawing of the library, and that the *oculi* were doubtless a fine thing, but that the amount of dust they would collect would be greater than the amount of light they would admit. Also, since the introduction of these windows required the walls to be raised by two *braccia*, this meant redoing the already completed roof. He also remarks, rather tartly, that on the subject of the colossus the pope meant it, and was not joking, and wanted it done and brought to perfection like everything else. Clement himself added a few words in his own hand:

You know that popes do not live long, and we could not wish more than we do to see or at least to know that the chapel with the tombs of our family and also the library are finished. Therefore we commend the one and the other to you, and meanwhile we will bring ourselves (as once you used to say) to a decent patience; praying God to give you the courage to carry everything forward with all haste. Never doubt that you will lack either work or reward while we live. Remain with the blessing of God and ours. (C.3.732.)

He signed this with his own name, Julius – which adds a note of pathos, since this is the name by which the young Michelangelo must have known him at the court of Lorenzo il Magnifico, where Giulio had grown up after his father Giuliano was murdered in the Pazzi Conspiracy a month before he was born. The pope was, in fact, just over three years younger than his artist.

Michelangelo's gentle ridicule settled the matter of the colossus. During the whole of 1525 work proceeded apace in both the Library and the Chapel. It is impossible to work out exactly how many men were employed on these works separately, but the number specified in the *Ricordi* as working on marble (presumably on the Chapel, since the stonework in the Library and the vestibule is the lovely grey-green *pietra serena*) was almost constant at between six and twelve, with a hard core of seven. On the Library, the numbers ranged from fifteen in March 1525 to thirty-eight in April, sixty-seven in May/June, ninety-eight in July, to a hundred in August 1525. After this date Michelangelo keeps the accounts differently. He lists each part of the interior stonework of the Library and the vestibule separately, with the price paid to the mason in charge of making it. Clearly by now he was no longer employing a large force of building labourers for the construction work. The last entry in the *Ricordi* for work in the *ricetto*, or vestibule, is in a folio for 23 June 1526. After this the *Ricordi* revert to being his personal account book – how much rent he received for property, how many barrels of wine or oil he got from a farm, how many *staia* of wheat he had sold. Even his payments for cloth for clothes, and for the wages of his housekeeper and his assistant, Antonio Mini, are listed.

On 17 June 1526 he wrote to Fattucci:

This coming week I shall have the figures that are blocked out in the Sacristy covered up, because I want to leave the Sacristy free for the *scarpellini* working on the marbles, as I want them to begin building in the other tomb opposite the one that is built in, which is aligned, or very nearly. And while they are building it in I thought the vault might be done and supposed that, with enough men, it could be done in two or three months, but I don't know. At the end of next week our Lord can send Messer Giovanni da Udine whenever he wishes, if he thinks the vault should be done now, as I shall be ready.

As to the *ricetto*, four columns have been built in this week – one of them was built in before. The tabernacles will be a little behindhand; however, I think it will be finished in four months from to-day. The framework of the floor should be begun by now, but the limes are not yet seasoned; we'll hasten the drying process as much as possible.

I'm working as hard as I can, and in a fortnight's time I shall get the other *Captain* [duke] started; then of the important things, I shall have only the four *Rivers* left. The four figures on the tomb chests [sarcophagi], the four figures on the ground, which are the *Rivers*, the two *Captains*, and *Our Lady* which is going into the Tomb at the top end, are the figures I want to do myself. And of these, six are begun. I feel confident about doing them within a reasonable time and having the others, which are not so important, done in part. I think that's all. Commend me to Giovanni Spina and beg him to send a note to Figiovanni to beg him not to call off the carters from here in order to send them to Pescia, because we should be left without stone, and likewise not to use his charms to ingratiate himself with the *scarpellini* here by saying to them, 'These people have no consideration for you, making you work until dusk, now that the nights last only two hours.'

We are hard put to it with a hundred eyes to keep one of them at work, and even that one has been spoilt for us by these bowels of compassion. Patience! God forbid that what does not displease Him should displease me! (c.3.752.)

Woodcut from Sigismondo Fante's *Trionfo di Fortuna*, published in Venice, 1527.

By this time Clement VII was in serious difficulties, political and hence financial. He had failed to maintain a coherent policy between France and the Empire of Charles V. What is worse, he had backed the losing side. Francis I of France was no longer in a position to support him, and his enemies were in command of Italy. On 17 July 1526, Fattucci wrote telling Michelangelo to cut down on expenditure for work on the Library by two-thirds, but to continue with the Chapel as before. On the 12 September he urges Michelangelo on, and in answer obviously to a suggestion of a present or reward for his own services, he says merely that a letter of recommendation to the pope would be reward enough. On 16 October, he thanks Michelangelo for reducing the number of his marble cutters to six, and says that work on the ceiling of the

Library must stop, but he is to continue to spend as much as is necessary for the Chapel and the figures.

Michelangelo began to see the desirability of keeping his options open. On 1 November 1526 he wrote to Fattucci:

I know that Spina has recently written very heatedly to Rome about my affairs regarding this Julius affair. If he made a mistake, in view of the times in which we are living, it is my mistake, because I implored him to write. Perhaps anxiety caused me to be too insistent. I had recently had a notification from Rome about the said affair of mine, which has filled me with alarm. This is because of the ill-will the relatives of Julius bear me – and not without reason – and because the suit is proceeding and they are demanding such damages that a hundred such as I would not suffice to discharge them. This has put me in a great turmoil and has made me wonder where I should find myself if the pope were to fail me, since I should be unable to exist in this world. This is the reason I got him to write, as I've said. Now I only want what pleases the pope; I know he has no wish to see me ruined and put to shame.

I have observed that building is being slowed down here, and I realize that public expenses are being curtailed, and I realize that a house is being rented in S. Lorenzo for me and that my salary is being paid as well – which are not slight expenses. If it would be advantageous to curtail these expenses also and to give me leave, so that I might begin something, either here or in Rome, for the said work of Julius, I should be very glad, because I desire to be rid of this obligation more than to live. None the less, I'm never disposed to depart from the will of the pope – provided that I comprehend it. So, as you know my mind, I beg you to write and tell me what the pope's wishes are and I won't contravene them. And I beg you to find out from him and to write and tell me on his behalf, so that I may the better and more readily obey, and also so that one day, should it befall, I may be able to justify myself by means of your letters. I think that's all.

If I haven't been able to make myself clear to you, don't be surprised, because I'm completely distraught. You know my mind; you will know his, who must be obeyed. Reply I beg of you. (C.3.760.)

Michelangelo also wrote, probably in December 1526, direct to Giovanni Spina, who had been responsible for all the payments required by the works at S. Lorenzo:

Realizing, as I've said, that the times are unfavourable to this art of mine, I do not know if I have any further expectation of my salary. If I were certain of not having it any longer, I should not cease on that account to work for the pope and do everything I could; but in view of the obligations that you know I am under, I should not go on keeping open house, as I have somewhere else to live with much less expense, and it would also relieve you of having to pay the rent. If however my salary is to be continued, I'll stay here as I am and do my best to fulfil my obligations. (C.3.769.)

On 21 December 1526 Fattucci wrote to him for the last time. It is one of his normal letters, encouraging Michelangelo to work, and urging him not to listen to rumours. The pope, he assures him, is concerned lest he be working too hard, but he also repeats the story that Figiovanni has written to Clement saying that Michelangelo is not working, to which the pope replied that Figiovanni 'is a brute, and would be well advised to gossip less'. He ends with the traditional 'I commend myself to you. God guard you from harm' (C.3.767).

At this point all correspondence with Rome stops. During the period when the last letters were written, Rome had undergone a first taste of the horror to come. After the total defeat of his allies the French at Pavia in February 1525, when Francis I himself was taken prisoner, Clement had been forced to submit to Spanish domination. Fatally, he then tried to change sides again. As a punitive act the Emperor Charles V encouraged the Colonna – a feudal family of immense power centred on the country between Rome and the borders of Naples – to attack Rome in September 1526. Clement took refuge in the Castel Sant'Angelo, from which he witnessed the pillaging of St Peter's.

When he emerged after a patched-up truce, one condition of which was a 'no victimization' clause for the Colonna, he immediately launched a revenge attack on them. The emperor, convinced that Clement's hedging and vacillation were proof of total unreliability, rather than evidence of his weakness, indecision and political ineptness – how unlike a Medici! – determined to punish him for his breaches of faith. He loosed against him a terrifying army composed of Spanish and German troops – the latter being the dreaded *Landsknechte*, who, being Lutheran, took a particular delight in assailing the papacy. This rabble army was unpaid and almost totally unprovisioned; they were expected to live off the land and to pay themselves by loot. By March 1527, they had reached Bologna; Florence put itself into a state of defence, and the marauding rabble passed by and descended upon Rome, where it arrived on 6 May 1527 and by evening had taken the virtually indefensible city.

The pope fled back to the Castel Sant'Angelo and from there had a clear view of the appalling pillage. The Spaniards attacked the palaces of prelates and nobles; the Lutherans sacked the churches, monasteries and convents; and for six weeks the richest, most splendid city of the West since Constantinople was given over to plunder, rapine and murder. After only a few days there was no more fresh food; Rome always depended on daily provisioning of food and firewood. Citizens were tortured to extract ransoms, no woman, nun or lay, escaped rape, and over the next seven months every imaginable indignity, and many almost unbelievable in their beastliness, were inflicted upon the hapless population.

Finally, almost inevitably, plague broke out, and before it the army retreated. The pope escaped to Orvieto, so poor that he had not even the wherewithal to buy a pair of shoes, and then moved to Viterbo. He made peace with the emperor; since even he, who had launched the horror upon Rome, was shocked at the deed he had licensed, and his own Spanish dominions were loud in their condemnation of his part in the fate of the holy city.

Meanwhile the Florentines, seizing the chance of reasserting their ancient freedoms, had driven out their Medici rulers. These were two youths, the

Print of 1555 representing a confrontation between Pope Clement VII and a herald of the occupying armies of Charles V in the Castel Sant'Angelo, during the Sack of Rome in 1527. It is based on Martin Heemskerck's very exact views of Rome, made during his stay in 1532–35. In front of the Castel Sant'Angelo was the great tower built by Alexander VI to guard the bridge over the Tiber; at the back on the left is Old St Peter's with its campanile, the bare arches of the new basilica rising behind it and the single wing of Bramante's new Vatican palace. The statues of SS. Peter and Paul were not placed on the bridge until after the siege, but Heemskerck has used them to good effect, turning St Peter to glare angrily at the *Landsknecht* who jeers at him, and St Paul to gaze down with anguish at the cannons threatening the pope.

sixteen-year-old Alessandro, bastard son of a mulatto slave woman and of either Lorenzo of Urbino or even (rumour had it) Clement himself, and Ippolito, the eighteen-year-old bastard son of Giuliano of Nemours. The deep personal affront which Clement felt at this led him to agree with Charles V on the subjugation of Florence – a pact sealed by the betrothal of Alessandro to Charles's own bastard daughter Margaret.

The republican Signoria in Florence had no illusions as to the penalty which would be exacted for their rejection of the Medici. The first necessity was to repair, rebuild, re-establish the fortifications. Michelangelo was in a very awkward position. He was a staunch Florentine of the older generation, and a strong believer in the city's right to self-government. At the same time, he was deeply involved with the papacy, and engaged on the exaltation of the Medici by his work on the tombs in the Medici Chapel, one of which was for the father of Ippolito. Despite his divided allegiance, Michelangelo immediately offered to work on designing the fortifications, and after working on them wholeheartedly and gratis for over a year, he was appointed in January 1529, in a document containing the most fulsome commendations, 'superintendent and procurator general over the construction and fortification of the city walls as well as over all defensive operations'.

150

Since the city lies astride the Arno, it was more necessary to defend it from the north, in that a river crossing would be hazardous for the enemy. The hill of S. Miniato was the most vulnerable point, since artillery sited there could have battered the city at leisure. Michelangelo fortified the hill, only to find when his back was turned that his defences were dismantled by order of the Gonfalonier, Niccolò Capponi. Part of the trouble lay in Michelangelo's previous connections; because he had been so closely allied to the papacy there were many who distrusted him. In July 1529 he was sent to Ferrara to inspect the famous fortifications built by Duke Alfonso d'Este – the same Alfonso who had climbed the scaffolding of the Sistine Chapel to examine and admire the Ceiling. He was well received and shown all that he required. After his return to Florence Michelangelo became deeply suspicious of the integrity of the *condottiere* whom the Signoria had hired to command the Florentine forces. This was Malatesta Baglione, and once he was convinced that Baglione would betray the city, Michelangelo went to the Signoria and set out the reasons for his suspicions. But the Signoria turned on him with abuse,

... reproaching him with being timid and too suspicious ... When Michelangelo perceived that little value was attached to his words and that the city was bound to be ruined, he used his authority to have the gate opened for him and he went out with two companions and proceeded to Venice. (AC.61.)

Actually, there were three of them: his assistant Antonio Mini, the goldsmith Piloto, and Rinaldo Corsini. It would appear that he was induced to fly by threats of assassination, which an informer passed on to him – a ruse employed by Baglione to get rid of him. In September 1529, he wrote from Venice to Battista della Palla in Florence:

I left Florence, as I believe you know, and intended to go to France, but when I reached Venice and made enquiries about the route I was told that going from here one has to pass through German territory which is difficult and dangerous. I therefore decided to find out from you ... whether you were any longer disposed to go, and ... to inform me if you are and where you wish me to wait for you, and we'll go together. I left without taking leave of any of my friends ... but although, as you know, I wanted to go to France in any case, and several times asked permission, but never got it, it was not because I had not resolved to see the war through first without any fear whatsoever. But on Tuesday morning, the 21st day of September, someone came out from the S. Niccolò gate to the bastions where I was, and whispered in my ear that to remain any longer would be to risk my life. And he came home with me till he got me out of Florence, assuring me that this was for my good. Whether he were god or devil I know not. (C.3.798.)

Battista della Palla of Lucca was Francis I's agent in Italy for buying works of art for his collection. He answered Michelangelo's letter on 24 October, 1529.

By Bastiano, stonecutter ... I sent you a letter of my own, together with ten others from friends, and a safe conduct for the whole of November from our Signori, for which, for security, though we do all we can to ensure that it arrives safely, herewith is a copy. But it does not seem necessary either to repeat what I said ... in two pages of writing, nor to endorse the friends who repeat the same, who all with one voice, without differences or doubts, have told you that immediately you receive this letter and the safe conduct, you should return to your country, in order to preserve it, your friends, honour and integrity, and to rejoice in and enjoy the fruits of those times which you have so much desired and looked forward to. If anyone had predicted to me that, without any fear, I could have borne to know that close to the confines of my country there would be an enemy army, I should have thought it so difficult as to have considered it impossible; and I tell you that not only do I find myself without any fear, but am filled with such hope of a glorious victory, and for the last few days with such joy in my heart, that if God for our sins or for whatever other reason ... did not leave this army broken in our hands I would feel that grief which one suffers, not when one fails to achieve a longed-for blessing, but when one loses one already acquired.... And thus again, as powerfully as I can from the fullness of my heart, I beg you, immediately you receive this, to come and take the road to Lucca where, because of my intense desire that you will not be lost to our country, nor our country lost to you, I have planned that you will find me ... and when I think of being willing to be away from and remaining even for a single day during the war outside the city, it seems to be a great hardship, but for love of you it will seem a light one to bear. (C.3.799.)

Battista was less worldly wise than Michelangelo. All his burning patriotism and high courage would end in his death in prison in the castle of Pisa, where he was poisoned by his captors, once Alessandro had regained his ill-gotten duchy. Michelangelo made his way back slowly. Battista waited for him in Lucca or Pisa until 19 November, when he returned to Florence. Michelangelo arrived there on 23 November, when the sentence of outlawry passed on him on 30 September was repealed. He once again worked untiringly on the city's defences, particularly at S. Miniato, where his device of hanging mattresses stuffed with fleece from the overhang of the tower so broke the impact of the enemy cannonballs at the end of their long trajectory that they were unable to do more than superficial damage, and thus saved the
148   position from falling into enemy hands. The siege was fought with desperate bitterness. The invading army, under Philibert of Châlons, Prince of Orange, was not large enough to invest the city totally, and the tactic which eventually settled the fate of Florence was to cut off, by fast armed raiding parties, the food convoys which sought to enter the city from the south. The heroic guerrilla warfare waged by Francesco Ferruccio to relieve the pressure on Florence by drawing off the enemy ended at the battle of Gavinana in the hills above Pistoia on 3 August 1530. The Prince of Orange was killed, and Ferruccio, desperately wounded, was taken prisoner and immediately murdered.

A few days later, Michelangelo's suspicions of Baglione were vindicated. Baglione had been in secret contact with emissaries from Clement, who, to give him his due, was appalled at the prospect of his own city being sacked with the same ferocity as Rome; and in any case by now the city was a prey to famine and plague. Perhaps Baglione – a Perugian from a family celebrated for its murderous treachery – was no more than a realist. On 12 August 1530 he compelled the Signoria to capitulate by turning his own cannon on the city. A treaty was signed with the envoys of the emperor and the pope, by which, after payment of a huge indemnity, the integrity of the city was guaranteed and an amnesty granted to those who had fought against the Medici. Baglione, with his Corsican mercenaries, held the city until 12 September, and then gave it up to a detachment of *Landsknechte* under a Spanish commander. Immediately and in breach of the treaty, the reprisals started; half a dozen of the most prominent members of the Signoria were beheaded, many were imprisoned or destituted, and Michelangelo found himself proscribed.

But then, when the enemy had entered the city by agreement and many citizens had been seized and killed the *corte* was sent to Michelangelo's house to arrest him; and the rooms and all the chests, even the chimney and the privy, were opened. But Michelangelo, fearing what was to ensue, had fled to the house of a great friend of his, where he remained hidden for many days without anyone except the friend knowing that he was in the house, and he saved himself; because when the furore had subsided Pope Clement wrote to Florence that Michelangelo was to be sought; and the pope's orders were that when he was found, if he were willing to continue the work he had already begun on the tombs, he should be treated with courtesy and allowed to go free. Learning of this, Michelangelo emerged, and although it had been some fifteen years since he had touched his tools [*sic*], he set about the project with such diligence that, impelled more by fear than by love, in a few months he made all [*sic*] those statues which appear in the sacristy of S. Lorenzo. It is true that none of them has received the final touches; however, they are all brought to such a stage that the excellence of the artist is very apparent, and the rough surfaces do not interfere with the perfection and the beauty of the work. (AC.63–4.)

With what bitter change of heart he must have returned to the work is clear from the two verses which sum up this tragic end to so grand an enterprise. A visitor to the Chapel, where around the floor the statues stood awaiting their final assembly on the tombs, thinking to give him pleasure hung a quatrain on the figure of *Night*.

140

> Night, whom you see so gently sleeping
> Was by an Angel carved from this stone;
> Because she sleeps, she lives. If you disbelieve me
> Wake her, and she will speak to you.

Michelangelo's reply is poignant:

> Sweet to me is sleep, and even more to be of stone
> While wrong and shame endure;
> Not to see, nor to hear is my good fortune.
> So do not wake me; oh! speak softly here. (V2.7.197.)

It was not until 1975 that an accidental discovery revealed the secret of Michelangelo's hiding-place. Under the altar space and its flanking *lavamani* in the Medici Chapel was found a tiny crypt, accessible only by a ladder under a trapdoor hidden under piles of abandoned furniture and rubbish. Here he must have lived, probably from mid-August immediately after the capitulation until the second half of October – a space of around two months. He owed his safety to Figiovanni, who, despite their earlier disagreements and despite also his own passionate pro-Medici feelings, accepted that the artist was not a man to be given over to sectarian vengeance as had happened, with

One of the drawings on the wall of the tiny crypt under the Medici Chapel clearly represents the lower half of the statue of Giuliano, Duke of Nemours.

151

such shocking breach of faith, to so many of his former colleagues in the anti-Medici party. Perhaps also the cynical betrayal of the city by Baglione was not an example he wished to emulate.

It can only have been during this period of enforced and wearisome idleness that the tremendous series of drawings on the walls of the crypt were executed. Many of the figures are life-size, and many considerably larger; many are connected with known works, such as the figures in the Chapel overhead; some, however, are for things which he elaborated much later – such as the drawing for the *Fall of Phaeton*. Some are whole figures, many are fragments, many are superimposed one on another. Their technique varies from a coarse charcoal to a greasy chalk, and some are in the red oxide usually associated with *sinopie* – the red under-drawing which lies beneath most frescoes. Too overt an acquisition of artists' materials might well have aroused suspicion, and Figiovanni was a cautious man.

Even after the disasters of the Sack and the Siege were over, peace brought no respite and no release from his worries. The business in which his favourite brother Buonarroto was a partner had failed, and in February 1528 Lodovico had sent Michelangelo a list of the creditors and debtors; in July 1528 Buonarroto had died of plague. During the siege Lodovico himself had been a refugee in Pisa, but he returned afterwards to Settignano, where he died in the autumn of 1531 at the age of eighty-seven. Two other brothers, Gismondo and Giovansimone, were both ill, as was Michelangelo himself, as a result of privations; and hardly was their father dead when Michelangelo once more had to complain that Giovansimone had gone about Florence speaking ill of him.

Then there were renewed battles over the Julius Tomb. Negotiations restarted in 1531; Fattucci had returned to Florence, and a new man was serving as negotiator on Michelangelo's behalf. This was Sebastiano Luciani, still not yet known as Sebastiano del Piombo. Sebastiano was a Venetian painter who had come to Rome in 1511 and worked first in the circle of Raphael before shifting his allegiance to Michelangelo, by whom he was deeply influenced. His involvement with the Tragedy of the Tomb began on 24 February 1531, when he reported to Michelangelo on, besides his own sufferings in the Sack of Rome, the sorry state of the house at Macel de' Corvi.

About your coming ... it does not seem necessary to me, unless you want to come for amusement; and you could restore your house to order, which in truth is in a bad way, even more than the things, such as the roof and other things. I think you know that the room where the framework [of the Tomb] was has collapsed with the worked marbles, which is a pity. This you could remedy and make some provision. For my part, I would take care of it to please you a little. (C.3.811.)

Lionardo Sellaio is nowhere again mentioned. Clearly he had either died or left Rome for good. Sebastiano wrote again on 29 April 1531:

On the way to Rome I went to Pesaro with a painter who works for the Duke of Urbino. He is called Hieronimo da Zenga [Girolamo Genga; Sebastiano's orthography betrays his Venetian origins].... he told me that you could easily satisfy the duke over the work for Pope Julius, which is very close to his heart. I told him that the work was proceeding well, but that 8000 ducats were lacking, and that there was no one responsible for those 8000 ducats. And he replied that the duke would provide them, but that he feared to lose the money and the work, and seemed to be very angry. But after many words he said, 'Would it not be possible to cut short this business in such a way that both parties were satisfied?'

I answered that it would be necessary to talk to you.... I believe that if there were something of this work to show they would be satisfied with everything, because they are more interested in some outward show than in the real truth. (C.3.813.)

In his next long letter of 16 June 1531, Sebastiano expatiated on how much Pope Clement cared for Michelangelo; he himself, too, was deeply caring.

About the Julius affair, ... I told His Holiness everything, and I also begged His Holiness to help you, and to side with you in this matter, which in truth would take twenty-five years off you. He ... answered that he would do it very willingly, and that it was of great concern to him; and he told me not to write to anyone connected with the duke without first finding out what you wanted. And he commissioned me to write to you, for you to let me know firstly your own wishes, and in what way you want to settle this matter, and also to let His Holiness know what he is able to offer on your behalf and promise to the agents, or rather the ambassador, of the Duke of Urbino.... Think very carefully what you want to do and study it carefully.

I have often wanted to write to you about your house. In truth, your things are in a very bad state. It is in the hands of a rogue who threatens and says he has possession and authority, so that you will have to restore at great cost, and they are ruining your house. Moreover, the framework has fallen below ground, so that it is badly damaged. It would be best to have it lifted out of the ruin and put those worked stones into the big workshop, although the roof leaks badly. It would be wise to see that those things don't get totally ruined since their making represents a great deal of time and money. (C.3.815.)

In Michelangelo's next attempt to extricate himself from the Tomb affair, Clement VII himself took a hand. Sebastiano wrote on 22 July 1531:

[I received] your last letter ... at the end of last month, in which you inform me of all that I have to present to the agents of the Duke of Urbino. And, so as not to disregard the orders

Woodcut of Sebastiano Luciani of Venice (Sebastiano del Piombo), from Vasari's 1568 *Lives*.

given by our Lord, I showed him your letter ... and he saw what you had a mind to do: which greatly surprised him, that you so positively offered 2000 ducats and the house so as to complete the Julius work in three years; which is really too much to offer and also too much damage to you.... This does not please His Holiness and he does not wish me to offer it at first, but has commissioned me, as if it came from me ... that I speak to the Duke's ambassador and to Messer Hieronimo Ostacoli, and that I see how they stand in this matter, and that I refer back their answers. And this I did.

I went to the house of the Duke's ambassador, there by chance I found Messer Hieronimo Ostacoli and as if from myself alone I told them all, and what I felt would benefit the work ... such as making it smaller, without offering a quattrino ... and I found the ambassador very satisfied and desirous in this matter. I think that one can do as one wishes with him, but I found Messer Hieronimo Ostacoli rather threatening, and he said, 'I know far better than you do what Michelangelo wants.' And he also said, 'Michelangelo would like to sell the house, and with the money shorten the work, and finish it as he likes; in which he is not honest. He has had 10,000 ducats; let him spend some of them and see if the work doesn't go forward, and if in the end, when one sees the work is being finished and the house is being sold for this purpose, then let it be sold.' And he said further that the house was not yours, that it belonged to Cardinal Aginense, and many other troublesome words. And he told me also that he had quarrelled with you and he had the contract for the work.

And the ambassador said to me, 'Michelangelo is out of favour with the pope, and no longer enjoys the favour which he formerly had, so that he is uncertain about this affair.'

I replied very energetically that you had no doubts either about the pope or emperor or of any other lord on earth, but that all you wanted you did for your honour and for the obligation you felt for the memory of Julius: so that with these words I appeased them both. And in conclusion I said that it would be far better for themselves and for the duke to submit to your wishes and do what you wanted either one way or the other, so that the work should be finished, than to stand on these punctilios and these arguments. And if by ill fortune, which please God won't happen, you were to die, the work would not be finished either one way or the other, because it doesn't rain Michelangelos, neither would they find any men who knew how to face it, much less to finish it. And then I did not know how one could get out of Florence the figures which have been made there for this work, so that they should be finished as they had been blocked out, if it were not by you.

These words pierced their hearts, and they confessed that I spoke the truth more from their side than from yours. And they deliberated how to persuade the duke to all that you wanted, and chiefly the ambassador; and he told me not to pay any attention to Messer Hieronimo's words, and that he would so work on the duke that he would agree to your wishes.... So that Messer Hieronimo has gone to Urbino and he has promised me that he would use his best offices. And all this I repeated to our Lord, who was very pleased....

I find the pope even more desirous of pleasing you ... and he has as much desire to satisfy you in this matter as you have to see an end to it. And he said to me that there was no need to tell the duke or his agents that you wanted to get it finished by others, that it would be quite enough if you made drawings and models and that you oversaw it, that they would be more than satisfied.

I ask you again, let me know how matters stand about the house, if it is yours or belongs to the cardinal's heirs, and also the amount of money you have received and the price of the whole work, because I don't know how to answer those that ask me, and also the pope. (C.3.820.)

The duke's ambassador was Giovan Maria della Porta, and his choleric and unsympathetic agent was Girolamo Stacculo, whose name Sebastiano always misspells, perhaps as an unconscious pun ('Mr Obstacles'). One of the few extant letters from Michelangelo to Sebastiano during this period is unsigned, possibly a draft datable in late November 1531, since the subscription is to Sebastiano after he was given the office of the Seal – the Piombo. It would also show that Michelangelo was in no hurry about the negotiations.

My dear Sebastiano – I'm giving you too much trouble. Bear with it patiently, reflecting that it is surely more glorious to raise the dead than to produce figures which appear to be alive.

Concerning the Tomb of Julius, I've thought it over several times, as you told me to, and it seems to me that there are two ways of freeing oneself from the obligation. One is to do it; the other is to give them the money to have it done themselves. Of these two courses, only the one agreeable to the pope can be taken. To do it myself will not, in my opinion, be agreeable to the pope, because I should not be able to devote myself to his things. Therefore they'll have to be persuaded – I mean whoever is acting for Julius – to take the money and get it done themselves. I would supply the drawings and models and whatever they want, together with the marbles that have been done for it. With the addition of two thousand ducats I think a very fine tomb could be produced; and among the young men there are some who could do it better than I could myself. If this latter course – that of giving them the money to get it done – is taken, I could put down a thousand gold ducats now and the other thousand somehow or other later on – provided they resolve on something that is agreeable to the pope. And if they're prepared to put this last into effect I'll write and tell you how the other thousand ducats can be raised, which I think will not be unacceptable. (c.3.824.)

Sebastiano wrote again, probably before 21 November, and in the letter tells Michelangelo, in a characteristically humorous way, about his having been granted the Seal. This was a profitable sinecure, in that he received a fee for affixing the lead papal seal to documents – hence his new name of Sebastiano del Piombo. It was a condition of the office that its holder should be a friar:

. . . the event which you may have heard about, how our Lord Pope Clement has given me the Seal and has made me friar in place of Fra' Mariano, so that if you saw me as a friar I'm sure you would laugh. I am the handsomest friar in Rome, which I never thought to be. . . .

Messer Hieronimo Ostacoli has returned to Rome and . . . spoke to me at the Cancelleria, and recounted all that he had negotiated with the duke . . . In conclusion he said he offered . . . that you are willing to finish the work . . . according to the contract made with Aginense, that is, the larger work, but it would be necessary to provide the rest of the money.

And the duke replied that he could not provide the rest of the money, but that he was more willing that you should do the work according to the second design, that is, that it should be made smaller according to the value of the money you have received. . . . When he had left Urbino, a man was sent post haste after him with a letter, that he should try . . . by all means that it should be done, but that the duke wanted . . . a drawing of how the work should be, and on this he would decide what he wanted.

I stoutly replied that you were not a man to give samples in drawing, nor models, nor similar trifles; that this was the way never to get anything done, and that the duke should be satisfied that you were willing to do the work in the second form, and that you were as tender of your honour as any other man of his.

And Messer Hieronimo answered, 'How can we do this,' and I replied, 'Thus: let the duke, with all the heirs of Pope Julius, agree to annul the contract made with Aginense . . . and make another contract.' That you would make a work to the value of the money you had received, and leave everything to your conscience. . . . And in the name of the duke Messer Hieronimo will annul the contract and make another as you wish, . . . to finish the Tomb according to the second way in three years, and to spend your 2000 ducats, counting the house, that the house be sold, and the money would suffice. . . .

I didn't want to offer more, and I think this is enough. . . . Send me a form of contract as you wish it to be . . . and a letter of administration, so that . . . I may annul the contract and make the second one . . . and I think that in this way you will be pleased and your mind will be at rest. . . . Our Lord will also be pleased . . . for he has said, 'This will rejuvenate him by twenty-five years.' –

PS. I have to tell you that . . . the Duke's agents agree to all you want, on this condition: that the figures which were done in Florence . . . come to Rome, and any framework which has been made, and that the tomb shall be finished in Rome and not in Florence, because they have it firmly in mind that there never be anything of the tomb, figures or other things, sent from Florence to Rome. And I have promised that you will send all the figures and the framework and marbles which belong to this work, so that they have said that if you will condescend on this point they will annul ... everything. But they believe that our Lord will impede everything; and to clarify things, I went on Saturday to ... the Belvedere and told him everything ... and that it would very easily be possible to satisfy them ... that is, to bring some figures, or some of the framework, whatever was satisfactory for you. ... And if some of those statues which have been made were suitable for His Holiness, it would suffice for His Holiness to say, 'I want this one or that one.' And the pope very firmly answered me that the figures made for that tomb would not answer his purpose, and moreover ... even if they were suitable ... he would not take them, because they had not the same intention, nor even one stone which came from that Tomb. And he told me this also: that the workshop with the marbles and figures of Pope Julius were separate from his own where his works were, so that ... he brought it home to me that His Holiness was anxious that you should execute that work as well as his, purely for your own satisfaction. And he said again to me, 'We will rejuvenate him by twenty-five years.' And he also said that ... if you felt it necessary to come to Rome as a solace to remain a month or two so as to put your work in order, His Holiness would be well pleased ... because he realizes that you are working very hard and he does not wish you to labour so hard. ...

By a letter ... I have learned of the suspicions you entertain of our Lord in this matter. I promise you, as your true and faithful Sebastiano, and not a friar, that I find him so far away from the fantasies that you have ... that I am ashamed to speak of it. I beg you, remove these suspicions from your mind, because the pope is more yours than his own, and let the gossips chatter, who may indeed chatter, but should be treated as they deserve. It pains me not to know how, with a pen, to make you understand this matter as I could by word of mouth. (c.3.833.)

However, they were by no means out of the wood, since Michelangelo was still making difficulties. Clearly, he was sick of the whole enterprise and fought to be free of it. Sebastiano's next letter is of 5 December 1531:

On the first of this month I received a letter from you ... saying that you wish the agent of the duke ... to have the Tomb made, and you will pay ... the agreed money, and will give information about the men who can do it, and will help as much as you can with drawings and models, but that you do not want the job of having it done, and that the work should not depend on you. These last four words ruin everything, and worried me so much since I thought I had done a good job. So today, being very upset ... I went to see our Lord, and ... His Holiness was also upset and said to me, 'The agents of the duke will never agree to this, if so openly ... it appears that Michelangelo wishes to abandon the work altogether, and not to have to think any more about the matter; if we were to revive all the antique masters who ever were, they would never agree.'

You are harmed only by yourself ... to me it seems that unless there is a little of your shadow, we will never bring them to what we want; and it seems to be a very easy thing, ... that is models and drawings, you can easily allocate ... the work to whom you please. ... It only needs a little of your shadow. ... And if they complain and say that Michelangelo isn't working with his own hands, they should look at the work you are doing for our Lord, where other people also work, and thus they will be quiet, even if they don't want to be.

Our Lord is of the opinion that your coming here would be very useful in this matter, and it would be more easily settled. ... And it seems to be right that if His Holiness has made a knight of Signor Cavaglier, and me a friar, it would be right indeed if he made you a duke or a king, or really that you should get your share of this papacy, of which you are the master, and you can have whatever you want done ... he [the pope] is giving orders that [the heirs and] the agents of the duke will all come before him to deal with this matter. ... For the love of God, take care not to succumb to any counsel of melancholy humour, which has always ruined things. (c.3.838.)

By 5 December 1531 Michelangelo had decided to come to Rome, and of the several invitations he received he accepted that of Benvenuto della Volpaia, Keeper of the Belvedere, on 18 January 1532, Even so, as late as 15 March 1532 Sebastiano was still trying to overcome Michelangelo's reluctance to undertake any more work on the Tomb himself, or even (it seems) to turn over his work in progress to the duke's agents. Sebastiano's pleading takes on a note of desperation.

... you can send whatever you like, even if it were only two blocked out pieces of stone – they don't really know what there is – so long as it appears to be something for the work. I know that all these ideas are contrary to your will, and I have never tried to find out exactly what you wanted, since I saw that the matter involved such discrepancies. But I have thought of a way ... that you find a man whom you think is good enough to do the work ... and get the duke's agents to commission the work from him ... without naming you in the contract ... and that you will give what is done by you in Rome and send something from Florence, purely to gain your objective of getting out of this affair ... particularly as you have our Lord on your side and in all your affairs as a perfect shield, ... because the pope has made it clear to everyone that he does not wish you to work for anyone but His Holiness. Forgive me, I entreat you, if I speak to you with too much assurance; I love you as my own soul, God knows. And I can say something else with assurance, that if you were to lose this chance of the favour, or truly of the shield, of the pope, I don't know how things would go. They would turn on you like serpents, and I can imagine the things which, may God prevent, would happen. You would be the most unhappy man in the world, because you would have to deal with people who would hold you in so little respect that I can't find decent words to explain it to you. I leave it to your judgment, but ... while good fortune is with you and since with very little you can get out of this business, get out of it, because your glory doesn't consist in this work, nor in the figures which are part of it. ... Everyone knows that it wasn't your fault. O God, how much it pains me that I can't reason with you for an hour, for I know that you would understand me quite differently! Patience. Take my words in good part; be advised by those who love you as themselves and believe me, this time. (C.3.854.)

Michelangelo arrived in Rome in April 1532, and the new contract was signed in front of Pope Clement on 20 April. Like the other contracts, this one (M.702–6) exists in both Latin and Italian, and in it Michelangelo is described as *magister Michael Angelus de Bonarrotis, civis florentinus, pictor et statuarius in Urbe* – Maestro Michelangelo di Buonarroti, Florentine citizen, painter and sculptor in Rome, the fullest description yet. By its terms, the heirs of Pope Julius withdrew all claims against him in respect of the 8000 ducats he had received; he agreed to make a new model and promised to supply for the Tomb the six statues either in Rome or in Florence, finished by his hand, and to complete the Tomb within about three years, beginning in August, and to pay 2000 ducats in respect of the house in the Macel de' Corvi and for the work still remaining to be done. The pope undertook to allow Michelangelo to come to Rome for two months or thereabouts in every year to supervise the Tomb, but if he failed to honour the terms of this agreement he would be liable for the execution of the preceding contract, as if this one had never been concluded.

Michelangelo took steps to raise the money. Back in Florence, he wrote to his friend Andrea Quaratesi in Pisa in May or June 1532:

I wrote and told you about a month ago that I had had the house surveyed and the amount for which it could be offered in these times assessed. I also wrote and said that I did not think you would manage to sell it. As I have to pay out two thousand ducats for my affair in Rome, which, with some other items, will amount to three thousand, I meant to sell houses and lands and to let them go at half price in order not to be stark naked, but I did not and have not managed to do so. I think, therefore, that it will be better to wait than to rush ahead. (C.3.876.)

By this date, only Duke Francesco Maria della Rovere, and Donna Felice della Rovere Orsina, survived from the original heirs and executors (Cardinal

132

Santiquattro had died in 1531), but because they did not know exactly what there was in Florence, Michelangelo had a free choice of what he was to use for the new project. The Duke's agent wrote to his master that the six largest statues would be chosen, probably settling for the *Moses* and the two *Slaves* still in Rome, and possibly the four unfinished ones in Florence. The bronze reliefs – the 'histories' – were abandoned, and it was left undecided whether Michelangelo or an assistant should do the group of the *Madonna and Child*.

What would the 1532 project have looked like? This last contract lacks the descriptive insert which was such a feature of earlier ones; only a model and a drawing are mentioned. The one thing that survived almost intact from earlier designs was the architectural framework of the façade of the lower stage; a framework based on a Roman triumphal arch of the type of the Septimius Severus or Constantine arches. Originally double arches in full depth had been envisaged; these had progressively shrunk to a single arch and then to a mere façade, totally out of keeping with the statues which had originally been made for it. The *Moses* still stood in the Roman workshop together with the two *Slaves*, but these were now much too large for their original sites under and in front of the terms, and – being only two – had lost their original significance. The four *Slaves* still in Florence seem at this stage to have been largely ignored, and no one knew about the *Victory*, also in Florence, except Michelangelo who does not appear to have offered it. The group of the *Madonna and Child* had not been begun, nor had the figure of Julius on his sarcophagus. It seems likely that the niches, too small for the two *Slaves*, were to be filled now with two female figures (which had in fact appeared as early as the 1513 drawing); these later developed into the *Leah* and *Rachel* – personifying the *Active* and *Contemplative Life* – of the present tomb. No final solution had yet been reached. It would appear that Michelangelo left Rome for Florence on the day the new agreement was signed, to continue work on the Medici Chapel and its tombs. As his Florentine contract permitted, he was to return to Rome in the autumn and winter of 1532–33.

To save time a considerable number of statues that were to be included were allocated to various other sculptors. Michelangelo allocated two of them to [Niccolò] Tribolo, one to Raffaello da Montelupo, and one to Fra Giovanni Angelo of the Servites; and he assisted these sculptors in the work, making for them the rough clay models. . . . Meanwhile Michelangelo had the Library itself attended to. Thus the ceiling was finished with carved woodwork, executed from Michelangelo's models by the Florentines Carota and Tasso, who were excellent carpenters and masters of wood carving, and similarly the bookshelves were designed by Michelangelo and executed by Battista del Cinque and his friend Ciappino, who were skilled in that kind of work. (v2.7.203.)

Lorenzo of Urbino's tomb had probably been finished by 1526, which precluded any of the alterations suggested by Salviati for combining the tombs of the two dukes so as to admit a double tomb for Leo and Clement. Giuliano of Nemours' tomb was probably done only in 1531–33. The group of the *Madonna and Child*, planned for a niche in the double tomb of the two Magnifici on the end wall, was not among the statues worked in the Chapel itself, but was almost certainly carved in the house rented for Michelangelo nearby. The double tomb, of which this *Medici Madonna* was to be the centrepiece, was not even begun until August 1533, and never got beyond the architectural framework. The project for the double papal tomb came to nothing. The site in the *lavamano* was too small; Clement proposed a site in the choir of S. Lorenzo itself, but although Michelangelo made a design for it, the project dwindled away. The ciborium so often mentioned in the letters was

Portrait of Andrea Quaratesi, the only portrait known from Michelangelo's hand, probably done in 1532. Andrea (1512–85) was a member of the banking family, and had known Michelangelo from childhood.

never made, but Michelangelo did eventually design a tribune, or balcony, for the exposition of the church's relics over the main door. This was executed only after he had left Florence for good and had little to do with him.

146   All work on the Library had stopped when money ran short in 1526. When, in August 1533, Michelangelo wanted to leave Florence, Clement consented only on condition that Michelangelo arranged for the completion of the staircase and the decorative work in the Library. In 1533–34, twelve carpenters were at work, and a contract was signed on 20 August 1533 with five masons for the completion of the staircase and for two doors into the Library. This contract called for the staircase to be made

> ... according to the method, shape and size, not so much of the drawings kept in the cloister, but according to the small terracotta model made by Michelangelo which each of the above named masters has seen.... The steps of the staircase shall be fourteen each, to be of one piece, particularly the first seven with the *rivolte*, without any joint being visible. (M.707.)

Steps with *rivolte* refers to the central ones, where there are small scroll-like returns at the ends next to the balustrade in the centre.

Only one of the two doorways was done – that from the vestibule into the Library. This double-sided doorway corresponds fairly closely, though not absolutely, to Michelangelo's own scale drawings in the Casa Buonarroti, made probably in 1525–26. The major variation is that on the Library side, the outer part of the double doorframe has its own segmental pediment, within which is fitted the triangular pediment of the inner part of the frame; the doorway at the head of the staircase, except for a few minor decorative details, is the same as Michelangelo's 1526 drawings. The second door projected was the outside one from the cloister walk (the cloister at S. Lorenzo is on two storeys, and the Library is reached from the upper walk of the cloister) into the vestibule; the inside of this door was completed as part of the lower stage of the vestibule architecture. Although all the stonework for this doorway was cut and brought to the site, it lay abandoned in the vestibule, and when about 1687 an entrance door was commissioned the architect ignored – or perhaps knew nothing of – the ready prepared stonework and merely repeated the shape of the inner side of the doorway, and added a segmental pediment over it. The abandoned stonework lay in the vestibule until, in all probability, it was removed in 1811 to the villa of Poggio Imperiale and used in the foundations.

Before Michelangelo left Florence in September 1534, the figures of the two dukes were placed in their respective niches, but neither of the dukes had yet been buried in his sarcophagus. The allegories – also presumably the two patron saints and the *Medici Madonna* – were scattered about the floor of the Chapel. After the murder of Duke Alessandro in January 1537, his successor Duke Cosimo I took steps to get the Chapel finished and usable. The bodies of the two dukes were transferred to the sarcophagi designed for them, and the murdered Duke Alessandro was also put into Duke Lorenzo's tomb. The four allegories of the *Times of Day* were then placed on the lids of the sarcophagi, as Michelangelo had intended – *Night* and *Day* for Duke Giuliano, and *Dusk* and *Dawn* for Duke Lorenzo. Tribolo and Montelupo finished what carving was still required, and in 1545 the Chapel was opened to visitors. A large sarcophagus was assembled from pieces of marble and mouldings in the workshop, the two Magnifici were transferred into it from the Old Sacristy, and it was placed on the entrance wall in 1559, with the two patron saints and the *Madonna* standing upon it. Despite the unfinished state of the Chapel, the

Masses for the dead and the intercessory prayers established by Clement VII's charter in November 1532 had been celebrated regularly ever since its foundation.

All work on the Library stopped again when Michelangelo left Florence in 1534, and when Clement died almost immediately afterwards there was no incentive to continue. An effort was made in 1549 to do something about the staircase. Tribolo, who had worked under Michelangelo, was given the job by Duke Cosimo, but after erecting four steps against the wall he ran into the difficulty that more steps would have impinged on the architectural scheme of the vestibule. Not knowing how to go on, he went to see Michelangelo in Rome to try to get him to help, but Michelangelo, almost certainly annoyed at finding that Tribolo was not trying to follow his own original design but was trying to substitute one of his own, and of a type which Michelangelo had long before abandoned as unsuitable, declared that he could remember nothing about it. Knowing that the original design still existed, five years later Cosimo got Vasari to approach Michelangelo, this time with success.

A letter of 18 February 1559 from Ammanati to Duke Cosimo I says:

Since I have seen that Your Illustrious Excellency was resolved to supply the staircase in the vestibule of the Library, and that your opinion was that it had to be like the model from the hand of Michelangelo Buonarroti, which I showed you, and I also thought the same, and because Michelangelo has since written to me that this was the way he first thought of it, and I trusted so much to his good feeling which is always to do what is pleasing to Y.I.E., and also in the affection which he has always by his deeds shown that he bears me, I drew the site, with both forms of staircase, writing to him and asking him to let me know which was the true one of the two. He did not limit his goodness to sending me a letter with good instructions, which Y.I.E. will see, but also with his own hand he made me a model, which makes clear all his thoughts, which, with my own, I now send to Y.I.E., asking you that when you have decided you will be good enough to send them both back to me, and as soon as I have the order from you I will, with the maximum diligence and speed that I can, set to work on it, to show to Michelangelo that the faith he has in me, as far as I possibly can will not prove false. And because he writes that he is of the opinion that the ceiling, the desks and the doorway would be better in a fine walnut, and also because I believe that it would look less cumbersome than stone, if Y.I.E. wishes, on your instruction that I ask him, when it seems good to you, about the ceiling, the *ricetto*, and the model for the façade, I will do so, because I am certain he will do as he has done for the staircase, and will add something, which would be very useful to me, since he believes that Y.I.E. has put me in charge of this work. (G.3.11.)

On 19 February 1559, Francesco di Ser Jacopo also wrote to Cosimo:

Bartolomeo Amannati, with his patience and goodness, has worked so hard that he has now obtained from Michelangelo Buonarroti a model of the staircase of the Library of S. Lorenzo, which is being sent in a little box in the way it arrived from Rome. Your Excellency will see it, and if Y.E. wishes this stair to be made, if you would give an order for four scudi a week from now until the end of June, it will be done and built.

The said Michelangelo Buonarroti has written to Amannato, and says that if this stair were done in a fine walnut it would not be unsuitable; however if dry and seasoned walnut cannot be found and if unseasoned it would split and would be unsuitable, but whatever Y.E. orders will be done. (G.3.12.)

These letters resulted in two replies, both sent from Pisa on 22 February 1559. Francesco di Ser Jacopo was told:

... that His Excellency has seen the model of the staircase of the Library of S. Lorenzo, and has given it to Luca Martini who will return it to Ammanato, adding that the staircase be made of

This tiny sketch in the margin of a letter to Vasari of 28 September 1555 is one of the few indications of Michelangelo's final ideas for the staircase of the Laurenziana.

stone and not of walnut. . . . So far as concerns the staircase H.E. is pleased to give an order of four scudi per week. (G.3.13–14.)

Ammanati received the same message, with an interesting aside:

As to the staircase at S. Lorenzo, he says to order it; concerning the ceiling of the *ricetto* and the model of the façade, that it will not be impossible to extract from Bonarroti whatever we can get. . . (G.3.13.)

How far from Clement's delicate consideration of Michelangelo is the crude reference to 'extracting' from him what they wanted, and even the misspelling of his name! The spelling of Ammanati's name remains confused, even to this day. Ammanati used the stones cut under Michelangelo's direction, which, like those of the unbuilt doorway, were lying around in the vestibule, and only needed small adjustments for the change in the placing of the landing. The curved stones of the central flight were cut in 1533–34, and only the rectangular steps of the outer flights and the balustrade were made to Ammanati's designs.

The superb ceiling of which Vasari speaks was designed by Michelangelo in 1525, but had not been started when work stopped in 1526. In 1533 Clement wanted the ceiling and the desks done, but how far work had got by September 1534 is unknown. The present ceiling follows one of Michelangelo's drawings, though the dolphins introduced into the corners of the central panel point to its having been reworked under Duke Cosimo after 1537, since dolphins were among his emblems. The benches, or desks, may have occupied the twelve carpenters hired in August 1533, but how much was then accomplished in the remaining year is impossible to tell. They follow Michelangelo's original design for them, and were finished in Cosimo I's campaign, and the inlaid tiled floor was certainly done in 1547–55. The windows include stained glass panels with the arms and devices of Clement and Cosimo I, and are dated 1568. The scroll over the door commemorates the completion of Clement's great project, without mentioning him, as a work of Cosimo I, with the date 1571, when the Library was opened to scholars and a medal was struck to commemorate the event.

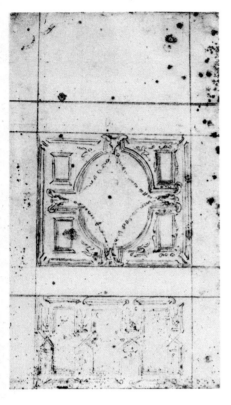

Drawing by Michelangelo for the design of the *intarsia* ceiling of the Laurenziana Library. When it was executed, for Cosimo I in 1549–50, the design was slightly elongated and Cosimo's emblem of the dolphin was inserted.

S. Lorenzo was the parish church of the Medici family, whose palace lies to the right, just out of the picture in this view taken from the top of the campanile of Florence cathedral. The church itself is Brunelleschi's design of 1419–60, and the dome of his Old Sacristy can be seen behind the library which Michelangelo built on the upper part of the long wing projecting from the left transept. The tall block at the beginning of the library range is the *ricetto* or vestibule. (This was finished in the twentieth century, not to Michelangelo's design.) Michelangelo's New Sacristy, the Medici Chapel, was built on foundations laid by Brunelleschi for a structure matching the Old Sacristy on the other side of the church. The huge dome at the back of the church is the Cappella dei Principi, the megalomaniac burial chapel for the later Medici, designed in 1602. The dome attached to the centre of the library wing is the addition built in 1841 by Poccianti.

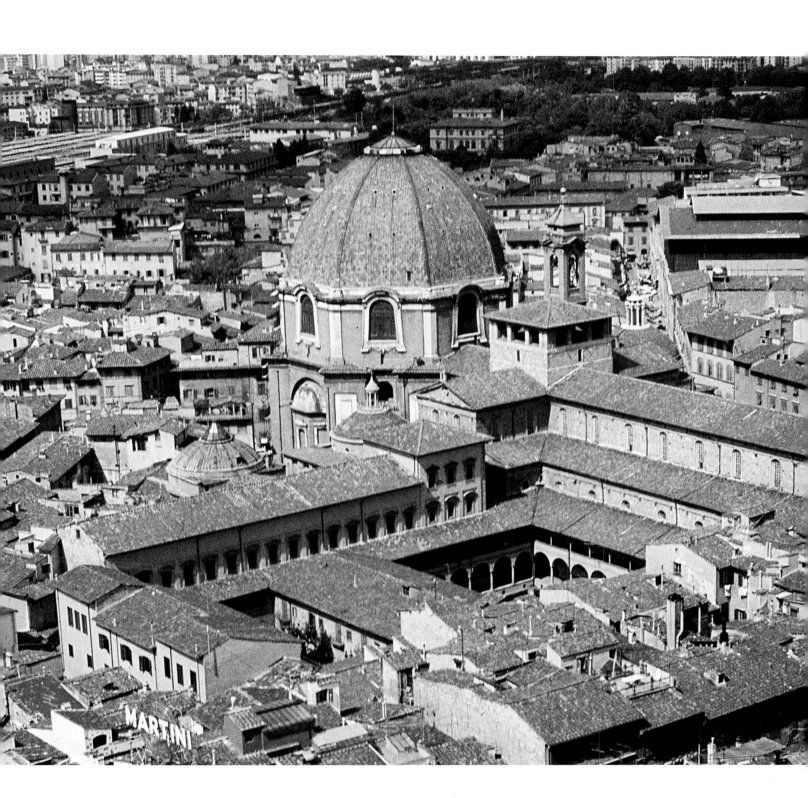

Leo X

Giovanni de' Medici, son of Lorenzo il Magnifico, was elected pope in 1513 and took the title of Leo X; he is seen here in a drawing by Giulio Romano. In 1516 he diverted Michelangelo from the Julius Tomb and commissioned him to build a façade for S. Lorenzo. Like the Julius Tomb, this was to have no less than forty statues by Michelangelo on it; another Herculean and indeed virtually impossible labour. A wooden model, now thought to represent his intentions at a late stage in the design, shows how he moved from a pattern of a high nave with lower aisles (as in the drawing, below) to a complete screen wall (bottom). Michelangelo spent years on the project, but in 1520 it was abruptly and outrageously cancelled, for reasons never completely explained. A photograph (right, below) shows the bare keyed brickwork as Brunelleschi left it in 1460, and as it still is. To the right are the houses which formerly abutted on the church and the Medici Chapel, and which were removed from 1938 onwards.

The Medici tombs

The second of Leo X's projects for S. Lorenzo, pursued during the papacy of his cousin Giulio (Clement VII) after 1523, was a funerary chapel for Lorenzo il Magnifico, his brother Giuliano, his son Giuliano, Duke of Nemours, and his grandson Lorenzo, Duke of Urbino. On the sarcophagus of Duke Lorenzo lie figures of *Dusk* and *Dawn* (left, above, and above); on that of Duke Giuliano lie *Night* and *Day* (left). The four figures have no relevance to the lives or personalities of the two dukes but express the symbolism of Life, Death and Resurrection.

The two dukes

The effigies of the two Medici dukes, in the niches above
their sarcophagi, are idealized figurations of the Active and
Contemplative Life, combined with attributes of power
and majesty. The face of Giuliano de' Medici, Duke of
Nemours, is shown here on the left, below; that of
Lorenzo de' Medici, Duke of Urbino, below. Neither
bears the slightest resemblance to the features of its subject
as shown in contemporary portraits (far left and near left).

The Medici Chapel

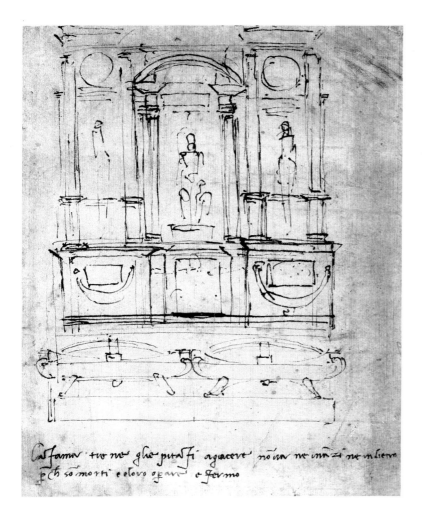

The altar is placed so that the celebrant faces the *Medici Madonna* on the opposite wall; the two dukes look the same way (far left), to complete the hermetic system of the chapel. When the door was shut all meaning was concentrated on the commemorative rites, with only the dead for congregation. The *Medici Madonna* herself (see p. 82) was to be part of the unexecuted double tomb of the Magnifici, Lorenzo and Giuliano (drawing, near left), between figures of SS. Cosmas and Damian.

Art students came to treat the Medici Chapel as earlier generations had treated the Brancacci Chapel. The little sketch (below) is by Federico Zuccaro; the drawing of *Dusk* (bottom), by Tintoretto, was made from a replica of the figure.

The Laurenziana

Work on the Library of S. Lorenzo was concurrent with that on the Medici Chapel. Below are some of Michelangelo's working drawings. The desks, on Clement VII's instructions, are of walnut. The triangular 'private library', for the most precious manuscripts, was designed to fit into the available space at the far end of the library. It was never built; it could have served in 1841, when the Elci donation of some 8000 volumes had to be housed, and Poccianti's domed addition was built half-way along Michelangelo's library (its entrance is seen on the right in the photograph, right). Michelangelo's drawing for the doorway shows the papal arms of Clement VII, which the pope rejected, insisting on Medici arms only. Michelangelo's drawings for the stairway in the *ricetto* or vestibule, leading up to the library from the upper cloister, show a variety of solutions. The stairs were not finished until the later 1550s, under Cosimo I, by Ammanati, who persuaded Michelangelo to provide a model for the present free-standing structure. By one of the architectural refinements that characterize this astonishing building, the central stair has one step fewer than the flanking flights.

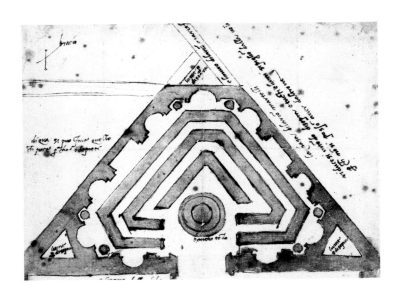

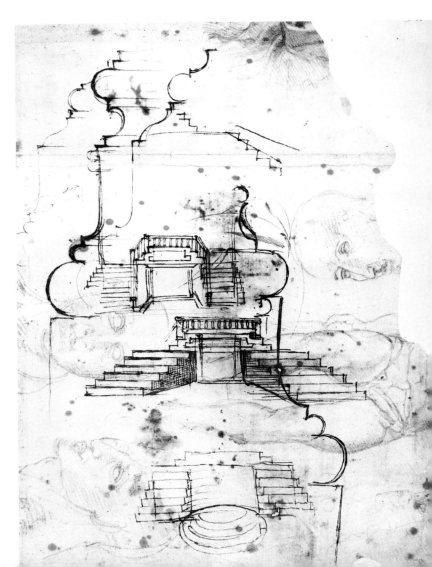

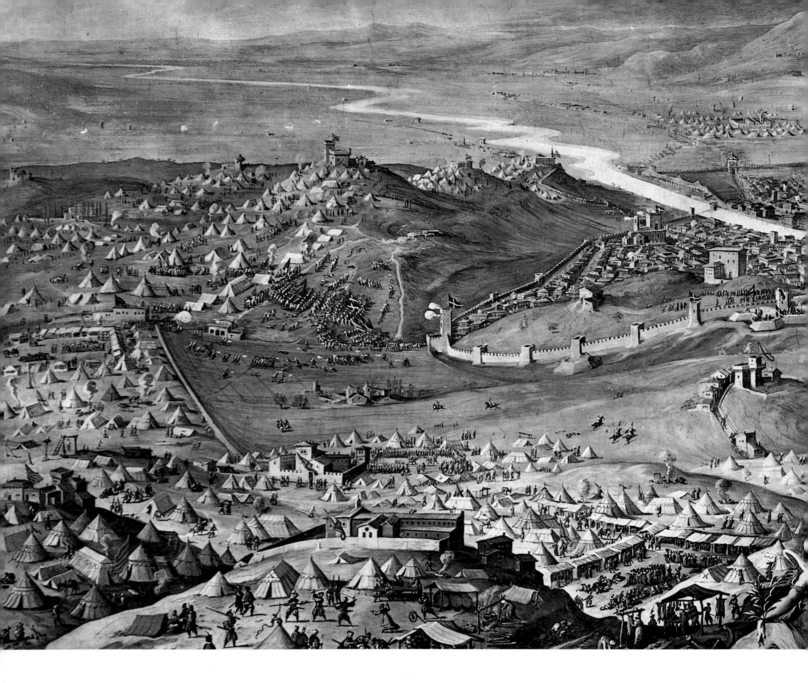

Florence besieged

Michelangelo Directing the Building of the Fortifications (left), by Matteo Rosselli (1615), is part of the posthumous glorification of the artist undertaken by his grand-nephew Michelangelo the Younger for the gallery in Casa Buonarroti in Florence. For this he commissioned pictures from a number of capable but uninspired painters, who created fanciful interpretations of incidents in Michelangelo's life. The historian Baldinucci recorded that the figures in this picture are all portraits of members of the Buonarroti family, that of Michelangelo himself being a portrait of Buonarroto, brother of Michelangelo the Younger.

In 1527 Florence cast off the Medici yoke in the person of Alessandro, detested son of Duke Lorenzo of Urbino. In 1529 Clement VII, now reconciled with the Emperor Charles V whose soldiery had sacked Rome in 1527, set out with Imperial help to reduce the city to obedience. Michelangelo, a Florentine patriot and a republican, gave his services as engineer to the defenders. Vasari's fresco of the *Siege of Florence*, painted in 1556–62, when he was redecorating the state rooms in Palazzo della Signoria, shows the city and the camp of the Prince of Orange, general of the Imperial forces, who was killed in one of the engagements. Lack of troops forced the besiegers to invest only the south of the city, and, since taking it by storm was impossible, it was decided to cut off food supplies from

Pisa and the surrounding hills by means of raiding parties. The siege lasted from the autumn of 1529 to August 1530, when the starving city surrendered to avoid being sacked. Vasari recorded how he chose his viewpoint with great care, and worked out the distances. He particularly picked out the elaborate fortifications designed by Michelangelo, and the posts of the commanders of the besieging armies. In this view, S. Miniato and Michelangelo's fortifications are on the extreme right; on the left, inside the walls, is the massive block of Palazzo Pitti with the fortifications of the Fortezza di Belvedere; in the foreground on the left is the Charterhouse of Galuzzo in the Val d'Ema; in the middle are Poggio Imperiale and the hills of the Pian de' Giullari, and on the hilltop to the left is the castle of Bellosguardo.

Engineer and fugitive

During the restoration of republican rule in Florence, which followed the expulsion of the Medici in May 1527, Michelangelo stopped work at S. Lorenzo and designed some of the fortifications (below) for the defence of the city. They were carefully worked out, not only to resist assault, but to provide lines of fire which left no part uncovered. When the Medici were reinstated in 1530, Michelangelo found it prudent to go into hiding. Drawings discovered in the substructure of the Medici Chapel by Dr Paolo dal Poggetto in 1975 have been credibly attributed to him and dated to this time. The tiny crypt in which Michelangelo was probably hidden can be entered only through a trapdoor in the little room on the left of the altar; it was lost for many years because the room was filled with lumber. Some of the drawings done during the two months in the autumn of 1530 when Michelangelo lived in the crypt are in charcoal and red earth pigment, some in red earth only, applied with the brush, as was common for the preparatory stage of frescoes (the *sinopie*); others are in sepia, again done with a brush, and most are very large in scale. All are very free in handling, and some are for subjects, such as the *Fall of Phaeton* and *Leda and the Swan*, which Michelangelo later developed in detailed small drawings, or in cartoons for other painters to execute. Other drawings are for the still unfinished sculpture in the chapel, and some are for projects such as the fresco of the *Resurrection* planned for one of the lunettes. Many were superimposed, as the artist ran out of space or light. In one corner is a well, and presumably food was supplied by the Prior, Giovanni Battista Figiovanni.

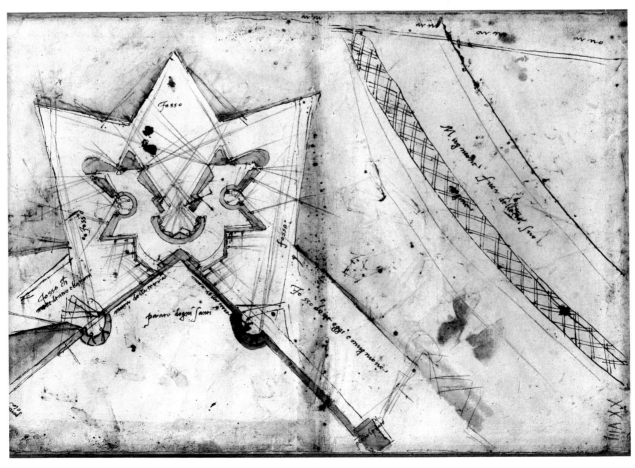

After the return of the Medici in 1530, and the ensuing terror, Michelangelo emerged from hiding with a papal pardon. As a considerable property-owner, however, he still had to keep on the right side of those in power; and so he accepted a commission from Baccio Valori, the Medici

henchman who had actually directed the purges, to carve the figure known as the *David/Apollo*. Its pose recalls the *Victory* (p. 195) and one of the crypt drawings (p. 150). It remained unfinished in his workshop when he left for good in 1534.

PART FOUR

LAST JUDGMENT

1532–1547

IT WAS WHEN MICHELANGELO was back in Rome in the late autumn of 1532 that he first met Tommaso Cavalieri. Very little – indeed surprisingly little – is known about him. He is thought to have been born about 1518–20, and married about 1538; his wife was probably a relation (a niece, perhaps) of Cardinal Andrea della Valle, who was raised to the purple by Leo X in 1517 and died in 1534. His maternal grandfather is said to have been the Florentine banker, Tommaso Baccelli, who was probably the source of his unRoman Christian name, but it is not known how he and Michelangelo came to meet.

Cavalieri was not a nobleman, but a *Patritius Romanus* – a member of an ancient family of Roman gentlemen. Only a handful of letters survive between Cavalieri and Michelangelo, the most notable being the several drafts of Michelangelo's second letter, datable at the very end of 1532. On the elderly and solitary artist Cavalieri made a profound impression through his striking personal beauty, the charm of his manner, and his general distinction. Michelangelo had apparently written to Cavalieri, and drafted this further letter before he received a reply from the young man. None of the drafts appears to have been sent at all. The first of them is as follows:

Inadvisedly, Messer Tommao, my dearest lord, I was prompted to write to your lordship, not in answer to any letter I had received from you, but being the first to move, thinking, as it were, to cross a little stream dry-shod, or rather what was apparently, from its shallow water, a ford. But after I left the bank I found it was not a little stream but the ocean, with its overarching billows, that appeared before me; so much so that, had I been able, I would willingly have returned to the bank whence I came, to avoid being completely overwhelmed. But since I've got so far we'll take courage and go on. And if I haven't the skill to steer a course through the surging sea of your brilliant endowments, you will, on that score, forgive me and neither scorn the disparities between us nor expect from me what I do not possess, since he who is unique in all things can have no companions in any. Your lordship cannot therefore rest content with the work of anyone else, being matchless and unequalled – light of our century, paragon of the world. If, however, any one of the things which I promise and hope to perform were to please you, I should count that work much more fortunate than excellent. And if, as I've said, I were ever to have the assurance of pleasing your lordship in anything, I would devote to you the present and the time to come that remains to me, and should very deeply regret that I cannot have the past over again, in order to serve you longer than with the future only, which will be short, since I'm so old. That's all I have to say. Read the heart and not the letter, since 'affection exceeds the compass of the pen'.

I must offer my apologies for having expressed such wondering amazement at your rare quality in my first letter; which I do, as I afterwards realized the extent of my error, since there is no more cause for wonder that Rome should produce men who are divine, than that God should perform miracles. And for this the world can vouch. (C.3.897.)

Cavalieri, meanwhile, replied to Michelangelo's first letter:

I have received a letter from you, so little hoped for by me, hence so much more welcome; unexpected, I say, considering myself unworthy that one such as yourself should deign to write to me. Concerning those things which Pier Antonio said to you in my praise, and those works of mine for which you appear to show me no small affection. I reply that they were not sufficient that a man so excellent as you are, and without any who approaches you, if not without peer on this earth, should wish to write to a young man hardly born into this world, and for this reason as ignorant as it is possible to be. Nor do I wish to say that you are lying. I really think, I am certain even, that from the affection you have for me the reason is this, that, being yourself full of virtue, or better still, virtue itself, you are moved to love those who follow virtue and love it, among whom I count myself, and in this, as far as I can, I give place to few. I promise you, indeed, that from me you will receive an equal, and maybe a greater exchange, who never cared for any man more than for you, nor ever wanted any friendship more than yours; and if in nothing else, at least in this I have very good judgment. And you would see the effect, except that fortune is against me only in this, that now that I might enjoy your company, I am unwell. I truly hope, if ill fortune does not again torment me, that within a few days I shall be cured and able to pay my dues in visiting you, if you are agreeable. Meanwhile, I shall pass at least two hours a day in the pleasure of contemplating two of your drawings which Pier Antonio has brought me, which the more I look at them the more they please me, and will appease in great part my sickness, thinking of the hope that Pier Antonio has given me of enabling me to see other things of yours.

So as not to weary you I will not write at greater length, only to remind you, in ceasing, that I am yours to command. And to you I always commend myself, your lordship's most affectionate servant. (C.3.898.)

The go-between was Pierantonio Cecchini, who lived in the household of Cardinal Niccolò Ridolfi. He was a minor sculptor, to whom Michelangelo appears to have given some instruction. Michelangelo's reply was on 1 January 1533:

Most inadvisedly I was prompted to write to your lordship, and had the presumption to be the first to move, as though I had a debt to pay in replying to a letter of yours. Afterwards I recognized my error the more, so much did I enjoy reading your reply, for which I thank you.

Far from being a mere babe, as you say of yourself in your letter, you seem to me to have lived on earth a thousand times before. But I should deem myself unborn, or rather stillborn, and should confess myself disgraced before heaven and earth, if from your letter I had not seen and believed that your lordship would willingly accept some of my drawings. This has caused me much surprise and pleasure no less. And if you really esteem my works in your heart as you profess to do in your letter, I shall count that work much more fortunate than excellent, should I happen, as I desire, to execute one that might please you.

I'll say no more. Many things that might be said in reply remain unwritten, lest you be wearied and because I know that Pierantonio, the bearer of this, can and will supply what I lack. On the, for me, happy first day of January.

[PS.] Though it is usual for the donor to specify what he is giving to the recipient, for obvious reasons it is not being done in this instance. (C.4.899.)

The friendship which thus ceremoniously began was long and fruitful. Cavalieri became, like his father before him, a member of the Roman *Conservatori* – one of the few offices open to members of the laity in ecclesiastical Rome. He was later involved with the architectural re-planning of the Capitoline Hill, which Michelangelo redesigned, but which was not carried out until after the artist's death. Cavalieri's youth was thus a positive benefit, in that it lengthened the continuity between the artist and the commissioning body. Cavalieri did not die until June 1587, by which time the greater part of the work was completed, though not all of it was according to Michelangelo's original designs.

That either Michelangelo or Cavalieri would have distorted their relationship into an association with sexual overtones may be dismissed out of hand. It was soon after this period that the artist became the friend and associate of Vittoria Colonna, and of Cardinals Pole and Contarini, and others dedicated to the reform of the Church in the years which preceded the Council of Trent. It is unreasonable to suggest that any member of this high-minded, austere, and deeply religious community would have tolerated double standards of morality, even if it were not equally unreasonable to attribute them to Michelangelo, whose deep religious commitment and its bearing on his life is attested not only by his works but also by his poems.

Michelangelo was in Florence from the end of June or early in July 1533. Bartolommeo Angelini, or Angiolini, a customs official in Rome who took over the care of Michelangelo's house and its contents, as Lionardo Sellaio had once done, and who also served as a 'post office' for the distribution of his letters to his Roman friends, wrote to him on 12 July:

Since your departure I haven't written to you, nor have I had letters from you, and all here want them. Your house is continually guarded every night, and frequently visited during the day by me. The hens and the lordly cock triumph, the cats lament your absence, although it doesn't prevent them eating.

The journey of our Lord is daily more certain, and it's said that Filippo Strozzi will leave for there on Monday, and will escort the Duchessina to Nice. (C.4.907.)

The Duchessina was Caterina, the fourteen-year-old daughter of Duke Lorenzo de' Medici, whom Pope Clement was to marry to the second son of Francis I of France, the Duke of Orleans (later Henry II), at Marseilles on 28 October 1533.

Michelangelo was in a very distressed state of mind after his return to Florence. He wrote to Angelini, probably late in July – the letter is badly mutilated and undated – but in it he speaks of his unhappiness at being so far away from Cavalieri, and also of his uncertainty about why the pope wanted to see him during his journey to France. On 28 July he wrote to Cavalieri:

Had I not believed that I had convinced you of the immense, nay, boundless love I bear you, the grave apprehension shown by your letter that I might have forgotten you, as I haven't written to you, would seem to me neither strange nor surprising. But there is nothing unusual in this, nor in being alarmed, when so many other things go wrong, lest this too should come to grief; since what your lordship says to me, I would have said to you. But perhaps you did this in order to try me, or in order to kindle anew a greater flame, if a greater were possible. But be that as it may, I realize now that I could [*as soon*] forget your name as forget the food on which I live – nay, I could sooner forget the food on which I live, which unhappily nourishes only the body, than your name, which nourishes body and soul, filling both with such delight that I am insensible to sorrow or fear of death, while my memory of you endures. Imagine, if the eye were also playing its part, the state in which I should find myself. (C.4.916.)

Cavalieri replied on 2 August. They are both still using the very formal *Vostra Signoria* mode of address, better rendered by 'You', rather than by 'your lordship'.

I have received one from you which gave me great pleasure. By what I have heard You were rather grieved about the forgetfulness I wrote about. I answer you that I didn't write to you because You had not sent me anything, nor to rekindle your flame, but I only wrote to tease you about it, which I believe I can do; so don't grieve because I am certain you won't forget me.

Concerning what You write to me about the young man of the Nerli family, he is a close friend, and since he had to leave Rome, he came to ask me if I wanted anything from Florence; I said No, and he asked me if I would allow him to go on my behalf to commend me to You, purely because of his desire to speak to you. I don't know what more to write about, except that You should return soon, because in returning you would free me from prison, because I fly from bad company, and wishing to flee from it, I cannot possibly frequent any other than yours. That's all. To You I commend myself many times. Yours more than his own. . . . (C.4.919.)

Angelini had written to him on 26 July 1533 (a Saturday):

Since Monday the pope has done nothing but cry out with the gout, but now he is better. His departure for Nice will not be before September, because before leaving he wants to have news of the consummation of the marriage of the Duchessina, after which he will leave at once. (C.4.915.)

A nice thought, seeing that the pope was going to Marseilles in order to marry her to her bridegroom! The negotiations had been long and difficult and a matter of hard bargaining. What the pope was waiting for was the formal conclusion of the negotiations and the ratification of the contract. Angelini wrote on 2 August:

Your house is, as always, in a good state, and the muscat grapes are nearly ripe, and when they are I will send their share to Messer Tomao [Cavalieri] and to Fra Bastiano [del Piombo], if the thrushes haven't eaten them all, as they have begun to do by stealth, but I have surprised them with birdscarers, if these work. (c.4.921.)

Clement eventually left Rome in September, and on his orders Michelangelo met him on the 22nd at S. Miniato al Tedesco, a small town a few miles west of Empoli between Florence and Pisa. There is no record of what they discussed; the works at S. Lorenzo were far from complete, but the problem there was one of money. Since the Sack and the Siege, Clement no longer had the resources for private works himself, nor could he force Duke Alessandro to pay for them. Moreover, Michelangelo no longer wished to stay in Florence. Not only was the Julius Tomb, after the new contract of 1532, a pressing obligation, but there were other factors: one was his mounting, even if it were illusory, fear of being murdered by Duke Alessandro; the other was that he grieved over the separation from Cavalieri. Despite his commitment to the work at S. Lorenzo, his heart was no longer in it. But Clement, who could not fund works in Florence, could fund works in the Vatican. Sebastiano del Piombo had hinted at this in a letter to Michelangelo of 17 July 1533:

His Holiness has . . . reread and considered the last paragraph of your letter, which he answers by saying 'Be of good heart,' for he has decided, as soon as you return to Rome, to work so well for you in what you have done and will be doing for His Holiness, and will give you a contract for such a thing as you have never yet dreamed of. These words are not just talk between us. His Holiness has told me to write to you on his behalf, and note it well, these are words which mean a lot. And you know how Pope Clement takes care not to promise in this way. So now you can be clear and have your mind at rest. (c.4.910.)

This is a very clear indication that a large work had been discussed. It is most likely that this would have been the altar wall of the Sistine Chapel, since a project for the replacement of the Perugino altarpiece was being mentioned while Michelangelo was still in Rome early in 1533. Agnello, the Mantuan envoy to the Vatican, who was then in Venice, reported on 2 March 1534 that there was a report by the Imperial Ambassador in Venice, as early as 20 February 1534, that Clement 'had persuaded Michelangelo to paint in the Chapel, and that over the altar a *Resurrection* is to be done, and the scaffolding for it is already made'.

There is no evidence that anything more than a replacement of the Perugino *Assumption* was being considered. The Perugino had to be replaced, since there is a report that in 1525 draperies at the side of the altar had caught fire and the altarpiece had been damaged. Also, it may be conjectured that during the Sack in 1527 more damage might have occurred, when the Chapel was used as a stable, particularly if the marauders included Lutherans, for whom the subject of the Virgin of the Assumption would have invited attack. A *Fall of the Rebel Angels* had also been discussed earlier as a replacement for the final pair of frescoes of the older 1481 series of the Lives of Moses and Christ, at the other end of the Chapel, because they had been badly damaged in 1522 by the collapse of the pediment of the entrance door. But what Clement and his artist decided is not known; they never met again.

Clement's words, 'as soon as you return to Rome', in Sebastiano's letter, have to mean 'when you have finished the works at S. Lorenzo'. Michelangelo now went back to Florence and continued with them for another year. It is not known what prompted him to leave when he did.

Michelangelo arrived in Rome on 23 September 1534; Clement VII died on 25 September. His death seemed to set Michelangelo free at last to finish the tomb of Julius II. But the new pope was Alessandro Farnese, Paul III. He forthwith commanded that Michelangelo should work for him, and when the artist protested that he was under contract to the Duke of Urbino, Paul is said to have lost his temper and declared:

'For thirty years now I have wanted to have Michelangelo work for me, and now that I am pope, why should I not have my wish? Where is this contract? I will tear it up.' (AC.72–3.)

Condivi records that the pope, with eight or ten cardinals, visited the workshop at Macel de' Corvi, and 'wanted to see the cartoon, made in Clement's time, for the altar wall of the Sistine Chapel' (AC.73.). What was this cartoon? The visit was probably made during the winter of 1534–35, and the decisions must have followed quickly, for the scaffolding for the destruction of all the paintings, the filling in of the windows, the removal of the balcony on the altar wall, was paid for on 16 April 1535. On 1 September 1535, Michelangelo was appointed chief painter, architect and sculptor to the Vatican Palace with a yearly stipend of 1,200 scudi partly secured on a ferry over the Po at Piacenza. He also became a member of the papal household (the *famiglia*) with the right to a seat at table. In the grant, the *Last Judgment* is specifically mentioned on the altar wall.

About 1512, for Julius II, Michelangelo had done a magnificent drawing of a *Resurrection* for the altar wall. The idea foundered, partly because the wall was still undamaged, partly because Michelangelo's *Risen Christ* is of an uncompromising nudity. He could never accept that the resurrected body should be garbed in conventional draperies. Did not St John's Gospel itself say (20.5) that the disciples 'looking in, saw the linen clothes lying'? Since there is clear evidence that a *Resurrection* was projected during Clement's last years, is it impossible that a cartoon might have been based on the 1512 project?

The decision to paint the whole wall instead of just replacing the altarpiece can only have been taken at one of three moments: when Michelangelo was still in Rome until June/July 1533; when he met Clement at S. Miniato al Tedesco in September 1533; immediately after Paul III's visit to the workshop in the Macel de' Corvi. There are two other *Resurrection* drawings by Michelangelo – one of c. 1525/30, the other of 1532/33 – both of them compositions in breadth rather than height which would have fitted an area not extending above the balcony. It is believed that the series of 'papal portraits' which formed part of the 1481 campaign included a *Christ* flanked by *SS. Peter and Paul* in the central space between the windows, and under the *Jonah* of the Ceiling, who points downwards towards him. This arrangement would still have been logical: Christ emerging from the tomb would be seen in Glory at the upper part of the altar wall. The *Resurrection* would have fitted the iconography of the Chapel; the *Last Judgment* does not. Why was the subject changed?

The terrible experiences of the Sack had left their mark; for many years afterwards Romans – lay and clerical alike – had no taste for gaiety, and were still in a state of shock, a shock increased by the fulminations of preachers who declared the Sack to have been a judgment from God, a Divine punishment for the sins of the city. It is quite probable that, given a choice, which Michelangelo would not have been slow to propose, between a *Resurrection*

180

81

The Resurrection, a drawing which Michelangelo did about 1532–33, possibly for the altar wall of the Sistine Chapel, or for one of the lunettes in the Medici Chapel. It is the most perfect of Michelangelo's treatments of the theme and is unlike all earlier depictions of the event, in that Christ makes no effort to liberate Himself from the tomb, but glides effortlessly from the confines of death into everlasting life.

rising over half the wall and a *Last Judgment* extending over the whole wall, the idea of a *Last Judgment* may have been uppermost in Clement's mind at the moment of Sebastiano's letter, and at the meeting at S. Miniato al Tedesco.

The decision to use the whole wall not only meant the destruction of the frescoes from the earlier series; it also involved the destruction of two of the lunettes with the *Ancestors of Christ* which he himself had painted as part of the Ceiling. The arrangements for the preparation of the wall were left to Sebastiano del Piombo, who persuaded the pope that the work should be executed in oil paint rather than fresco, and without consulting Michelangelo he had the surface of the wall prepared for oil painting. Michelangelo said nothing, but when the wall was ready he said that oil painting was fit only for women and for lazy people like Fra Sebastiano, and ordered that the whole surface should be removed. That this was done is attested by the Treasury records, the removal of the top layer of plaster being paid for on 25 January 1536, and a fresh *arriccio* was applied by mid-April, 1536 (T.5.21.). This was the end of the friendship between Michelangelo and Sebastiano.

Michelangelo worked on the fresco alone, with the help only of Francesco Amatori, called Urbino, his servant and assistant, as a grinder of colours and to help apply the *intonaco* as it was required. Michelangelo began work in April/May 1536; the impatient Paul III visited the work on 4 February 1537, which must have been when the papal master of ceremonies, Biagio da Cesena, protested about the number of nudes, in revenge for which Michelangelo used him as a model for Minos at the mouth of Hell. 183

The scaffolding was lowered to the bottom half of the wall on 15 December 1540, and soon after this Michelangelo fell off it and injured his leg. He finished the huge work, which was unveiled on 31 October 1541, the Vigil of 182 All Saints, exactly twenty-nine years after he finished the ceiling overhead.

The interest evoked by the fresco was considerable. As early as 16 September 1537, when the general design must already have been established, Pietro Aretino wrote to Michelangelo offering advice about the content of the 181 work. The letter, which like all Aretino's letters was designed for publication possibly even more than as a communication to its recipient, begins with effusive compliments, laced with covert self-praise:

Just as it is disgraceful and sinful to be unmindful of God, so it is reprehensible and dishonourable for any man of discerning judgment not to honour you as a brilliant and venerable artist.... In your hands lives the idea of a new kind of creation, whereby the most challenging and subtle problem of all in the art of painting, namely that of outlines, has been so mastered by you that in the contours of the human body you express and contain the purpose of art....

I have never hesitated to praise or scorn the merits and demerits of many people and so now, in order not to diminish what worth I have, I salute you ... and it is surely my duty to honour you with this salutation, since the world has many kings but only one Michelangelo. (C.4.952.)

Then, after more extravagant eulogies, he proceeds to give his views of what the painting should depict:

I see Antichrist in the midst of the rabble.... I see terror on the faces of all the living, I see the signs of the impending extinction of the sun, the moon, and the stars ... I see Nature ... full of terror, shrunken and barren in the decrepitude of old age. I see Time, withered and trembling ... near to his end ... I see Life and Death in fearsome confusion. I see Hope and Despair guiding the ranks of the good and the throng of evil-doers. I see ... Christ enthroned among his legions, encircled by splendours and terrors.... [And so on and on, ending:] The vow I made never to see Rome again will have to be broken because of my desire to see this great painting. (C.4.952.)

To this Michelangelo returned a tactful and evasive reply on 20 November 1537:

To the divine Aretino: Magnifico Messer Pietro Aretino: my lord and brother, on receiving your letter I had joy and pain together. I was rejoicing greatly since it came from you, who are supreme in this world in virtue, and also I was deeply grieved, because having completed the greater part of the history, I cannot avail myself of your imagination, which is so made, that if the Day of Judgment were to have happened, and had you been present to see it, your words could not have pictured it better. Now, to answer you about your writing about me, I say to you that not only is it dear to me, but I beg you to do so, since kings and emperors are delighted that you should mention them. If in this, I have anything which would be agreeable to you, I offer it with all my heart. And to end, your not wishing to return to Rome, do not break your resolve in order to see the painting which I am doing: it would be too much. I commend myself to you. (C.4.955.)

Unfortunately, the matter did not rest there. The unlucky words, 'if I have anything which would be agreeable to you, I offer it with all my heart', prompted the acquisitive scoundrel to write again in April 1544 to beg drawings from Michelangelo, which he could then have displayed as homages to his own power and fame.

But if you are revered, thanks to public acclaim, even by those who do not know the miracles of your divine intellect; why should it not be thought that I too revere, who am almost able to respond to the excellence of your fatal genius? And to be made thus, in seeing the tremendous and venerable and fearfulness of your day of the *Last Judgment*, my eyes fill with tears of emotion. Now think of the way my tears would be shed in seeing the work which has come from your sacred hand. If that were so, other than revealing the spirits of living nature by the feeling colours of art, I would give thanks to God for having given me the gift of having lived in your time, a thing which I regard as the same as being alive in the days of Charles Augustus [Charles V]. But why, O Lord, do you not reward my burning devotion, which bows down before your heavenly qualities, with a few relics of those papers which you care least about? Certainly, I should appreciate two chalk marks on a sheet of paper more than so many cups and chains ever presented to me by this or that prince. But, even if my unworthiness were the reason why I do not achieve that wish, I should be satisfied with the promise which would give me hope. I will rejoice while I hope for them, and in hoping for them contemplate them; and in contemplating them I congratulate myself upon the good fortune I have to be able to satisfy myself with the promised thing, which can only be a dream if it is not changed into a vision. And I can also assure you of the adherence of my friend Titian, a man of excellent example and of a serious and modest life. He, a fervent advocate of your superhuman style, has testified by writing of it to you, with the respect due to his faith in deriving from it the benefice which he desires the pope to grant him for his son, and the favour which he expects from your sincere goodness, the idol both of him and me. (C.4.1021.)

This revolting effusion, which begins by begging on his own behalf, and ends by suggesting that Michelangelo shall be a broker for Titian's desire for preferment for his son Pompeo, got no answer at all. Undaunted, he returned to the attack in April 1545: This time he began his letter without honorific salutations, merely 'To Buonaruoto':

In the beneficence of the salutations which you sent me in the letter from [Jacopo] Cellini, my spirits experience that joy which, singularly divine Michelangelo, resembles the flocks of birds which feel themselves awakened by the sweetness of spring . . . but with a certain modulation of joy agreed among them, similar to the harmonization renewed in their throats . . . I take up my pen so that I write to you as I know how – since as I should, I cannot – and in writing to you confess myself as surprised that the gift of drawings does not correspond with the promise. Because he who does not obtain what he desires attributes the fault to having desired what he should not. . . . But if to anyone you should be generous, I am among the number, it happening that Nature has infused such power into the letters which she inspires in me, which are able to blazon the admirable marbles and the stupendous walls existing by virtue of your chisel and your art, in every part and for all centuries. . . . If you will now gratify my expectations with the reward which its urgent prayer so strongly desires, not because I already think myself to be that which has prompted me to praise myself, nor the pride displayed in having so spoken, but the supreme longing of obtaining some of the marvels which are continually brought to birth from the divinity which impregnates the intellect. (C.4.1040.)

What Michelangelo felt on finding himself bespattered with this perfumed manure has not been recorded. Again he did not answer. Aretino's next missive, in November 1545, was of a totally different character; it may well rank as one of the nastiest letters ever written, and goes far to explain why, as early as 1525, Michelangelo was complaining about the taunts which afflicted him over the Julius Tomb.

On seeing the complete sketch of the whole of your Day of Judgment, I was able to perceive the noble grace of Raphael in the lovely beauty of its invention. Nevertheless, I, as one baptized, am ashamed of the licence, so harmful to the spirit, which you have adopted in the expression of the concepts where is set out the end to which every sense of our supremely truthful faith aspires. And so, that Michelangelo so stupendous in fame, that Michelangelo so outstanding in wisdom, that Michelangelo whom we admire for his conduct, has been willing to show to people no less impiety of irreligion than perfection of painting? Is it possible that you, who as a divine being do not condescend to the society of men, should have done such a thing in the foremost temple of God? Above the main altar of Jesus? In the most important chapel in the world, where the great cardinals of the Church, where the reverend priests, where the Vicar of Christ with Catholic devotions, with sacred rites, and with holy prayers, bear witness to, contemplate, and adore His body, His blood, and His flesh?

If it were not a wicked thing to make such a comparison, I would boast of the judgment shown in the *Treatise on Nanna*, preferring the wisdom of my discernment to your faulty conscience, since I in lascivious and immodest subject matter not only use restrained and polite words, but tell my story in pure and blameless language. But you, in a subject matter of such exalted history, show angels and saints, the former without any of the decency proper to this world, and the latter lacking any of the loveliness of Heaven.

Remember that pagans in the statues – I don't say of Diana clothed, but in the naked Venus – made them cover with their hands the parts which should not be revealed; and one who is a Christian, because he values art more than the Faith, displays as a genuine spectacle not only absence of decorum in the martyrs and virgins, but also the gesture of the man dragged away by his genital organs, a sight to which eyes would be shut tight even in a brothel. What you have done would be appropriate in a voluptuous whorehouse, not in a supreme choir. Hence it would be a lesser vice if you were an unbeliever, rather than that, believing in such a manner, you diminished the belief of others.

But even here the excellence of such outrageous marvels should not remain unpunished, since the miracle of their being is the death of your fame. But you could revive your good name by making the flames of fire cover the shame of the damned, and that of the blessed with the rays of the sun, or imitate Florentine modesty which under a few gilded leaves covered that of its beautiful colossus; and this stands in a public square, not in a sacred place. So thus may God forgive you, as I do not say this because of the contempt which I have for the things I desire; because satisfying what you undertook to send me should be attended to by you with all dispatch, since in such an act you would silence envy, which says that only Gherardi and Tomai [Gherardo Perini and Tommaso Cavalieri] can dispose of them. But if the treasure which Julius left you so that you should place his remains in the receptacle of your carving was not sufficient to make you keep the promise, what hope then can I have? Though not your ingratitude, nor your avarice, great painter, but the grace and merit of that great Pastor is the reason for it; although God wills that his eternal fame shall live simply in having been himself, and not in a proud machine of sculpture created by your art. In this matter your failure to honour your debt is attributed to you as a theft. For our hearts have more need of the feeling of devotion than of the liveliness of art, may God inspire the Holiness of Paul as it inspired the Blessedness of Gregory, who wished at first to strip Rome of the superb statues of idols which took, by their beauty, reverence from humble images of saints. To end, if you had accepted the advice, in composing the Universe, the Abyss, and Paradise, with the glory, the honour and the terror sketched out for you from the instruction, the example, and the wisdom of my letter, which the century has read, I dare to say that then Nature and every benign influence would not repent of your having been given so clear an intellect that today your supreme ability has made you into a simulacrum of the marvellous, but the providence of the One who rules everything will take account of such a work, without making use of his own laws in governing the hemispheres.

[PS.] Now that I have somewhat given vent to my anger against the cruelty with which you repay my devotion, and having, it appears to me, made you see that, if you are divine, I am not made of water, tear this up, just as I have reduced it to bits, and remember that I am such that even kings and emperors reply to my letters. (C.4.1045.)

There was no answer to this either. The pamphlet on Nanna, which Aretino holds up as a suitable comparison to the style of the *Last Judgment*, was a set of instructions from a woman to her daughter, about to enter upon the profession of a whore, on her conduct and on the treatment she would find meted out to her. Neither is there any evidence that the *David* was ever garlanded to preserve the modesty of Florentine passers-by. But Aretino had one more shot in his locker, and before firing it he gave Michelangelo, in April 1546, one more chance:

Anselmi, Messer Antonio, truly the mouthpiece of your praise and soul of my affection, besides saluting you in my name, who adores you, will excuse no more no less my importunity towards you, by my extreme desire for some of the drawings with which you are prodigal to the flames but so miserly to me. Stay well. (C.4.1062.)

No drawings were sent. Aretino then revenged himself by rewriting his letter of November 1545, and sending it to Alessandro Corvino, one of the secretaries of Duke Ottavio Farnese, the pope's nephew. The odd thing about the second version, as Aretino published it, is that it refers to a new pope; the letter is dated 1547, and Paul III did not die until 1549. The letter in its version to Corvino was published in Aretino's *Fourth Book of Letters* in 1550, so that the published version must have been amended to concord with the general chorus of criticism now being heard about the *Last Judgment*. The last sentence sums up the man:

But if our immortal intellect [Michelangelo] should resent hearing what I write, I shall bear it by saying that in such matters it is better to displease him by speaking of them than to offend Christ by keeping silent. (c.4.1045n.)

Cries of complaint were heard almost immediately the fresco was unveiled, in 1541, and Biagio da Cesena may well have orchestrated some of them before the fresco was finished. Most of them stemmed from the powerful body of reformers in the Church, who felt that displays of nudity were undesirable in themselves and even more so in the major papal chapel. The chorus of denunciation was matched by an equally passionate acclaim, so that two camps formed; the clergy who wanted the nudities done away with, the artists who extolled the painter's genius and hailed a new masterpiece.

The violence of the protests is puzzling in one respect in particular. Overhead, on the ceiling of the same Chapel, is one of the most splendid displays of nudity ever seen. It is true that the first of the 'spiritual' popes, Hadrian VI, had disliked it and called it a 'brothel' (*stufa*); but none of the critics of the *Last Judgment* ever seems to have raised his eyes to the Ceiling. Does the reason for this difference of response lie in the fact that for the Ceiling Michelangelo clearly had the help of theologians who set out a programme which the artist was then able to treat as he thought fit, while in the *Last Judgment* he worked alone, inspired by Dante, by the *Dies Irae*, by the words of the Requiem Mass, by his vision of the horror and clamour of terror and rejoicing, expressed by his supreme ability to represent the human form in movement?

From the half-awakened, struggling blindly from the earth which opens to release them, rising in tumult towards the fulminating figure of Christ, and either merging among the elect or tumbling headlong, struggling, rebelling, fighting against the fate that awaits them below – no pose was so difficult, no foreshortening so extreme, that he could not accomplish it with what looks like ease. Very few drawings have survived – some studies of fragments of figures and a few sketches for the composition done while he was still working out the design. The rest – drawings and cartoons – were destroyed, hence Aretino's complaint about his generosity to the fire. On 19 November 1541, Nino Servini, agent for Cardinal Ercole Gonzaga, wrote to his master in Mantua, obviously in response to an urgent order to obtain a copy of the new work:

I have not found anyone with the courage to make drawings quickly of what Michelangelo has newly painted, because it is a large and difficult work, since it contains more than five hundred figures, and of such a kind that to copy even one of them would give the painter pause for thought; even though the work is of such beauty as Your Illustrious Lordship may imagine, there are not lacking those who damn it. The Theatine fathers are the first to say that it is not good to have nudes displaying themselves in such a place, even though he has paid great attention to this, and only in about ten out of so great a number can one see anything indecent. Others say that he has made Christ beardless and too young, and He does not have that majesty which is suitable for Him, and so there is no lack of talk. But Cardinal Cornaro, who spent a long time examining it, has spoken truly, saying that if Michelangelo would paint him a picture containing just one of those figures he would pay whatever he asked for it, and he is right, because to my mind it is something which it is impossible to see anywhere else.

76

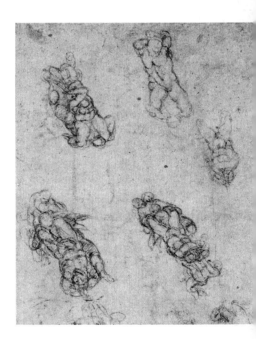

Detail of a sheet of tiny drawings, dating from about 1534, of ideas for the figures and groups in the *Last Judgment*.

163

The said Cardinal has a painter of his there copying it, and although he doesn't lose a moment he won't finish the whole in less than four months, and with all this I will do my best to have at least a sketch so that Y.I.L. will be able to see the arrangement he has made, which I do not think will be enough to satisfy you, and that Messer Julio [Giulio Romano, court painter to the Gonzagas] would have done it more honour, and it will be, when you see it, very different from what he thinks it is, because it is known that all his strength has gone to making bizarre figures in a variety of poses, and if I cannot send you the drawing I will endeavour to describe at least the composition and you will get from that what little pleasure you can. It is said that our Lord wants him to paint the other small chapel which His Holiness has had built. (P.12.659–60.)

On 4 December 1541, Sernini wrote again:

I have not failed to seek every possible way to obtain a drawing of the work ... but as I wrote to Y.I.L., because it is a very large and difficult thing to copy it takes a long time. Many continually draw it, among whom the best is said to be a Mantuan called Marcello [Venusti] whom Messer Julio must know, who is said to be diligent and for a young man works very well. I have spoken to him to come to some arrangement, so that he copies the whole thing, promising him that when Y.I.L. has seen his drawings you will return them, so that he can work on the copy I wanted, to help him to keep himself, because the poor man has no means of his own to live. He wants to serve you, but I fear that I will not get the drawings which, if you get them, you will value highly. He has worked for a month without losing any time and has hardly finished Charon's bark, in which there is a large number of figures. Y.I.L. may from this realize how long it will take to do the rest, because one can say that the bark is a finger of a whole body. (P.12.660.)

A typical example of the developing cult of Michelangelo can be seen in a letter written to him in January 1543 by Anton Francesco Doni, a disillusioned critic of post-Renaissance society, who denounced the injustice of the social structure and denied that humanist teaching could improve the lot of man or the conduct of rulers.

The fame of the *Judgment* sounds in my ear, so that I think, because of its beauty, that on the day Christ comes in glory it will deserve that He should order everyone to adopt those attitudes and show that beauty, and that Hell should maintain that darkness that you have painted, as being impossible to improve upon. (C.4.1006.)

Francisco de Holanda, a Portuguese artist who attached himself to the circle round Michelangelo, later wrote a treatise in which he gives accounts of conversations on art with Michelangelo and Vittoria Colonna, praising him fulsomely and recording notably Michelangelo's denigration of Flemish painting. But this treatise is held to be as much self-advertisement for his own social contacts as for his learning in art.

Vasari's first edition of 1550 contained a very long and detailed account of the *Last Judgment*, saying 'he shakes the hearts of all who are not knowledgeable as well as those who are knowledgeable in such matters', and later, 'This work makes chained prisoners of those who believe they know about art' (V2.7.215). It is not impossible that the popularity of Vasari's great work, and his unstinted admiration for Michelangelo and for this now highly controversial fresco, may have lain behind some of the bitterness of the attacks on it.

One of the most painful aspects of the controversy for Michelangelo was that many of the most virulent attacks emanated from the circle around Vittoria Colonna of which he was a member. This included many of the major religious reformers of the age: Cardinals Gianpetro Carafa (founder of the Holy Office, or Inquisition, and later Pope Paul IV), Gasparo Contarini, Spannocchi Cervini (later Marcellus II), Reginald Pole, all of whom were affected by the views and the rhetoric of the popular preacher and heresy-hunter Ambrogio Politi, known as Caterino. He published his violent attack on the *Last Judgment* in 1551, ten years after its unveiling, and drew painful analogies between the nudity of the figures and actual heresy.

In our time there is an excellent painter and sculptor, Michelangelo by name, who is admirable at rendering nude human figures and their private parts. I commend the art in this fact; the fact itself I vehemently deplore and detest. Yet there is everything to be seen, on altars and in the most splendid chapels of God, this most indecent nudity of the members. (DM.48.)

Bernardo Cirillo, a priest in the circle of Michelangelo's cardinals, who was also a correspondent of Aretino's, wrote in a letter in February 1549:

I esteem the miracle of Nature, in painting and sculptor, Michelangelo Buonarroti, but, if he had painted all those unbreeched and nude figures, which he has made in the Chapel as an ostentatious display of his art and his own prowess, in a garden loggia, it would have been much more seemly. (DM.49.)

Bernardo Cirillo, by Orazio de Sanctis.

The strictures of the professional theologian Gilio da Fabriano were current long before he finally published them in 1564 in his (to give it its abbreviated title) *Errori dei pittori*, which he wrote with particular reference to the *Last Judgment*, and in which he adumbrated an iconography of such orthodoxy that it becomes almost an Index of Prohibited Paintings. He criticized the *Last Judgment* for its wingless angels, for saints without haloes, that all were nude and thus made equal; he complained about the introduction of Charon and his bark, where Michelangelo quotes directly from Dante:

> Charon the demon with eyes of glowing embers
> Beckoning to them gathers them together
> And drives with his oar the laggards on the bank.

He objected to the standing Christ, who he said should be seated on His Throne of Glory, and to the angels with the trumpets all together in the centre where Revelation says they were sent to the four corners of the earth. Gilio, whose motto *Haud aliter* (In no other way) expresses the rigidity of his thought, was very influential. His detailed exposition of the painter's 'unhistorical' departures from the orthodox expectation of this final moment of future history formed part of the growing attitude that such divergencies were departures from orthodoxy itself – in other words, they were heresies. No one contradicted Gilio, and his ideas were crystallized by such things as the metal loincloth on Michelangelo's *Risen Christ* in Caterino's own church, 81 and in the metal chemises added to the nude figures of Guglielmo della Porta's tomb of Paul III in St Peter's in 1562. The result of this type of criticism can be seen in the anonymous letter of March 1549, now in the National Library in Florence:

There were unveiled the heavy and ugly figures in marble in Sta Maria del Fiore by Baccio Bandinelli, which are *Adam* and *Eve*, and which were generally condemned by the whole city. ... In this same month there was unveiled a *Pietà* in Sto Spirito, sent to that church by a Florentine, and it is said that the original derives from the inventor of filth, Michelangelo, who thinks only of art and not of devotion: who, of all modern painters and sculptors, in imitating such Lutheran fantasies, makes nothing for holy churches either in painting or sculpture but that which subverts faith and piety, but I hope that one day God will send His saints to throw down such idolatries as these. (DM.49.)

A copy of Michelangelo's St Peter's *Pietà* had been placed in a niche in Sto 37

Spirito in 1549, the work of Nanni di Baccio Bigio, son of the man who had been so jealous and obstructive during the works on S. Lorenzo.

Paul III had defended his artist, mostly by inaction, though at one moment he seemed to be listening to the party advocating destruction. The election of his successor, Julius III, in 1550, brought little comfort to the anti-*Last Judgment* party, since he so admired Michelangelo that he declared that 'he would give five years of his own life and his life-blood itself, to prolong his existence'. Aretino's publication of his vile attack in 1550 by no means began the persecution of the fresco; he merely found it a useful band-wagon on which to climb in pursuit of his almost unbelievable project of being made a Cardinal. Julius died in 1555. His successor, Marcellus II, though a friend and admirer of Michelangelo, was a strong critic of the fresco; but his papacy of twenty-two days is best remembered by his patronage of Palestrina, who wrote his *Missa Papae Marcelli* as a memorial to him.

With the election of Paul IV – Carafa – the fresco was in real danger, for Paul immediately sent Michelangelo a peremptory message that he should 'amend the fresco', to which the artist replied with equally angry abruptness, 'Tell the pope that this is a small matter and can easily be amended; let him amend the world and pictures will soon amend themselves' (v2.7.240); a flash of the fire that had made Leo X, all those years ago, say to Sebastiano: 'Michelangelo is terrible; one cannot deal with him' (c.2.474).

It was common knowledge that Paul IV hated the fresco, but his hand was stayed by an important consideration. On 1 January 1547 Paul III had appointed Michelangelo as supreme architect to St Peter's. Even Paul IV could recognize that Michelangelo's powers of design were equal to the tremendous task, that his probity in handling the contractors, which made him many enemies, was to the benefit of the work and the treasury, and that, since he gave his services free, it was hardly decent, much less politic, to destroy one of his major works. Moreover, Paul had other worries: a disastrous foreign policy and the mounting horror with which Romans were coming to regard the Holy Office. When he died in 1559, he was so loathed that he was hurried hugger-mugger into his grave, his statue was thrown down and rolled into the Tiber, the prisons of the Holy Office were stormed and its prisoners freed, his palace destroyed, and the civic authorities ordered that his arms should be defaced throughout Rome. Paul's successor was Pius IV, a Medici, not of the Florentine house to which he claimed to be related, but from Milan, and his chief adviser was his nephew Carlo Borromeo, who became a cardinal and later a saint.

Meanwhile the Council of Trent had been working steadily towards its last session in 1563, which was concerned with the role of art in churches, and it is clear that the *Last Judgment* was one of the main topics in the discussion. Revisions to the fresco were among the eleven urgent decrees on which it was decided to act at once. The commission which determined, on 21 January 1564, to proceed to the retouching of the nudes was presided over by a friend of Michelangelo, Cardinal Morone. By this time it was obvious that Michelangelo was dying. The insult of mauling his masterpiece was delayed until after his death, less than a month later.

The task of being wardrobe-master to the newly risen dead fell to Daniele da Volterra, close friend and admirer of Michelangelo. With the exception of the figures of St Catherine and St Blaise, who seem for some obscure reason to have been particularly detested and which, instead of merely clothing them, he destroyed down to the *arriccio*, he managed his unenviable labour with scrupulous care and delicacy. It did not prevent his being nicknamed

Pope Paul IV, Gianpietro Carafa: one of the few surviving effigies of this unpopular pope. He was among the most vehement Reformers, but was deflected from his real mission by his disastrous foreign policy.

Detail of presumed portrait of Cardinal Spannocchi Cervini, later Pope Marcellus II. Had his pontificate lasted more than a few weeks, Marcellus might well have had the *Last Judgment* destroyed.

'Breeches-maker'. Pius IV died in 1565, and the election of Pius V, who had long expressed his detestation of the work, once again endangered it. Although two more 'breeches-makers' were appointed, it may well have been the influence of Vasari, Pius' favourite painter, which restrained him from further damaging the work.

181

Gregory XIII, who succeeded in 1572, also considered destroying the fresco. The involvement, at this moment, of El Greco has been contested, but he was in a thoroughly ambivalent position. He became a member of the Accademia di S. Luca, the artists' official body and one strongly pro-Michelangelo, and he was closely associated with another passionate admirer of Michelangelo, the miniaturist Giulio Clovio, who was his sponsor in the Farnese Palace. When it became known that the *Last Judgment* was to be destroyed because of what Gregory described as 'the obscenities and low-class figures' of the remaining nudes, El Greco declared that 'if it were thrown down he would paint another with honesty and decency and equal to that one in quality of painting' (DM.42). The result for El Greco was his speedy departure to Spain, where he too came face to face with incomprehension and rejection. The dreadful saga continued: Sixtus V after his election in 1585 employed yet another hack to mutilate the work. Clement VIII (1592–1605) was only dissuaded from demolishing it by the prayers of the *Principe*, or president, of the Accademia di S. Luca who besought him in tears and on his knees not to commit a crime against humanity. The painting survived; it was merely decided to allow it to perish by neglect and casual damage.

228

The blame for all this lay partly in the fact that for the popes, prelates and clerics of the age which succeeded the Renaissance nudity was equated with indecency. In an age when privilege and social status became even more entrenched, the utter lack of distinction in the fresco between resurrected humanity, saved or fallen, and the body of saints and martyrs – no haloes, no glories, no flames, no radiances, no winged angels, no Michael weighing souls – was, as Gilio had laid down, to be equated with a denigration of spiritual truths and hence equated with heresy.

In 1538, before the *Last Judgment* was finished, Francesco Maria of Urbino died. The new duke, Guidobaldo, was in such deep trouble politically that he was tactful enough not to enrage Pope Paul III by complaining about the new interruption to the completion of the Tomb. He was, he assured Michelangelo confident that the moment the artist had finished the painting he would, as a man of honour, proceed with the Tomb. But even this relaxed attitude did not help. The moment the *Last Judgment* was finished, Paul insisted that Michelangelo should paint two frescoes in his newly constructed private chapel – the Cappella Paolina.

186

Michelangelo was now in his seventies and weary, yet he offered to supervise the completion of the Tomb with the *Moses* which the Pope had admired when visiting Michelangelo's workshop, and which Cardinal Gonzaga of Mantua had suggested would be perfectly adequate in itself as a memorial to Julius. On 20 July 1542, Michelangelo, to put the whole dreadful affair on a proper legal footing, petitioned Pope Paul to get him released from any contract existing between himself and the Duke of Urbino.

88

Messer Michelangelo Buonarroti, having undertaken a long time ago to execute the Tomb of Pope Julius in Santo Piero in Vincola, in accordance with certain terms and conditions, as by a contract drawn up by Messer Bartolomeo Cappello, under date, the 18th day of April 1532 appears: and being afterwards required and constrained by His Holiness our Lord, Pope Paul the Third, to execute the painting of his new chapel, and being unable to attend to that and to the finishing of the Tomb, he came, through the mediation of His Holiness, to a new agreement with the Illustrious Lord Duke of Urbino, to whom the charge of the aforesaid Tomb has fallen, as from one of the duke's letters, dated the 6th day of March I542 is evident; whereby of six statues that are to be built into the said Tomb, the said Messer Michelangelo might allocate three to a good and approved master to finish and to build into the said work; and the other three, including the *Moses*, he had himself to finish with his own hand, and, similarly, he was obliged to have the architectural frame completed, that is to say, the rest of the ornament of the said Tomb, in the style of the first part that had been completed. Whence, in order to give effect to the said agreement, the aforesaid Messer Michelangelo allocated the finishing of the said three statues, which were well advanced – that is, one of *Our Lady* with the *Child* in her arms, standing, and one *Prophet* and one *Sibyl*, seated, to Raffaello da Montelupo, a Florentine, recognized as being among the best masters of the present time, for four hundred scudi, as by the written agreement between them appears; and the rest of the architectural frame and ornament of the Tomb, with the exception of the crowning pediment, he allocated in like manner to Maestro Giovanni de' Marchesi and to Francesco da Urbino, *scarpellini* and stone carvers, for seven hundred scudi, as by the written undertaking between them appears. It remained to him to finish the three statues by his own hand, that is, the *Moses* and two *Captives*; the which three statues are almost finished. But because the said two *Captives* were executed when the work was designed to be much larger, and was to include many other statues, which work was afterwards in the above-mentioned contract curtailed and reduced; for this reason they are unsuited to the present design, nor would they by any means be appropriate for it. Therefore, the said Messer Michelangelo, in order not to fail to honour his obligation, began the other statues to go in the same zone as the *Moses*, the *Contemplative Life* and the *Active*, which are well enough advanced to be easily finished by other masters. But the said Messer Michelangelo, being again required by His said Holiness, our Lord Pope Paul the Third, and urged to begin work on his chapel and to carry it to completion, as stated above, the which is a great task, which requires his personal attention complete and undistracted by any other concern, the said Michelangelo, being an old man, and desiring to serve His Holiness with all his powers; being also constrained and compelled by him in the matter, and being unable to do so, unless he is first released entirely from this work of Pope Julius, which keeps him in a state of physical and mental suspense, petitions His Holiness, since he is resolved that he should work for him, to negotiate with the Illustrious Lord Duke of Urbino for his complete release from the said Tomb, cancelling and annulling every obligation between them, on the following unequivocal terms. First, the said Michelangelo requests permission to be allowed to allocate the other two statues that remain to be finished to the said Raffaello da Montelupo, or to whomsoever else His Excellency pleases, for a fair price to be determined, which he thinks will be about 200 scudi; and the *Moses* he wishes to deliver, finished by himself. And further, he is willing to deposit the full sum of money that is to go into the finishing of the said work – notwithstanding the inconvenience it will be to him, and much though he has contributed towards the said work – that is, the balance that remains outstanding of the amount he has not yet paid to Raffaello da Montelupo to finish the three statues allocated, as above, which is about 300 scudi, and the balance outstanding, which he has not yet paid for the working of the architectural frame and ornament, which is about 500 scudi; and the 200 scudi, or whatever will be needed to finish the last two statues, besides a hundred ducats, which are to go to the finishing of the crowning pediment of the said Tomb; which in all amounts to between I,I00 and I,200 scudi, or whatever shall be necessary, which he will deposit in Rome in a suitable bank, in the name of the aforesaid Illustrious Lord Duke, in his own name, and in that of the work, with the express condition that the sum is to be used to finish the said work, and for nothing else, nor is to be touched or removed for any other purpose. And he is agreeable, besides this, as far as he is able, to superintend the said work on the statues and ornamentation, so that it may be finished with that diligence which is required. And in this way His Excellency will be assured that the work will be finished and will know where the money is to be found to effect it, and will be able, through his agents, to press for the continuance of the work, and to have it brought to completion. This is much to be desired, because Michelangelo is very old and is fully occupied on work which he will with difficulty have time to finish, let alone to do anything else. And Messer Michelangelo shall remain entirely free and shall be able to work for and to fulfil the wishes of His Holiness, whom he hereby petitions to cause a letter to be written to His Excellency, requesting him to give the requisite order here, and to send a mandate empowering his release from every contract and obligation existing between them. (C.4.993.)

On 20 August 1542, a final contract was negotiated, recording that Michelangelo was impeded in this previous contracts by having to paint in the Sistine Chapel, and now also in the Cappella Paolina for Pope Paul III, and the 1532 contract was annulled. The new contract survives only in Italian, and rehearses the facts as set out in Michelangelo's petition to the pope. The Duke therefore agreed that it should be as if no contracts had ever been signed, and that a perpetual silence should be imposed on the subject of any negotiations for the Tomb. It records that Michelangelo has paid 1400 ducats for the completion of the work by other hands, confirms him in total ownership of the house – subject of so much dispute – and stipulates that no alterations shall be made to the text of the contract (Michelangelo complained bitterly in a long letter of October or November 1542, probably to Cardinal Alessandro Farnese, that after he had left Rome when the 1532 contract was signed, the lawyers had materially altered the terms of the contract without his knowledge or consent). In a further contract, of 21 August, between the Duke's agent and Michelangelo's assistants, Raffaello da Montelupo and Francesco Urbino, Raffaello is to finish the statues begun by Michelangelo, and Urbino to complete the framework and, oddly, to ensure that Michelangelo himself retouches the face of Pope Julius in his effigy, and also the heads of the terms, as he thinks fit.

The Duke was to ratify the contract with Michelangelo within fifteen days, but he refused to do so because he wanted Michelangelo himself to finish the *Leah* and the *Rachel*, and this Michelangelo was forced to do in November 1542; the ratification finally arrived sometime in April 1543. The last figures were moved out of Michelangelo's workshop to S. Pietro in Vincoli in February 1545, and the last payment was made for the work on 3 February 1545.

Unfortunately, the upper part does not match the lower in many ways. The colour is very different; the lower stage is in a marble with an ivory tinge, while the upper part is in a cold, greyish white, veined marble; this accentuates, despite the dim lighting, the contrast between the highly decorative and enriched lower structure and the almost stark upper part, a conflict reinforced by the contrast between the splendour of the *Moses* (together with the affecting simplicity of the *Leah* and *Rachel*) and the very pedestrian quality of the statues in the upper part. 87

However disappointing the result may have been to the artist, however distressing the backward view from the 1545 monument, brought to its dragging conclusion after so many years in a climate poisoned by recrimination, accusations of cheating, peculation and dishonesty, at least he was now free. Condivi's last words on the Tomb, after a long eulogy of its marvels, are probably Michelangelo's own final apologia:

Never was a man more eager about his work than Michelangelo was about this, both because he realized how great a reputation it would bring him and because of the memory he always retained of the blessed soul of Pope Julius, for whose sake he had always honoured and loved the Della Rovere family, and principally the Dukes of Urbino for whom he put up a fight against two popes who wanted, as had been said, to take him away from that undertaking. And this is Michelangelo's complaint: that, in place of the gratitude that was his due, what he received for it was odium and disgrace. (AC.77.)

One may well wonder what must have passed through the sculptor's mind as he surveyed in February 1545 the finished tomb in the transept of S. Pietro in Vincoli. He had begun it forty years before in a time of optimism and enthusiasm, when the arts were reaching a climax of grandeur and splendour, in a world where the gathering storm clouds were still only a distant threat. But then had come the devastation of one invasion after another, culminating in the destruction of Florentine political integrity and liberty, and the frightful Sack of Rome. At the age of seventy, as he smoothed the last chisel marks on the effigy of Julius II, he must have remembered with poignancy the man of thirty who had stood before this most vital and commanding of popes, had honoured him, defied him, served him, and then recognized bitterly, in front of this object, that this was also the tragedy of his own life.

186

The Cappella Paolina formed part of the new suite of state apartments in the Vatican, built for Paul III by Antonio da Sangallo the Younger from 1538 onwards. It lies at right angles to the Sistine, with which it is linked by the Sala Regia, a state reception room reached by a main staircase from the courtyard of the palace guardroom. The first Masses were said in the chapel in January 1540, although it was then entirely undecorated.

Originally, it was lit by two large semicircular windows in each of the main walls of the nave, and the shallow choir probably also had a small semicircular window over the altar. In 1609, when a long nave was added to St Peter's, the choir of the chapel, which abutted on the new work, was rebuilt, and one of the two large windows of the nave was blocked up because the new façade of St Peter's was built against it.

Paul III must have determined, probably at the planning stage of his new private chapel, that there were to be two large wall spaces which Michelangelo was going to have to paint, despite the contract for the Julius Tomb. Immediately the *Last Judgment* was finished Paul pacified the young Duke Guidobaldo of Urbino, materials were accumulated, the scaffolding was erected, and the wall prepared for fresco. No contracts exist, because Michelangelo was a member of the papal household. Painting started in November 1542; Michelangelo's work was interrupted by an illness in the summer of 1544.

The first fresco was seen by the pope on 12 July 1545, and was probably the *Conversion of St Paul*. Before the *Crucifixion of St Peter* was begun in 1546, there must have been a change of plan, in that the obvious parallel subject was the *Charge to Peter* – which is the moment of the founding of the Church. The martyrdom of St Peter does not fit iconographically. But the *Charge to Peter* already existed in the 1481 series in the Sistine Chapel, in the beautiful fresco by Perugino. In his 1550 edition of the Life of Michelangelo, Vasari says:

When this [the *Last Judgment*] was finished, he was given another chapel to do, where the sacrament will be kept, called the Paolina, in which he painted two scenes . . . one where Christ gives the keys to Peter, the other the awe-inspiring *Conversion of St Paul*. (VI.2.987.)

Now Vasari was only intermittently in Rome during the preparation of the first edition of the *Lives*, so that he was probably well informed about the original project, but not in a position to know about later changes. Who suggested the change of subject is unknown, but it is not impossible that it was Michelangelo himself, who by the new treatment of this unrewarding subject, usually shown in static and repellent imagery, gave it a new and revitalized form.

The *Ruolo di famiglia* is a list of the members of the papal household having emoluments and dining rights. It dates from the pontificate of Paul III, who appointed Michelangelo to his household on 1 September 1536. The list includes a number of the official birdsnarers (*uccellatori*), the pope's astrologer, his tailor, his gardeners, his architect Messer Antonio (da Sangallo), and also Messer Michel Angiol Bonarotto – misspelt.

The circular movement in both frescoes is reminiscent of the *Last Judgment*, but on a changed plane. In the *Conversion of St Paul* the composition seems as unplanned, as confused, as the event. On the ground all the movement is from the centre outwards; in the heavens it rushes inwards. In the *Crucifixion of St Peter* the crowd turns in a concentric wheeling round the formidable menacing figure in the centre who twists himself upwards as if to call to witness the supreme price he is willing to pay for his cry of faith, 'Thou art the Christ, the Son of the Living God!' Here are no ecstasies, no angels bearing palms and crowns of celestial reward; there is gloom and terror, curiosity, derision, and indifference.

184
185

Paul just failed to live to see the completion of the work; he visited it for the last time on 13 October 1549. The Florentine ambassador wrote in a despatch:

His Holiness is so hardy that this morning he climbed a ladder of ten or twelve rungs to see the painting which Buonarroto has made in the chapel. (s.55.)

Paul III was broken in spirit by the tardy realization of the crimes of the numerous relatives whom he had unwisely favoured. He died on 10 November 1549, and the fresco was either finished before 26 November or not completed until February or March of the following year, since the Conclave for the election of Paul's successor began on 29 November, and the Chapel would then have been in constant use until the election of Julius III on 8 February 1550 after one of the longest Conclaves known.

Critical opinion varied about the frescoes. For the ever-faithful Vasari, faced with the austerity of the works, and their anomalies of movement and scale, his comment is brief – brief enough to suggest that it conceals a sense of shock.

As has been said elsewhere, Michelangelo concentrated his energies on achieving absolute perfection in what he could do best, so there are no landscapes, nor any trees, buildings or other embellishments. . . . These scenes . . . were the last pictures he did and they cost him a great deal of effort because painting, especially in fresco, is no work for men who have passed a certain age. (v2.7.216.)

For the painter and writer on artistic theory, Paolo Lomazzo, writing in 1590, they represented the lowest stage of Michelangelo's progressive decline. Gilio da Fabriano, who criticized the *Last Judgment* on almost every count, found the figure of Paul, blinded by the dazzling light from Heaven, acceptable because here the painter had adhered to the historical account in the Acts of the Apostles, and had not intermingled profane literature, as he had done in the *Last Judgment* by drawing on Dante. There were no denunciations on the score of nudities or indecencies, because of the artist's notable discretion in the posing of his angels in the *Conversion*, the rendering of the 'light from Heaven that shone about him' so that it encompasses also the figure of Christ and provides a nimbus; in the *Crucifixion* the only nude figure is that of the martyr. Was it perhaps as a subtle revenge that Michelangelo used the antique figure of the reclining hermaphrodite for one of the angels in the group swirling above Christ?

Michelangelo's circle of friends was never a wide one. He was not a social man and feared involvement in the lives of others. He had first met Vittoria Colonna almost certainly in 1536. She was the daughter of Prince Fabrizio Colonna and granddaughter of the great *condottiere* Federigo da Montefeltro, Duke of Urbino. She married Ferrante d'Avalos, Marquis of Pescara, possibly the ablest of the Emperor Charles V's generals; he was seriously wounded at

178

the battle of Pavia in February 1525 and died in the following December, leaving behind him great renown for military valour, though a less savoury reputation in political matters. His widow grieved deeply for him, and her early poems are dark and gloomy, reflecting her personal sufferings and also the generally depressed Italian, and particularly Roman, state of mind after the horrible events of 1527, not just in the Sack but in the trail of devastation which preceded it and followed it through the length and breadth of Italy. Normally, she lived in a convent attended by her own servants, not taking the veil yet participating in the life of the community, and joining in the religious controversies which were the main preoccupation of the society she moved in. She spent much of her time at Viterbo, where Cardinal Pole lived as Governor of the Patrimonium Petri – the estates of the Church – and this saintly man, stricken by Henry VIII of England's persecution of his family, became her religious adviser. Only a tiny handful of letters between her and Michelangelo has survived – two of his, five of hers, all undated. His appear to be from early in their friendship, probably during the winter and spring of 1538–39.

Before taking possession, Signora, of the things which your ladyship has several times wished to give me, I wanted, in order to receive them as little unworthily as possible, to execute something for you by my own hand. Then I came to realize that the grace of God cannot be bought, and that to keep you waiting is a grievous sin. I confess my fault and willingly accept the things in question. And when they are in my possession I shall think myself in paradise, not because they are in my house, but because I am in theirs; wherefore I shall be under an even greater obligation to your ladyship than I am, if that were possible.
  The bearer of this will be Urbino, my assistant, whom your ladyship could inform when you wish me to come and see the head of Christ you promised to show me. I commend me to you. (c.4.984.)

The letter was accompanied by one of his sonnets. The 'something ... I wanted ... to execute for you' must refer to the drawing of the *Crucifixion*, which he sent to her unfinished for her comments:

Signora Marchesa – Seeing that I am in Rome, I do not think it was necessary to have left the *Crucifix* with Messer Tommao [Cavalieri] and to have made him an intermediary between your ladyship and me, your servant, to the end that I might serve you; particularly as I had desired to perform more for you than for anyone on earth I ever knew. But the great task on which I have been and am engaged has prevented me from making this known to your ladyship. And because I know that you know that love requires no task-master, and that he who loves slumbers not – still less had he need of intermediaries. And although it may have seemed that I had forgotten, I was executing something I had not mentioned, in order to add something that was not expected. My plan has been spoilt.
  '*Mal fa chi tanta fè...*' (c.4.967.)

The 'great task' to which Michelangelo refers was the *Last Judgment*; the quotation is from Petrarch, 'He does ill who so much faith so quickly forgets.' Vittoria Colonna had written to him:

I beg you to send me the *Crucifixion* for a while, even if it is not completely finished, because I want to show it to some gentlemen of the Cardinal of Mantua [Ercole Gonzaga]; and if you are not working today, you could come at your convenience to talk to me. (c.4.966.)

For her he executed some of his most beautiful and poignant presentation drawings: the tragic *Pietà*, the *Crucified Christ* (which seems to be the one mentioned in her letter), the so-called *Madonna of Silence*. All these drawings have the delicacy of handling, as if the forms were breathed on to the paper,

179

The *Madonna of Silence* is one of the drawings which may have been made for Vittoria Colonna. The complex iconography reflects the use of symbolism familiar in her erudite circle. The pose with crossed legs re-uses the unusual feature of the *Medici Madonna*; the drooping figure of the Christ child deliberately echoes a *Pietà*; the hourglass is half run through, possibly a reference to Michelangelo's own attitude to life; the thoughtful St Joseph recalls the gloomy Jeremiah of the Ceiling; the Baptist, hooded in a lionskin, enjoins silence.

which is characteristic for the whole series. This is true not only of those made for her, but also of the ones done for Cavalieri – the *Phaeton*, and *Ganymede*, the *Tityus* – and of the mysterious *Archers, Children's Bacchanal*, and *Dream of Human Life*, subjects which have never been elucidated, all made for unknown recipients. The lovely series of *Teste Divine* ('divine heads') is almost certainly earlier, probably done towards the end of his years in Florence. They show more use of line, though the shading is of the utmost delicacy. Considering that he made the presentation drawings when he was working on the *Last Judgment*, as is known from his letter to Vittoria Colonna, it is astonishing that he could find the time during this huge undertaking to make these infinitely delicate and detailed drawings, in such a laborious technique as stippling, and on such abstruse subjects, and that they make such stylistic and technical contrasts to the *Last Judgment*, and yet show the same vigour in the handling of form.

His closest friend in these years was Luigi del Riccio, the head of the Strozzi-Ulivieri Bank in Rome, and through him he was in contact with other Florentine exiles, such as Donato Gianotti, writer and humanist, who tells the story in his *Dialoghi* of the occasion when, after spending the morning in conversation with him and Luigi del Riccio and another friend, Del Riccio invited them all to dine at his house that evening. Michelangelo declined, saying:

'I am a man more inclined than anyone who ever lived to care for people. Whenever I see anyone possessed of some gift which shows him to be more apt in the performance or expression of anything than others, I become, perforce, enamoured of him and am constrained

190
193
192

to abandon myself to him in such a way that I am no longer my own, but wholly his. (EHR.2.XVI.)

Only by being alone again could he be restored to himself. It was Del Riccio who removed him to the Strozzi palace when he fell ill in 1544 and again in 1546 and nursed him back to health, and the frequent letters that passed between them speak of quiet intimacy and warm-hearted friendship. Del Riccio, who was childless, had a young kinsman whom he had adopted and to whom he was devoted, Cecchino Bracci. The boy was apparently of great personal beauty, charm and winsomeness, and to the elderly exiles 'pining by Tiber for their lovelier Arno' he epitomized their hopes for the future. The boy died suddenly at the age of sixteen in January 1544, and Del Riccio was broken-hearted. Michelangelo composed many sonnets and verses in celebration of the boy, designed for him a tomb in Sta Maria Aracoeli which Urbino executed, and did all in his power to console his friend for his loss. Del Riccio on his side was Michelangelo's advisor, guide and mediator in the long and frustrating negotiations over the Julius Tomb. When he died suddenly in the autumn of 1546, Michelangelo was distraught. The loss of Luigi del Riccio was followed closely by another shattering loss: Vittoria Colonna died on 25 February 1547, at the age of fifty-seven, having been ill for some time.

In particular, he greatly loved the Marchioness of Pescara, with whose sublime spirit he was in love, and she returned his love wholeheartedly. He still has many of her letters, filled with honest and most sweet love, and these letters sprang from her heart, just as he also wrote very many sonnets to her, full of deep thought and tender longing. She often travelled from Viterbo to Rome . . . for no other reason than to see Michelangelo, and he in return bore her so much love that I remember hearing him say that his only regret was that, when he went to see her as she was departing this life, he did not kiss her forehead or her face as he kissed her hand. Because of her death he remained a long time in despair, and as if out of his mind. (AC.96–7.)

One of her last letters to him from Viterbo gives some idea of her personality: serious, yet not without humour.

I did not reply earlier to your letter because it seemed to me a reply to one of mine, thinking that if you and I continued to write according to my obligation to you and your courtesy, I should have to leave the Chapel of St Catherine without keeping to the set hours of these sisters, and you would leave the Chapel of St Paul without finding yourself in the morning before dawn all day in sweet discourse with your paintings, which in their own voices will not speak differently to you than those of the real live people who surround me. So that I to the brides, and you to the Vicar of Christ would both fail. However, knowing your faithful friendship and linked in a Christian knot of secure affection, I do not strive by mine to obtain the testimony of your letters, but I await with an attentive mind a real occasion to be of service to you, praying to that Lord, of whom with such ardent and humble heart you spoke to me when I left Rome, that I may find you on my return with your imagination so revived, and with true living faith in your heart as you have so well depicted it in my *Samaritan*. I commend myself to you and also to your Urbino. (C.4.1012.)

The drawing of *Christ and the Woman of Samaria* is lost.

Michelangelo's poetry is virtually untranslatable. The subjects of his sonnets and madrigals range widely: disillusion with Pope Julius, rueful complaints over his physical sufferings when painting the Sistine Ceiling, grief over the fate of Florence or the faithlessness of friends, the splendour of Dante, the fugitive nature of happiness, and, increasingly as he grew older, weariness and the growing strength of his faith and his expectation of death. One of his most important sonnets was addressed to Vittoria Colonna and is a

Detail of the tomb of Cecchino de' Bracci.

proclamation of his artistic creed as a sculptor: '*Non ha l'ottimo artista alcun concetto*', it begins. A bald translation of the first verse, which is the vital one, reads:

> The greatest artist never conceived an idea
> Which a block of marble does not itself contain
> Within its shell, and only the hand that obeys
> The intellect will attain to it. (MR.151.)

In 1547, Benedetto Varchi, humanist, historian and critic, gave a lecture to the Florentine Academy on the problems which this poem stated. Varchi followed this first lecture with a second, on the question of whether painting or sculpture was the superior art, and they were published in 1549 as *Due Lezioni*.

The lectures mark a turning point in the history of Michelangelo's fame, for Varchi begins by remarking that Michelangelo is so well known as to require no explanation of who he is talking about. Varchi's first aim is to compare the potential which may be, as a realizable concept, within the marble, with the potential of the artist to release or reveal it, and he decides that if an inferior work results it is because the hand was not equal to the intellect. When in his detailed commentary, he comes to discuss the meaning of Michelangelo's words *ottimo artista* he justifies Michelangelo from the example of Dante, thus by inference placing Michelangelo as a poet on a similar plane to the greatest of Italian poets and among the greatest figures in Florentine culture. And this during Michelangelo's lifetime, and also during the uproar over the *Last Judgment*.

Michelangelo acknowledged the compliment he had received in his letter to Varchi of March 1547:

Messer Benedetto – So that it may indeed be evident that I have received your treatise, as I have, I will make some attempt to reply to the question asked of me, unlearned though I am.

I admit that it seems to me that painting may be held to be good in the degree in which it approximates to relief, and relief to be bad in the degree in which it approximates to painting. I used therefore to think that painting derived its light from sculpture and that between the two the difference was as that between the sun and the moon.

Now, since I have read the passage in your paper where you say that, philosophically speaking, things which have the same end are one and the same, I have altered my opinion and maintain that, if in face of greater difficulties, impediments and labours, greater judgment does not make for greater nobility, then painting and sculpture are one and the same, and being held to be so, no painter ought to think less of sculpture than of painting, and similarly no sculptor less of painting than of sculpture. By sculpture I mean that which is fashioned by the effort of cutting away, that which is fashioned by the method of building up being like unto painting. It suffices that as both, that is to say sculpture and painting, proceed from one and the same faculty of understanding, we may bring them to amicable terms and desist from such disputes, because they take up more time than the execution of the figures themselves. If he who wrote that painting is nobler than sculpture understood as little about the other things of which he writes – my maidservant could have expressed them better.

There are an infinite number of things, still unsaid, which could be said of kindred arts, but, as I've said, they would take up too much time, and I've little to spare, because I am not only an old man, but almost numbered among the dead. I therefore beg you to have me excused. I commend me to you and thank you to the best of my ability for the too great honour you do me, of which I am undeserving. (C.4.1082.)

The argument about which of the arts was more noble than the others had been going on for a long time. Leonardo da Vinci had been one of the main figures in this futile polemic, though it was of great consequence at the time, since it affected the status of the artist; the contention being, baldly, that because a sculptor had to chip marble and get dirty in the process, he was closer to a workman – an artisan – whereas the painter, who dealt with refined and delicate colours, could sit at his easel in fine clothes while music was played. The argument died out after Michelangelo, largely because his own attitude was that it was the idea – the *concetto* – that marked out the artist, and the mechanics were therefore of no importance. But the argument resulted in a general agreement that the important thing was *disegno* – using the term in its wider sense of 'design', not in the purely literal sense of 'drawing'.

A second sonnet, of far greater poignancy, must have been written late in his life, since it begins '*Giunta è già'l corso della vita mia*', and – again, in bald translation of the words – may be crudely rendered:

> The course of my life has already reached
> Through a tempestuous sea, in its frail bark,
> To the common harbour where on arriving we account
> And excuse our every good or evil deed.
>
> So that the loving fantasy
> Which made art and idol and a king for me,
> I now well know with how much sin was laden;
> With that which all men desire against their will.
>
> The loving thoughts, once so vain and gay,
> What use to me now, as I approach two deaths?
> Of one I am quite sure, the other threatens me.
>
> Nor painting, nor sculpture, now can calm
> The soul that turns to that Divine love
> That on the cross opens its arms to receive us. (MR.285.)

This bronze portrait bust by Daniele Ricciarelli (Daniele da Volterra) was made after Michelangelo's death; a version of it stands on his tomb. It is based on Daniele's own beautiful portrait drawing (p. 227). Vasari describes Michelangelo thus: 'Michelangelo was of medium height, broad in the shoulders but well proportioned in all the rest of his body. . . . His face was round, the brow square and lofty, furrowed by seven straight lines, and the temples projected considerably beyond the ears, which were rather large and prominent. His body was in proportion to the face, or perhaps on the large side; his nose was somewhat squashed, having been broken . . . by a blow from Torrigiano; his eyes can best be described as being small, the colour of horn, flecked with bluish and yellowish specks. His eyebrows were sparse, his lips thin (the lower lip being thicker and projecting a little), the chin well formed and well proportioned with the rest, his hair black, but streaked with many white hairs and worn fairly short, as was his beard which was forked and not very thick.'

Vittoria Colonna

'Michelangelo Buonarroti, Patrician of Florence, in his seventy-second year. All that Art can do in Nature, and Nature can do in Art, he teaches, who is equal in Art to Nature.' So runs the Latin caption to Giulio Bonasone's engraving of 1546 (left). Since 1537 Michelangelo had been a devoted friend of the pious poetess Vittoria Colonna, dowager Marchioness of Pescara, who is seen in her richly crimped coif in the medal below.

RIME DE LA DIVA
VETTORIA COLONNA DE
pescara inclita Marchesana
NOVAMENTE AGGIVNTOVI
XXIIII. Sonetti spirituali, & le sue stanze,
& uno triompho de la croce di Christo non piu stampato con
la sua tauola.

IN VENETIA M D XXXX.

Vittoria Colonna lived partly in a convent in Viterbo, partly in Rome; in her circle Michelangelo met such reforming churchmen as Cardinals Pole and Contarini (see p. 189). Her early poems express her grief for her husband, Ferrante d'Avalos, who died after the battle of Pavia in 1525. Michelangelo's copy of her poems, including the gloomy later *Sonetti spirituali*, first published in 1540 (left), bears his signature on the last page (near right).

The drawings of the *Crucifixion* and *Pietà* were made about 1538–40, expressly for Vittoria Colonna. In her letter of thanks to Michelangelo for one of them, she praises both the concept – the *concetto* – and the detailed handling, which is all the more astonishing in that he was then at work on the *Last Judgment* in the Sistine. The concept of a living crucified Christ, as against the traditional form used since Giotto of a dead Christ on the Cross, is as new as the lamenting Sun and Moon are part of the old tradition. For this reason, the 'angels' and the hilltop and skull of Golgotha have even been believed to be later additions; this cannot be so, since they are technically identical with the figure of Christ. The *Pietà* drawing bears the cryptic inscription *Non vi si pensa quanto sangue costa*, from Dante's *Paradiso*, which may be translated either as 'no one thinks how much blood it costs' or as 'no one thinks how much blood costs'.

392
Ma quanto fece allor pungente strale
  Piu larga piaga, tanto oggi mi uanto
  Di noua gioia, e doue pianſi, or canto,
  E l'alma ſpoglio d'ogni antico male.
Voſtra mercè, Madonna, che rompeſte
  Il corſo al pianto, e d'aſpra indegnitade
  Sgombraſte il cor con note alte, e modeſte.
L'alme, ch'or ſan del ciel tutte le ſtrade,
  Crebbero al gioir lor ben mille feſte
  Piene di caſto amore, e di pietade.

IL FINE.

Last Judgment and censorship

Michelangelo's *Last Judgment*, on the altar wall of the
Sistine Chapel, was commissioned by Pope Paul III
(portrait, right, by Titian) soon after his election in 1534.
The initial project had probably been for a *Resurrection* for
his predecessor Clement VII. It is said that when Paul III, a
man of great qualities but no saint, saw the finished work,
he fell on his knees, saying: 'Lord, hold not my sins against
me!' The finished work (see following pages) was the
largest mural painting in existence (to be compared only
with the ceiling overhead, which is two and a half times
longer). Its colours (detail, right, below) have darkened;
Michelangelo's device of canting the wall forward so as to
avoid the accumulation of dust made it more vulnerable to
the effects of smoke from candles and censers.

The *Last Judgment* was unveiled, appropriately, on All Saints' Day, 1541, but quite soon there were mutterings about its 'indecency'. Paul III himself may have been affected by these; the climate was certainly changing, so that one of his successors, Paul IV (1555–59), had to be dissuaded from destroying the work. In 1545 the Venetian pornographer Pietro Aretino (seen as portrayed by Titian, left) wrote a savage – and thoroughly hypocritical – attack on the nudities as more suited to a brothel than a chapel. At the end of Michelangelo's life, and increasingly after his death, such attacks gave reason to fear that the fresco might after all be destroyed. To silence the criticisms (particularly of the figure of St Catherine), draperies were added. The artists who thus saved the work, including Michelangelo's friend Daniele de Volterra, were rewarded with the nickname *Braghettoni* (Breeches-makers). The original state of the fresco is recorded in a copy made in 1549 by Michelangelo's follower Marcello Venusti for Cardinal Farnese. A detail (left, below) is shown for comparison with the present state of the work (below). Recent restoration has shown that the figures of St Catherine and St Blaise, lower right, were not overpainted in *fresco secco*, Daniele's professed method, but destroyed and repainted on fresh plaster.

The Last Judgment

In the centre (far left) the beardless Christ judges the resurrected souls. He is surrounded by the martyrs, each with his or her identifying attribute, who clamour for justice against their persecutors. In the lunettes above are angels carrying the Instruments of the Passion. Behind Christ, who takes on the likeness of the thundering Jupiter, the Virgin cowers back. Below are the angels blowing the Last Trump, and the dead arise from their graves and surge upwards in a vast circulatory movement, some to fall again to Hell beneath, like the stunned and horror-stricken man who realizes as he is borne away that his fall is his own doing. Charon on his bark, 'with eyes like burning coals', as Dante describes him in *Inferno*, drives the reluctant damned towards their doom.

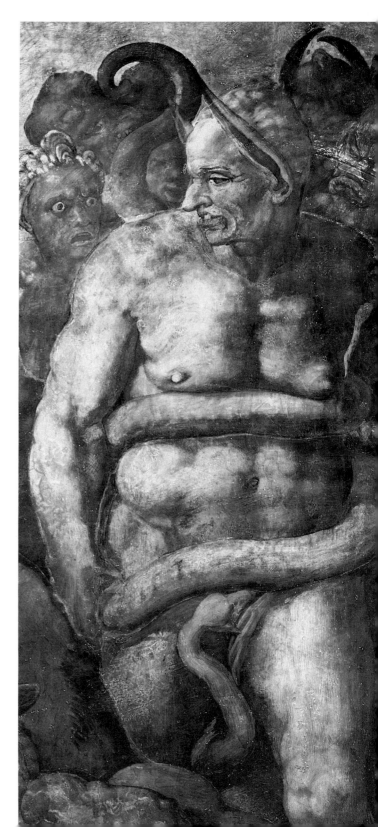

St Bartholomew's flayed skin (above) bears a self-portrait. Minos (right), ruler of Hell, has the face of the papal master of ceremonies, Biagio da Cesena. When Biagio demanded redress, Paul III is said to have answered that his writ ran in Heaven and on Earth, but not in Hell.

Last paintings

The frescoes in the Cappella Paolina were Michelangelo's last paintings. He was sixty-seven when he started, and when he finished in 1550 he was seventy-four, complaining bitterly over such hard labour at his advanced age. The two frescoes are high in colour, and the movement in both is a curiously circular one. In the *Conversion of St Paul*, on the left-hand wall, the horse from

which the blinded Paul has fallen plunges into depth;
Christ, in the vision which the saint cannot see, plummets
downwards with fearsome energy. One of the angels at the
top derives from the type of the Reclining Hermaphrodite,
of which there were at least two examples in Rome. In the
Crucifixion of St Peter, the Apostle glares out of the picture,
calling the spectator to witness the price paid for faith.

Cappella Paolina

When Michelangelo finished the *Last Judgment*, late in 1541, he expected to return at last to the Julius Tomb. Instead, Paul III decided that he should paint two frescoes, a *Crucifixion of St Peter* and a *Conversion of St Paul*, in the newly built Cappella Paolina, then as now the private papal chapel. The chapel is now too dark to see clearly by natural light, let alone to paint, the *Crucifixion of St Peter* under the window on the right-hand wall. This is because the window opposite was blocked when Carlo Maderno extended the nave of St Peter's along the wall of this building in the seventeenth century. The frescoes themselves (preceding pages) contain fascinating reflections of antique art. The St Paul is clearly reminiscent of a river god; and on the right of the St Peter, the man with crossed arms (left), whom William Blake made into his *Joseph of Arimathea*, is derived from figures of barbarians in Roman sculpture, including the lost work shown in the engraving below and those on the Arches of Septimius Severus and Constantine. Below left is the only cartoon by Michelangelo, for a work which he himself completed, to have escaped destruction. It is for the lower right-hand section of the *St Peter*.

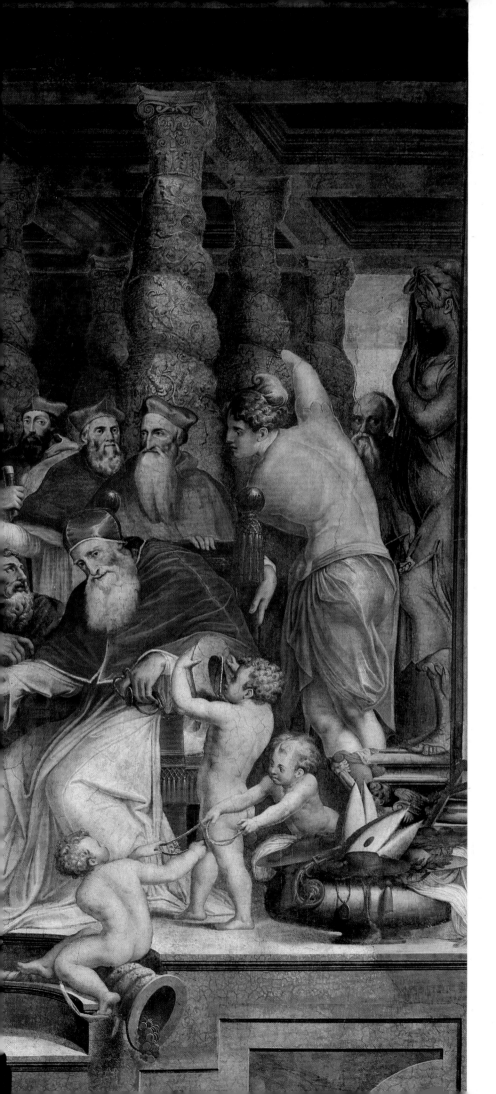

Paul III's Court

Giorgio Vasari early became a fervent admirer of Michelangelo, and imitated his style despite the fact that his own talents were unequal to the strain. He worked mostly in Florence, in the Palazzo della Signoria, and in the Sala Regia adjoining the Sistine Chapel in Rome. His best artistic work was done as an impresario, supervising architects such as Buontalenti (the Uffizi in Florence) or Vignola (the Villa Giulia in Rome). His greatest achievement was the founding of the History of Art, with *Lives of the Most Excellent Italian Architects, Painters and Sculptors . . .*, in 1550. In the Cancelleria, in Rome, he painted the frescoes of the Sala dei Cento Giorni, so called because he did the work in only a hundred days. ('And it shows,' said Michelangelo.) The scene of the court of Paul III (left) shows the pope accompanied by four prelates (in the background): Paolo Giovio, and Cardinals Reginald Pole, Gasparo Contarini and Pietro Bembo. Pole, a future Archbishop of Canterbury, Bembo and Contarini were members of the circle of Vittoria Colonna; in spite of the personal connection Contarini was a vehement critic of the *Last Judgment*. Michelangelo himself looks through the doorway on the left, behind an allegorical figure who clasps a column; Vasari himself is silhouetted between two columns on the right.

189

Presentation drawings

Michelangelo frequently made presentation drawings for his friends after moving to Rome in 1534. Their minute and laborious technique provides an equivalent to the flowery language of admiration and devotion in which he wrote the letter to accompany his gift of a drawing to Tommaso Cavalieri (right, below). Michelangelo's themes are both mythological and personal. Ganymede (left) was borne up to Olympus by Jupiter's eagle to serve as cupbearer to the gods; he symbolizes the exaltation of divinely inspired and spiritual Love. The sin of Phaeton (right) is Pride: he drove the horses of his father the Sun, lost control, and was stopped by Jupiter's thunderbolt; his grieving sisters were turned into trees. The figure of the god prefigures Christ in the *Last Judgment*.

The fate of Tityus (above) is the punishment of Lust. He attempted to rape Leto, mother of Apollo and Diana, and was thereafter chained to a rock in Hell with a vulture devouring his liver.

S mo Cavo

Se io nõ amessi creduto auerui facto certo del grandissimo &

smisurato amore che io ui porto nõ mi sare parmta cosa

strana ne misarei marauigliato del sospetto & uoi mostra

te p la uostra amore a uinto & io nõ ui dimēti chi ma nõ

e cosa nuoua me da pigharne amiratione andando tante

altre cose alcõtrauio fue questa uadi arrouescio a chella

192

Beauty and allegory

Many presentation drawings by Michelangelo are less manifest in their intention than *Phaeton* or *Ganymede*. The seven female *Teste divine* ('divine heads', far left and below) have no apparent purpose outside themselves. They are images of ideal beauty, unconnected with any of the other works. They show an interest in fantastic hair arrangements which recalls the late fifteenth-century drawings of Leonardo and Verrocchio. The so-called *Dream of Human Life* (near left) is less explicit still. Man, supported precariously by the world of illusion and surrounded by the temptations of sin, is awakened by the trumpet of an angel; but only six of the Deadly Sins are represented, suggesting that the stimulus to human activity is Pride. Might the man then be a personification of Pride itself, aroused by the trumpet of Fame? The *Archers Shooting at a Herm* (below left) is hard to square with any known poem, myth or theme, whether classical or Renaissance. The archers shoot arrows but have no bows; and the only figure who has a bow is stringing it the wrong way round. Their gestures of violence are directed at an unresponsive carved figure. Love sleeps oblivious of the violent activity behind him, while other *putti* fan the flames. Do they allude to the childish sources of hectic adult energy?

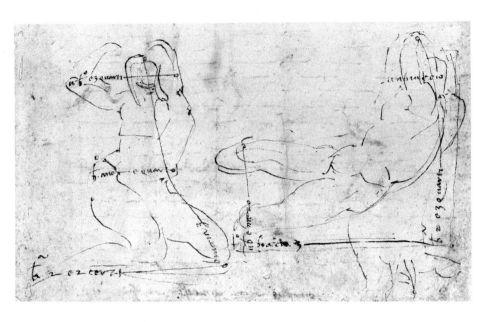

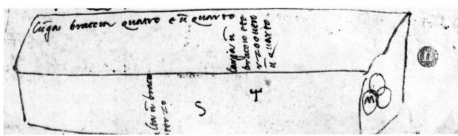

Technique

The development of a piece of Michelangelo's sculpture can be traced from the initial drawings he prepared to determine the measurements of the block required, and those he did for the quarry masters who had to match the block to the dimensions and grain indicated (far left). The block was then roughly shaped to the figure which he proposed to 'free' from it. This stage was important since it avoided transporting superfluous marble. He prepared small wax models for his own use, as with the *Hercules and Cacus* which was eventually done by Bandinelli (centre); or, for his assistants, a large clay model on an armature, such as those of the *River Gods* planned, but not executed, for the Medici Chapel (far left, below). When he began carving, he attacked the block from the front. Many pieces, including the *Brutus* of 1540 (below), still show his handling of different types of chisel, particularly his favourite claw chisel. He allowed his assistant Tiberio Calcagni to work on the partly finished *Brutus*. The *Victory* (left), carved in Florence in 1530–33, was almost certainly intended for a late version of the Julius Tomb, and shows his superb finish in those areas which he completed.

Sebastiano Luciani, later called Sebastiano del Piombo, was about ten years younger than Michelangelo. Venetian by birth, he was much influenced by Giorgione, after whose death in 1510 he moved to Rome. There he worked at first in Raphael's circle, but soon became Michelangelo's faithful follower and friend, executing in oil paint (a medium which Michelangelo disliked using) pictorial ideas worked out by the older man, occasionally in conscious rivalry with Raphael. Sebastiano's *Flagellation* (above right) was one of the resulting works; a drawing of 1516 (above left) shows an early stage of the design. A drawing perhaps done for the Sistine *Eve* gave Sebastiano the pose for a *Pietà*.

Sebastiano's major work is the huge *Raising of Lazarus* of 1517–19 (above right), intended by Cardinal Giulio de' Medici, later Clement VII, for his cathedral at Narbonne as a pendant to Raphael's *Transfiguration* (which never reached Narbonne). Michelangelo designed the work (above left), in deliberate competition with Raphael; but,

as Raphael died in 1520 before completing his painting, the contest remains a draw. The drawing below was recognized by Johannes Wilde as preparatory to a cartoon which Michelangelo gave in 1522–23 to Jacopo Pontormo, and which has never been traced. Pontormo's *Venus and Cupid* exists in several versions; this must be the earliest.

When the Emperor Charles V arrived on a visit to Rome in April 1536, the Capitol or Campidoglio lay on the route of his procession, and its neglected state prompted some efforts at tidying up. The statue of Marcus Aurelius originally stood near St John Lateran and had survived destruction in medieval times because it was thought to represent Constantine. It was moved to the Capitol in 1538, and Michelangelo made a pedestal for it. The state of the site is seen in a drawing made as late as 1554–60 (top left), which shows the municipal Senate, the Roman Tabularium, at the back, crowned with a medieval bell tower, and the Palazzo dei Conservatori, or town hall, at the right. The drawing also shows the beginnings of alterations to the Senate façade, where Michelangelo had designed a splendid stairway crowned by a baldachin (never executed). The scenic effect can be seen in Dupérac's engraving of 1568. The medieval town hall was to disappear behind a new façade, to a design by Michelangelo, and a similar building was to face it (the present Capitoline Museum, not built until the following century). Michelangelo's friend Tommaso Cavalieri himself designed part of the complex, adhering as far as possible to Michelangelo's designs. The Senate façade, and the completion of the Conservatori, are by Giacomo della Porta, who could never resist altering Michelangelo's designs – as here when he inserted an extra wide window in the centre and doubled the end bays. The pavement, also changed by Della Porta and restored in 1940 to Michelangelo's design, expresses both an outward and an inward movement, appropriate to a city that claimed to be the centre of the world.

The Farnese palace, a huge but rather characterless structure, was begun by Antonio da Sangallo the Younger about 1517. Sangallo died in 1546, leaving a design for the cornice; but Paul III, a Farnese, held a competition for a new design. Michelangelo won. He raised the top storey (right, top) to compensate visually for his massive overhang, and added a recessed window and a coat of arms to provide a central accent below. His windows for the top storey in the courtyard (centre) display all his inventiveness in handling classical forms. The pediment, which in a first drawing (far right) forms part of the window framing, becomes entirely separate (below). For the frieze he designed a row of little grotesque masks. His assistant was almost certainly Vignola, the most conservative classicist of the next generation.

Vasari records that Jacopino del Conte painted a portrait of Michelangelo during his lifetime; they could have met either in Florence or in Rome, where Jacopino worked from 1538 onwards. Several versions of the portrait attributed to Jacopino exist; this one, in New York, may well be the original.

PART FIVE

ST PETER'S

1547–1564

Woodcut of Antonio da Sangallo in Vasari's 1568 *Lives*.

O N 2 JANUARY 1547, Paul III made Michelangelo the supreme architect of St Peter's in succession to Sangallo. One of Sangallo's most striking projects was for the amendment of Bramante's centrally planned church by extending it to provide, not a long nave but a concourse which should contain a benediction loggia – an obligation since it had to replace the existing one in the Piazza, from which popes were proclaimed on election, pilgrims were blessed, and the yearly blessing *Urbi et Orbi* – to the City and the World – was given, then as now. Sangallo's design had been given form as a huge model which Antonio Labacco had taken seven years to make. Vasari's account begins with Michelangelo being asked, and then ordered, to undertake the task.

Then one day he made his way to St Peter's to have a look at the model in wood that Sangallo had made, and to study the building itself. When he arrived he found there all the Sangallo faction who, crowding round him, said as agreeably as they could that they were delighted that he had been given responsibility for the building, and that Sangallo's model was certainly like a meadow where there would never be any lack of pasture. 'That's only too true', observed Michelangelo; and by this he meant (as he told a friend) to imply that it provided pasture for dumb oxen and silly sheep who knew nothing about art. (v2.7.218.)

Michelangelo's poor opinion of Sangallo's project is confirmed by his letter to Bartolomeo Ferratini, the Prefect of the Deputies in charge of St Peter's, of January 1547:

Messer Bartolomeo, dear friend – One cannot deny that Bramante was as skilled in architecture as anyone since the time of the ancients. He it was who laid down the first plan of St Peter's, not full of confusion, but clear, simple, luminous and detached in such a way that it in no wise impinged upon the Palace. It was held to be a beautiful design, and manifestly still is, so that anyone who departs from Bramante's arrangement, as Sangallo has done, departs from truth; and that this is so can be seen by anyone who looks at his model with unprejudiced eyes.

218

He, with the outer ambulatory of his, in the first place takes away all the light from Bramante's plan; and not only this, but does so when it has no light of its own, and so many dark lurking places above and below that they afford ample opportunity for innumerable rascalities, such as the hiding of exiles, the coining of base money, the raping of nuns and other rascalities, so that at night, when the said church closes, it would need twenty-five men to seek out those who remained hidden inside, whom it would be a job to find. Then, there would be this other drawback – that by surrounding the said composition of Bramante's with the addition shown in the model, the Cappella Paolina, the Offices of the Piombo, the Ruota and many other buildings would have to be demolished; nor do I think that the Sistine Chapel would survive intact. As regards the part of the outer ambulatory that has been built, which they say cost a hundred thousand scudi, this is not true, because it could be done for sixteen thousand, and little would be lost if it were pulled down, because the dressed stones and the foundations could not come in more useful and the fabric would be two hundred thousand scudi to the good in cost and three hundred years in time. This is as I see it and without prejudice – because to gain my point would be greatly to my detriment. And if you are able to persuade the pope of this, you will be doing me a favour, because I'm not feeling very well. (C4.1071.)

Subsequently, Michelangelo demonstrated the truth of his words with a model which he made himself, and which showed the building completed on the lines we can see today. This model cost him twenty-five crowns and it was made in a fortnight.... In contrast, Sangallo's ... cost four thousand and took many years. It became evident that the building had been turned into a shop organized for making money on behalf of those who were trying to monopolize the work, which they were dragging out indefinitely.... To get rid of the culprits ... he said to them openly one day that they should enlist the help of their friends and do everything in their power to prevent his being put in charge.... These words ... explain why they conceived for

Michelangelo a bitter hatred which grew daily more intense (as they saw him change all the plans, inside and out).... Every day, ... they thought up various new ways to torment him. Finally, the Pope issued a *motu proprio* putting Michelangelo in charge of the building, with full authority, and giving him power to do or undo what ever he chose ... and that all the officials employed there should take their orders from him. (v2.7.219–20.)

But from the first document of appointment to this second *motu proprio* almost three years had elapsed, for the second one was issued in October 1549. The salient clauses are as follows:

Forasmuch as our beloved son, Michelangelo Buonarroti, a member of our household and our regular dining companion, has remade and designed, in a better shape, a model or plan of the fabric of the Basilica ... which had been produced by other skilled architects and has done the same to the building itself ... without accepting the reward or fee which we have repeatedly offered to him.... We ratify and confirm the matters aforesaid ... since they contribute to the grace and beauty of that church.... We hereby approve and confirm the aforementioned new design and alteration, and all and several demolitions and constructions of whatever kind are caused to be done by the same Michelangelo or by his orders ... even if these things shall have been caused to be done at considerable expense and with damage to the destruction of the fabric; and these conditions together with the model or plan ... are to be observed and carried out in perpetuity, so that they may not be changed, re-fashioned, or altered. And moreover, trusting in the good faith, experience, and earnest care of Michelangelo himself ... we appoint and commission him the prefect, overseer and architect of the building ... on behalf of ourselves and of the Apostolic See for as long as he shall live. And we grant him full, free and complete permission and authority to change, re-fashion, enlarge and contract the model and plan and the construction of the building as shall seem best to him ... without seeking permission from the Deputies and those who shall be in office at that time, or from anyone else whatsoever. (EHR.2.308–9.)

The document continues by revoking any ordinances or privileges which may have been granted. No brief could be clearer; no authority more fully given. Unfortunately, Pope Paul died less than a month later. Michelangelo's troubles started again, and rapidly became so bad that Julius III in late 1550 was forced by, the volume of complaints to hold an enquiry over which he presided himself. It was argued that

The noble Basilica, planned by Bramante and most beautifully embellished by Antonio ... had been completely destroyed ... that vast sums of gold had been expended to no purpose ... and that everything had been thrown into confusion by the decisions of a single man, contrary to the feeling of the whole city. (EHR.2.309–10.)

Another criticism was that the lighting was insufficient, which provoked Michelangelo's famous retort to Cardinal Cervini.

'Monsignore, above these windows ... there will be three others.'
   'You have never informed us of this.'
   'I am not obliged, and I certainly do not intend, to tell either Your Eminence or anyone else ... what I propose to do. Your office is to provide the money and ... see to it that it is not stolen, and to leave the design of the building to me.' (v2.7.232.)

Julius renewed the *motu proprio* Paul had given.
   Perhaps one of the reasons for the bitterness of the opposition is to be found in an open letter to the overseers, who had been appointed by him:

You are aware that I told Balduccio that he was not to send his lime unless it was good. Now, having sent it when it was poor, without the expectation of having to take it back, it may be

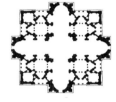

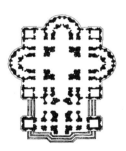

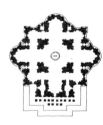

Ground plans of the successive designs for St Peter's, by Bramante (1506), Bramante and Raphael (1515–20), Sangallo (1539) and Michelangelo (1547–64). Each time the central piers were enlarged. Michelangelo demolished Sangallo's ambulatory and used its abutments to consolidate the dome.

thought that he was in league with the man who took delivery of it. This is playing into the hands of those whom I have dismissed from the fabric on like account. Whoever takes delivery of materials necessary to the fabric, but of inferior quality, which I have forbidden, does nothing but treat as friends those whom I have treated as enemies. This, I think, would be a new confederacy.

Promises, gratuities and presents corrupt justice. I therefore pray you, with that authority I have from the pope, henceforward not to take delivery of anything that is not suitable, even if it comes from Heaven, so that I may not appear to be what I am not – partial. (C.4.1159.)

Balducci supplied travertine stone for the building; the undated letter was probably written in 1548 or 1549, but has been put as late as 1550 to 1553.

It is enough to record that Michelangelo as diligently as he could had the work pressed forward in those parts of the building where the design was to be changed, so that it would be impossible for anyone else to make further alterations. This was a shrewd and prudent precaution, for it is pointless doing good work without providing for what may happen later; the rash presumption of those who might be supposed to know something . . . can easily, with the approval of the ignorant, have disastrous results. (V2.7.221–2.)

Julius III issued a further *motu proprio* on 23 January 1552, confirming Michelangelo in his position, and appointing three officials, the Bishop of Lipari (Baldo Ferratini), the Patriarch of Jerusalem, and the Auditor of Curial Pleas, who were partisans of Michelangelo, to protect him from further attacks. Work slowed down because of shortage of money from 1552 onwards, but by February of that year the great cornice below the dome was finished, and a banquet of all the workmen was held to celebrate the event. Vasari describes the cornice: 'nothing could appear more lovely, more splendid . . .'.

Vasari was also pressing him to accept the offers made by Duke Cosimo for a return to Florence. Michelangelo wrote to him on 11 May 1555:

I was forced to undertake the work on the fabric of St Peter's and for about eight years I have served not only for nothing, but at great cost and trouble to myself. But now that the work is advanced, that there is money to spend on it, and that I am almost ready to vault the dome, it would be the ruin of the said fabric if I were to depart; it would disgrace me utterly throughout Christendom and would lay a grievous sin upon my soul.

Therefore, my dear Messer Giorgio, I beg you to thank the duke on my behalf for the splendid offers of which you write to me, and to beg his lordship to allow me to continue here with his kind permission until I can leave with a good reputation, with honour and without sin. (C.5.m.475.)

During these years Michelangelo was beset by troubles. Julius III always protected him, but when Cardinal Cervini succeeded as Marcellus II in 1555 it seemed as if Michelangelo would have to pay dearly for the rebuff given to him when he was cardinal. He then seriously considered returning to Florence, but the pope died within the month. The succession of Paul IV brought difficulties in that, as Cardinal Carafa, he was disinclined to favour Michelangelo because of the *Last Judgment*, and he appointed Pirro Ligorio as papal architect, who insulted Michelangelo by declaring that he was in his dotage and totally incapable of directing the work. The pope, however, had the sense to confirm Michelangelo in control of St Peter's.

In the Vatican Archives is a letter from Michelangelo which is, unfortunately, both undated and without any indication of who the recipient was. It has usually been given a late date – *c.* 1560 – and the recipient has been conjectured to have been Cardinal Pio da Carpi, who was a Deputy of the

Fabric, and the cardinal to whom Michelangelo addressed a letter resigning his office on 13 September 1560, because of the provocations of Pirro Ligorio. From a careful reasoning from the facts and content of the letter, and also from an examination of the handwriting, E.H. Ramsden has put forward the theory that the letter was written probably in December 1550, and its addressee was Cardinal Cervini, with whom he had had the sharp brush over who was responsible for what in the work at St Peter's. The letter is fairly sharp in tone itself – a no-nonsense letter addressed by a professional to a learned man but one with only a purely theoretical knowledge of architecture. The central feature referred to must in fact be the dome, which even as early as this Michelangelo must have considered to be independent of the supporting structures, which themselves must be the 'diverse parts' which are to have the same character.

Most Reverend Monsignore – When a plan has diverse parts all those that are of the same character and dimension must be decorated in the same way and in the same manner; and their counterparts likewise. But when a plan changes its form entirely it is not only permissible, but necessary, to vary the ornament also and [that of] their counterparts likewise. The central features are always as independent as one chooses – just as the nose, being in the middle of the face, is related neither to one eye nor to the other, though one hand is certainly related to the other and one eye to the other, owing to their being at the sides and having counterparts.

It is therefore indisputable that the limbs of architecture are derived from the limbs of man. No one who has not been or is not a good master of the human figure, particularly of anatomy, can comprehend this. (c.5.m.490.)

It is one of Michelangelo's very few statements on the aesthetics of his profession.

The disastrous policies of Paul IV, including a war with the Colonna which he lost, led to a shortage of funds, and between 1556 and 1561 building work was halted. It was now evident that Michelangelo would not live to see the completion of the dome, and his friends urged him to establish his intentions once and for all. In November 1558 he began a model, ten feet high to the apex of the interior vault, which was completed exactly three years later. Vasari in 1568 describes it minutely, saying:

If it should ever happen (which God forbid) that his work were impeded now that Michelangelo is dead by the envy and ill-will of presumptuous men (as it has been hitherto), these pages of mine . . . . may be able to benefit those faithful men who will execute the wishes of this rare artist, and also restrain the ambition of those evil men who might wish to change them. (v2.7.249–50.)

221

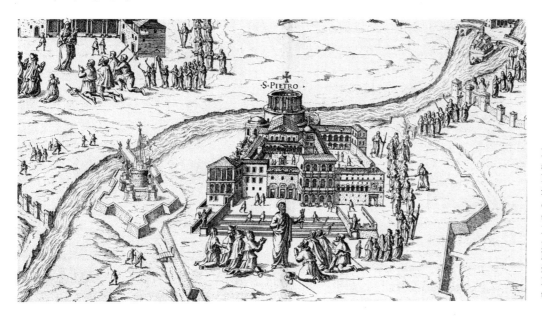

Detail from Lafreri's *Speculum romanae magnificentiae*, 1575. It shows Old St Peter's with the new basilica rising behind it, the huge atrium with the antique pine-cone fountain (removed by Michelangelo to the Cortile del Belvedere), Alberti's Benediction Loggia in front facing the piazza, the Madonna della Febbre on the left of Old St Peter's, and a rather inaccurate view of the Vatican palace (cf. Heemskerck's far more accurate view in the engraving of the Sack of Rome, p.122).

Vasari's fears were based on bitter experience. It seems fairly clear from the few small sketches Michelangelo made that he began by planning a slightly pointed dome; he even sent to Florence for details of Brunelleschi's great dome, which was built with a pointed, virtually Gothic shape dictated largely by the need to bring its downward thrust within the buttressing area of the existing choir and transept apses. But at the time of the foundation medal of 1506, Bramante is supposed to have said that he wanted to raise the dome of the Pantheon on the arches of the Temple of Peace – that is, on the Basilica of Constantine, the largest Roman classical building with Christian connotations (however ill-founded). Michelangelo discarded Bramante's imitation of the stepped outline of the Pantheon dome, but over the years he also abandoned the idea of a pointed dome, and his thickening and strengthening of the supporting piers (every successive architect over the years had done this too) may well have been in expectation of their having to withstand the greater stresses of a hemispherical dome.

It seems fairly certain that when he took over the building of the dome in 1588, under Sixtus V, Giacomo della Porta remade the outer shell of the model, and his own design was executed in the actual dome. The best record of what Michelangelo intended is in the engravings by Dupérac. Della Porta raised the dome by about 25–30 ft (8–9 m), to give it a pointed silhouette; he made the ribs lighter and narrower; raised the height of the frieze with its delicate garlands; and raised also the height of the lantern. The dome has a far greater 'spring' than Michelangelo's design; this has its advantages, in that it helps to counterbalance the visual effect of the lengthening of the nave by Maderno between 1607 and 1623.

To add to the vexations at St Peter's, he had private griefs. He wrote to his nephew Lionardo on 30 November 1555:

In your last letter I had the news of the death of Gismondo, my brother, but not without great sorrow. We must be resigned; and since he died fully conscious and with all the sacraments ordained by the Church, we must thank God for it.

Here I'm beset by many anxieties. Urbino is still in bed and in a very poor condition. I do not know what will ensue. I'm as upset about it as if he were my own son, because he has served me faithfully for twenty-five years and as I'm an old man I haven't time to train anyone else to suit me. I'm therefore very grieved. So if you have some devout soul there, I beg you to get him to pray to God for his recovery. (C.5.m.283.)

On 23 February 1556, he wrote to Vasari, who had written to him concerning the S. Lorenzo Library staircase:

My dear Messer Giorgio, – I am hardly able to write, but at least I'll make some attempt to answer your letter.

You know that Urbino is dead; through whom God has granted me his greatest favour, but to my grievous loss and infinite sorrow. The favour lay in this – that while living he kept me alive, and in dying he taught me to die, not with regret, but with a desire for death.

I have had him twenty-six years and found him entirely loyal and devoted; and now that I had made him rich and that I had expected him to be a support and stay to me in my old age, he has vanished from me, and nothing is left to me but the hope of seeing him again in Paradise. And of this God has given me a sign in the happy death he died; for he was far less grieved at dying than at leaving me here in this treacherous world with so many burdens; though the greater part of me has gone with him, and nothing but unending wretchedness remains to me.

I commend me to you and beg you, if it is not a trouble, to make my apologies to Messer Benvenuto for not replying to his letter, because in thoughts such as these I am so overwhelmed with emotion that I cannot write. Commend me to him and to you do I commend myself. (C.5.m.477.)

219

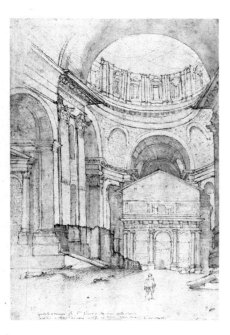

Anonymous drawing, attributed to Ammanati, made 1559–62, looking west up the nave to the small edifice erected by Bramante to enable services to be held at the high altar over St Peter's tomb. The ropes criss-crossing the open space of the dome were part of the tackle used for lifting the blocks of stone.

The Benvenuto was Cellini. Michelangelo's nephew Lionardo came to Rome in the early spring of 1556; Michelangelo wrote to him in March:

I learn from your letter of your safe arrival, which gave me great pleasure, especially as Cassandra and the others are well. Here I remain in the same state in which you left me, and as to regaining my due, nothing has yet resulted but prevarications. I'll wait as long as I can to see what happens. (c.5.m.286.)

Michelangelo's stipend attached to his appointment at St Peter's was 1200 scudi a year, half of which was secured on the dues payable at the ferry across the Po at Piacenza. It gave him endless trouble, and finally he was deprived of it by the Emperor Charles V, who had come into possession of the area. In 1548 Paul III granted him another 'office of profit', but Paul IV took it away from him, and he never succeeded in regaining it.

In his later years persistent and tempting offers were made to him, mostly through Vasari, to entice him back to Florence. He evaded them all with skill, protesting his involvement with the work at St Peter's as his reason for not following the inclinations of his heart. He may indeed have longed to return to his own land, but he could never bring himself seriously to consider a return to the city where his memories of its past as a free republic would have been overlaid by the oppressive presence of a Medici who was no longer a citizen 'first among equals', but an absolute ruler exercising untrammelled power. Neither could he ever forget the weeks spent in hiding in 1529 before he was pardoned at Pope Clement's insistence, on condition that he completed the tombs of the now destested Medici in the New Sacristy of S. Lorenzo. But he owned considerable property in Florence, and a brusque rejection of Duke Cosimo's overtures might have provoked unfriendly retaliation. He wrote to his nephew Lionardo on 13 February 1557:

When he came to see me here in Rome about two years ago Messer Lionardo, the agent of the Duke of Florence, told me that his lordship would be greatly pleased if I were to return to Florence and he made many offers on his behalf. I replied to him that I begged his lordship to concede me enough time to enable me to leave the fabric of St Peter's at such a stage that it could not be changed in accordance with some other design which I have not authorized. I have since continued with the said fabric, not having heard anything to the contrary, but it is not yet at the said stage; furthermore, I am obliged to make a large model in wood, including the cupola and the lantern, in order to leave it completed as it is to be, finished in every detail. This I have been begged to do by the whole of Rome, and particularly by the Most Reverend Cardinal [da] Carpi; so that I think it will be necessary for me to stay here for at least a year in order to do this. For the love of Christ and of St Peter I beg the duke to concede me this length of time, so that I may return to Florence without this goad, in the knowledge that I should not be obliged to return to Rome any more. As regards the fabric being closed down, there is no truth in this, because, as may be seen, there are still sixty men working here, counting *scarpellini*, bricklayers and labourers, and doing so with the expectation of continuing.

I would like you to read this letter to the duke and to beg his lordship on my behalf to grant me the necessary grace mentioned above, which I need before I can return to Florence, for if the form of the said fabric were changed, as envy is seeking to do, I might as well have done nothing up till now. (c.5.m.302.)

Already by 1557 Michelangelo had become one of the sights of Rome. A letter of 4 January 1557 to Vincenzo Borghini, Prior and *Spedalingo* of the Innocenti in Florence, says:

How much difference there is between one man and another! These German gentlemen had a great wish just to *see* Michelangelo, and I introduced them; he received them very kindly to their great satisfaction. (G.2.419.)

Detail from a drawing by Federico Zuccaro, c. 1560, showing Michelangelo in old age on horseback pausing to watch Federico's brother Taddeo painting the façade of the Palazzo Maffei.

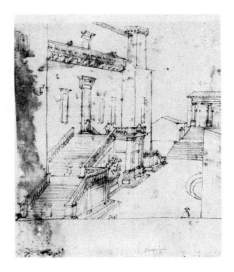

Dosio's drawing of the Capitol, done between 1561 and 1564. Michelangelo began planning the reconstruction of Rome's civic centre in the late 1530s. He designed the splendid staircase of the Senate, which was finished by 1552. The arched loggia at the head of the steps at the back of the drawing was built by the end of 1553; the cantilevered balcony across the front of the Senate was rebuilt in 1554, but demolished in Della Porta's reconstruction in 1573–79. See p.198.

199

Michelangelo was responsible for directing six other architectural works in Rome, besides St Peter's.

The people of Rome, with the consent of Pope Paul [III], were anxious to give some useful, commodious, and beautiful form to the Capitol, and in order to embellish the district. . . . For this purpose they sought advice from Michelangelo, who made for them a very rich and beautiful design in which on the side of the Senator's palace he arranged a façade of travertine and a flight of steps ascending to the centre of the palace hall. . . . Then . . . he mounted on pedestals in front of the steps the two ancient figures of recumbent river gods . . . each eighteen feet long, intending to have a niche containing a statue of Jupiter between them. On the southern side, to bring the Conservators' palace into line he designed for it a richly adorned façade, with a portico . . . and all around are various ornaments of doors and windows, some of which are already in place. . . . Below the Aracoeli there is to be another similar façade, and in front of this . . . an almost level ascent of shallow steps with a balustrade. And here will be the principal entrance to the piazza. . . . In the middle of the piazza, on an oval base, has been erected the famous bronze horse bearing the figure of Marcus Aurelius, which Pope Paul had removed from the Piazza di Laterano, where it had been put by Sixtus IV. Today work on this whole enterprise is yielding such beautiful results that it is worthy of being numbered among Michelangelo's finest achievements; and under the supervision of Tommaso de' Cavalieri (a Roman gentleman, one of the greatest friends Michelangelo ever had) is now being brought to completion. (v2.7.222–3.)

The niche with the Jupiter was changed in 1588 to a fountain, fed by the waters of Sixtus V's Acqua Felice, and Jupiter was replaced by a diminutive antique of Minerva in a porphyry robe.

Antonio da Sangallo's palace for Cardinal Alessandro Farnese has a long and complicated building history. It was started in 1517; work stopped during the long troubles of Clement's reign, started again when the cardinal became Pope Paul III, and with intermittent interruptions continued until the death of Sangallo in September 1546. Sangallo's palace – an enormous island block – had an almost characterless façade thirteen bays long, all exactly alike except for a larger central window on the main floor. Its great beauties were the entrance vestibule, coffered *all'antica*, and the splendid courtyard, derived from the theme of Roman theatre design, with tiers of arcades (now glazed in). In 1546 the top storey of the façade was partly built and needed a cornice. Designs were put forward by Perino del Vaga, Sebastiano del Piombo and Vasari; Michelangelo won the contest after mounting a wooden mock-up of

Three views of the vestibule of the Farnese palace, about 1560. On the left, a view into the courtyard with the garden beyond shows that that wing of the palace had not yet been completed. To the left of the arch a niche contains the antique *Farnese Hercules*. On the right, a view from the courtyard shows the massive red granite columns of Sangallo's majestic entrance, with its contrasts of semicircular and flat vaulting systems. Inset below is a glimpse of the street outside looking across the piazza towards the Campo de' Fiori.

his design, to the alarm of the builders, on the completed section of wall. Vasari's account places the competition for the cornice before, rather than after, Sangallo's death, but he is right when he says:

Michelangelo made the great marble window with the beautiful columns of variegated stone ... surmounted by a large marble coat of arms, of great beauty and originality.... Within the palace over the first storey of the courtyard Michelangelo continued the two other storeys, with their incomparably beautiful graceful and varied windows, ornamentation and crowning cornice.... At the same time, Michelangelo made designs for a bridge crossing the Tiber in a straight line with the palace, so that it would be possible to go direct to another palace and gardens that they owned in the Trastevere, and also from the principal door facing the Campo de' Fiori to be able to see at a glance the courtyard, the fountain, the Strada Giulia, the bridge, and the beauties of the other garden, all in a straight line as far as the other door opening on to the Strada di Trastevere. This was a marvellous undertaking which was worthy of that pontiff and of Michelangelo's talent, judgment and powers of design. (V2.7.223–5.)

199

Unfortunately, this splendid project was never carried out. The palace and gardens on the Trastevere were the former villa of Agostino Chigi, and became the Farnesina only in 1580. In any case, it does not lie in quite the direct line that Vasari makes out.

The church of Sta Maria degli Angeli was made out of the tepidarium of the Baths of Diocletian from 1561 onwards, but everything he did was so altered by Luigi Vanvitelli in the eighteenth century that nothing of his work remains. The Porta Pia was another very late work, from 1561–65, and was never finished; the medal represents an early rejected design. The curious attic storey may have been built, but is said to have collapsed soon after. The present top storey was built in 1853 by Virginio Vespignani after the gate had been struck by lightning and badly damaged, and is his design, not Michelangelo's. The varied shapes of the windows and the main doorway are consistent with Michelangelo's striving for expressive form in architecture.

223

The projects for the Florentine church in Rome, S. Giovanni dei Fiorentini, were done because the existing Florentine church was a very poor affair and was not felt to express national pride adequately. Michelangelo wrote to Duke Cosimo on 1 November 1559:

Most Illustrious Lord Duke of Florence – The Florentines have often before had a great desire to build a church to S. Giovanni here in Rome. Now, in your lordship's time, being in

Left: Dosio's drawing, c. 1565, of the interior of the Baths of Diocletian, where Michelangelo designed the transformation of the huge *tepidarium* into Sta Maria degli Angeli (1563–66).

Below: The vestibule and chancel of Sta Maria degli Angeli before Vanvitelli's alterations of 1749 destroyed Michelangelo's design. Across the floor is the meridian line laid in 1702, known as the *Linea Clementina* after Clement XI.

expectation of better facilities, they are resolved upon it and have appointed five men to take charge of it, who have asked me, nay begged me several times, for a design for the said building. Knowing that Pope Leo began the said church, I replied that I did not want to turn my attention to it without the permission and commission of the Duke of Florence.

Now, as it afterwards transpires, I have received a most kind and gracious letter from your most illustrious lordship, which enjoins me by express command to turn my attention to the above-mentioned church of the Florentines, from which the great pleasure you have in it is manifest.

I have already done several designs suited to the site for this building, which the above-mentioned Deputies have shown me. They, being men of great judgment and discretion, have selected one of them, which I frankly think is the most imposing. This will be copied and drawn out more clearly than I am able to do myself, because of old age, and will be sent to your most illustrious lordship. What ensues will be as your lordship deems best.

I regret in this instance that I am so old and so ill-attuned to life that I can promise little of myself to the said fabric; albeit from my own house I will endeavour to do what is asked of me on behalf of your lordship, and may God grant me not to fail you in any way. (c.5.m.487.)

The trouble with all three of Michelangelo's very fine designs was that they were for a large church, and the site was restricted by the river and would have required building on piles out into the bank. All three are variations on the fascinating theme of the central plan. One got as far as a model – where it may be noted that the dome was also hemispherical – but the money soon ran out, and, to Michelangelo's annoyance, the project faded away. The designs were made between 1559 and 1560, and the model is only known from engravings made in 1607, since it was destroyed in the eighteenth century. The present church was begun by Giacomo Della Porta in 1582, and finished by Maderno in 1614 with a traditional long nave and a dome on the crossing.

The Sforza Chapel in Sta Maria Maggiore was designed in 1560 or thereabouts, but remained unfinished because of the deaths of the commissioner, Cardinal Ascanio Sforza, and of Michelangelo in 1564, and also of Tiberio Calcagni, whom Michelangelo put in charge of the work, in 1565. The design is curious, very complicated and sophisticated, but the execution was careless and clumsy. The most unusual feature is the variegated vaulting system – three different kinds are used in this tiny space – and the projection into the central space of the supporting piers. The original entrance by Della Porta has been destroyed.

Although Michelangelo continued to labour on the works at St Peter's he was becoming increasingly frail. On 7 July 1559 Cardinal Sforza's secretary Giovan Francesco Lottini wrote to Duke Cosimo I, who was still making efforts to entice Michelangelo back to Florence:

Michelangelo Buonarroti is in fact so old that even if he wished he could not move more than a

Rome in 1575, showing the sweep of the Tiber around the 'horn' of the city. The Castel Sant'Angelo with Alexander VI's tower guarding the bridge, the grim prison of the Tor de' Specchi (no. 93), and in the foreground the mean structure of the church of S. Giovanni dei Fiorentini – almost on the river bank – are all clearly shown. In the river are moored two of the many floating watermills which ground the city's flour.

few miles, and for some time now goes little or rarely to St Peter's. Other than which, the model will need many months to complete it, and he is under the obligation, and the desire, to finish it. When I made him Your Excellency's offer, he wept with feeling, and it is clear that he would wish to serve you if it were in his power, but in fact he cannot, being afflicted, besides suffering with the stone, with other very troublesome ills. (G.3.14–15.)

Vasari wrote to the Duke on 9 April 1560, when he accompanied Cosimo's second son, Giovanni, to receive his cardinal's hat:

I immediately went to see *il mio gran Michelagnolo*. He did not know of my coming and with the tenderness of a father unexpectedly finding a long lost son he threw his arms round my neck and kissed me a thousand times, weeping with pleasure, so glad was he to see me and I him.... He regretted not being able to visit [the new Medici cardinal], but he now goes about very little, and has become so very old that he gets little rest, and has declined so much that I believe he will only be with us for a short while, if he is not kept alive by God's goodness for the sake of the works at St Peter's which certainly need him. He made me astonished in realizing that the ancients are surpassed by the beauty and grace of what his divine genius has been able to achieve. (G.3.29–30.)

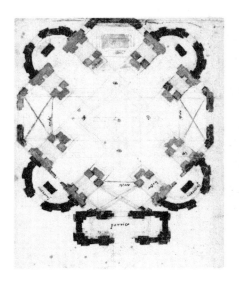

One of Michelangelo's designs for S. Giovanni de' Fiorentini, 1559.

In 1562, Nanni di Baccio Bigio, who had always been a thorn in Michelangelo's side, endeavoured to displace him, and succeeded in being appointed as overseer. Michelangelo was so driven by anger and despair that he confronted the pope (Pius IV by this time) on the Piazza di Campidoglio and asked for his discharge. On discovering the intrigues that had been going on, the pope dismissed Nanni forthwith and confirmed Michelangelo in all his appointments. He also gave him an independent deputy to cope with day-to-day business which Michelangelo, at his great age (he was then eighty-seven), could no longer do himself.

Michelangelo died on 18 February 1564. He had been failing for some time, so that his death was not unexpected. At his bedside were Daniele da Volterra, Tommaso Cavalieri, his servant Antonio and his doctors. His body was removed the same day to SS. Apostoli, and news of his death was sent to Duke Cosimo by Michelangelo's doctor.

This afternoon that most excellent and true miracle of nature, Messer Michelangelo Buonarroti passed from this to a better life, and being together with other doctors attending him in his illness, I discovered that his wish was that his body should be carried to Florence; but since there was no relative here at all, and since he died, I think, intestate, it occurred to me immediately to give You notice of it, since You bore great affection for his rare virtues, and also so that You may arrange that the wishes of the deceased may be followed and that, moreover, Your beautiful City shall be ornamented with the most noble bones of the greatest man who was ever in the world.

Gherardo Fidelissimi of Pistoia
Through the grace and liberality of Your
Illustrious Excellency, Doctor of Medicine (G.3.126–7.)

The duke's ambassador, Averardo Serristori, wrote on 19 February:

Having written last night to Your Excellency . . . I have nothing else to relate, except the death of Michelangelo Buonarroti, who died last evening of general debility; and this morning as I had ordered I sent to the Governor the inventory of all the goods that were there, which were few, and no drawings. They then listed what was there and the important thing was a coffer sealed with several seals, which the Governor had opened in the presence of Messer Tomaso del Cavaliere and Maestro Daniello da Volterra, who were there, summoned by Michelangelo before his death, and in it were found between 7 and 8000 scudi which have been ordered to be deposited with the Ubaldini.... The governor will not fail to have the members of his household questioned to find out if anything was removed, which is not thought to have happened, because as regards the drawings it is said that he had already burnt what he had; whatever is there on the arrival of his nephew will be given to him, and Your Excellency may inform him of this.

Included in this is a letter from Maestro Nanno, Florentine architect, in which he begs Your Excellency to support him with our Lord, so that he obtains the place of the aforementioned Michelangelo in the work at St Peter's, as earlier he wrote to Your Excellency and which you promised to do when Michelangelo should die. (G.3.127–8.)

It is clear that the duke must have alerted the ambassador that when Michelangelo died a particular search was to be made for any drawings relating to the works at S. Lorenzo; but Michelangelo had forestalled him. The letter from Nanni di Baccio Bigio was particularly disgraceful. He had in 1562 tried to enlist the Duke's help in getting Michelangelo removed from the control of St Peter's, and the duke had told him plainly that

We shall never do you such an office while Michelangelo is alive, because it would too much disparage his merits and the love we bear him; but we promise you that at an opportune moment we will not fail you. (G.3.66.)

Nanni hardly waited until Michelangelo's body was cold before he wrote to the duke, 'It having pleased our Lord God to end the days of Messer Michelangelo Buonarroti, to the great displeasure and harm of the world ...', to solicit his support, reminding him of what had seemed to him the promise given in 1562. He also adds the words. 'besides being certain that this is desired by everyone' (G.3.129.). Vasari comments on his earlier attempt: 'This was the end of Nanni in the works at St Peter's; he was driven out with very uncivil words from the works in the presence of many gentlemen.' Now he had the effrontery to declare that he was 'desired by everyone'. At first the job was given to another of Michelangelo's *bêtes noires*, Pirro Ligorio, but he tried to make changes in the design and was immediately dismissed; he was succeeded by Giacomo Vignola, who held the appointment until his death in 1573, when Giacomo della Porta was appointed, on the recommendation of Cavalieri.

Michelangelo left a considerable fortune, the result of shrewd investment of his income as an artist. His sole heir was his nephew Lionardo, whose character may be judged by two incidents. Immediately before the unveiling of the *Last Judgment* Michelangelo offered to pay his expenses so that he could visit Rome worthily, and sent him fifty ducats as an advance, and promising him as much more for the journey. Lionardo said he'd sooner have the money; Michelangelo never forgot the slight. When news reached him that the old man was dying, Lionardo rushed to Rome, not to visit the dying man nor to attend his death bed, but merely to assure himself that no property that Michelangelo owned in Rome should be lost to his inheritance. The group of properties which Michelangelo had accumulated in the Via Ghibellina in Florence eventually became the site of the Casa Buonarroti, and is now the museum housing much of the archives, many of the drawings, and some of the works. The direct male line of the family endured until 1858, when Cosimo Buonarroti bequeathed the house and its contents to the city of Florence. There are still descendants from collateral branches of the family living today.

Michelangelo expressed at one time a desire to be buried in S. Maria Maggiore; was this because he did not wish to share the honours of the Pantheon with Raphael? But he was too precious a Florentine relic to be left to the Romans. Lionardo wrote to the Duke from Rome on 22 March 1564:

It having pleased the Lord God to take to himself the good soul of Michelangelo Buonarroti ... since the said Michelangelo has asked in death to be buried in the church of Sta Croce ... and since nothing of his has been found in his house, as was my hope, so that I might present it to Your Excellency, and since he has gone without leaving much, except the things in Florence in Via Mozza, which if they pleased Your Excellency it would be the greatest favour to be allowed to present them; and since if from here there is nothing to recover, I will endeavour to be of service to you. (G.3.131–2.)

The workshop in the Via Mozza, now Via S. Zanobi, must have contained the four unfinished *Slaves* and the *Victory*. which came into the ducal collections at that time. A Florentine memoir, recorded by Gaye, says:

10 March 1564: Friday at twenty hours [2 p.m.] there arrived in Florence the corpse of Michelangelo Buonarroti secretly carried off from Rome by Lionardo his nephew in a bale of merchandise. It was found uncorrupted in a wooden coffer lined with lead, and was dressed in a robe of black damask, with boots and spurs on his legs, and on his head a silk hat *all'antica*, with a drapery of plush with a long pile. He was immediately taken to the Company of the Assumption behind S. Pier Maggiore. On 12 March he was taken to Sta Croce. (G.3.133.)

It does not appear that any objections were made to the removal of the body from SS. Apostoli, nor that any special arrangements had been made for a funeral in Rome. When the body arrived, Vasari, to whom the bale was addressed, was notified that it was being held at the Customs House. He at once had it taken to the oratory of the Company of the Assumption, and on the Sunday the Academicians met and decided to carry the coffin in a torchlight procession to Sta Croce. They assembled at sunset with a velvet pall to cover the coffin: the sight of the grave and reverend signors of the Academy carrying the body of the world's most famous artist through the streets attracted a huge crowd, and by the time they reached the church, instead of its being deposited quietly in the sacristy the church itself had to be opened to admit them all. Moreover, since Vasari had had the coffin sealed in the Customs House, an official had to be sent for to cut the seal when it was decided to open the coffin so as to verify that it was indeed the body of Michelangelo, and to gratify those who had never seen him alive. In the account of the Obsequies, published immediately afterwards, this moment is described:

We all, and he too, believed that we would find the body putrefied and disfigured because it had been in the coffin 22 days or more, and from the day of his death 25 days had passed. [Actually, it was only 22]. But after opening it they found no bad smell whatever and you would have sworn that he was resting in a sweet and quiet slumber. The same features of the face, the same mien except for the colour, which was that of death. Not one limb decayed or revolting. When touching his head and his cheeks, which everyone did, they found them to be soft and life-like, as if he had died only a few hours before, and this filled everyone with amazement. (W.74–7.)

On 9 March 1564 Duke Cosimo wrote to Benedetto Varchi:

The affection which we bore to the rare qualities of Michelangelo Buonarroti makes us desire that his memory shall be honoured and celebrated in every way possible. Therefore it would

ESEQVIE DEL DIVINO
MICHELAGNOLO
BVONARROTI
Celebrate in Firenze dall'Accademia de Pittori, scultori, & Ar- chitettori.
Nella Chiesa di S.Lorenzo il di 14 Luglio
M D L X I I I I.

IN FIRENZE
Appresso i Giunti 1564.
Con Priuilegio.

Frontispiece of the account of the ceremony of Michelangelo's obsequies on 14 July 1564, in S. Lorenzo in Florence.

be pleasing to us that for love of us you should undertake the charge of making the oration, which is to be recited at his obsequies, according to the order made by the deputies of the Academy, and it would be most pleasing if it were recited by your voice. (w.66–7.)

After many arguments at the Academy, which had only been founded in 1563, two painters, Vasari and Bronzino, and two sculptors, Cellini and Ammanati, were to organize the funeral and its artistic side, and another sculptor, Lastricati, was to control the financial and practical matters. The first date chosen, immediately after Easter (2 April), was far too soon for such a complicated affair, and in any case Lionardo only returned to Florence in early May. To add to the complexities, the old argument whether painting or sculpture was the major art broke out again with renewed fury and bitterness, over the positions on the catafalque of the effigies of the arts. Finally, Cellini was so enraged that sculpture was to be on the left, which he regarded as a deliberate slight, that he refused to have anything more to do with the arrangements, and even made an abusive attack on Vasari and Borghini. The funeral was to be treated as a manifestation of the arts, with not only the contested effigies on the catafalque, but paintings by the younger artists of Florence round the church. The choice of younger artists was an expedient designed to cut the cost of the affair – they were to be rewarded by fame, and by being able to sell their pictures afterwards; unfortunately, no one wanted to buy them. Older, established artists would have had to be paid.

232 The ceremony was finally held on 14 July 1564, and Vasari sent Duke Cosimo a full report. Although Varchi, in his oration, mentioned Francesco de' Medici as present, this was not so. No Medici came, and probably none was expected, but the young prince had taken over power from his father, Cosimo, at the beginning of May when Cosimo retired, and possibly the flattering reference was no more than adroit policy in so autocratic a state.

The ceremony began with a solemn Requiem, with the huge catafalque in the nave and the high pyramid of candles behind it. After the Mass was finished, Varchi climbed up into the bronze pulpit and gave his oration. This was extremely long – at least two hours – full of the most elaborate rhetorical flourishes, such as his hair standing on end as he thinks of one man mastering all three arts, and his embarrassment at addressing the assembled Academicians – 'flowers of the most faultless genius, the most ingenious spirits, the most sparkling, most bizarre, most rare, and extravagant brains, which exist today or which perhaps were ever known to painting, to sculpture or to architecture', and so on and so on.

Then in the approved fashion, he divided his discourse into three parts: Michelangelo as perfection in all three arts; his life and work as a good poet, good philosopher and good theologian; and an exhortation to rejoice for his life rather than mourn his death. In the section on his life he depended, although he began by promising not to, on Vasari and Condivi, though he adds some details which he may perhaps have had from personal knowledge. He says that Michelangelo made his own tools for sculpture so that he could have exactly what he wanted (Michelangelo's use of the claw chisel suggests that this was in fact made specially for him), and that in the cartoon for the 47 *Battle of Cascina* some parts were sketched in in charcoal and others more fully finished, and some modelled with touches of white. When he mentions the 46 *David* he ranks Florence above Rome for the possession of a priceless and timeless masterpiece which excels the productions of the ancients – a very popular sentiment. He returns to Vasari in tracing the rise and importance of Florence in the development and flowering of the arts, and then at the end he speaks of death as a liberation, echoing Michelangelo's own sentiments in his sonnet which begins 'The course of my life has already reached, Through a tempestuous sea, in its frail bark...', though Varchi develops the thought at greater length and with less felicity.

Vasari wrote to Duke Cosimo on 14 July itself:

This morning ... were performed the obsequies of the divine Michelangelo Buonarroti to the satisfaction of all, so that S. Lorenzo was filled with persons of quality, besides many noble ladies and a great number of strangers. It was a marvellous thing; and all passed with great quiet and good order which was maintained at the doors by the Otto family, and by the Bargello in the church with his guards, besides the guards of the captain of the Lances who were around the catafalque and took care that the doctors and the lawyers and the Academy of Letters had their places, and so all the citizens, as well as taking care that all the Academy and Company of Design were placed in the eminent position, the Lord Lieutenant having been placed in the middle in front of the pulpit, surrounded by the consuls and the three deputies on the dais, who were Bronzino, Giorgio Vasari and Bartolommeo Ammanati; Benvenuto [Cellini] did not wish to be there, nor did Sangallo [Francesco, son of Giuliano], which caused a great deal of talk among the assembly. The family of Michelangelo were kindly used, since we arranged for Lionardo Buonarroti to be seated next to the Lieutenant, which act of piety towards the virtues of that old man gave great pleasure.... At the feet of the Academicians were some twenty-five young men who are all learning to draw ... It evoked great admiration this morning to see altogether eighty painters and sculptors, and it is not believed that at any time the arts were gathered together in such numbers and greatness. The catafalque was so successful that it is impossible to describe its size and majesty, and how well the figures appeared. (G.3.139–42.)

He goes on to describe the pictures round the church, many of which were later re-created by the team of painters employed by Lionardo's son Michelangelo for decorations in the Casa Buonarroti. (Michelangelo had always exhorted his brother and nephew to 'buy an honourable house', and in 1546 he wrote 'A fine house in the city honours one greatly.') Vasari's narrative continued:

230

148,231

The church had figures of Death on all sides ... and there was also a figure of Eternity with Death below, and everywhere a device of three garlands – his sign – but simply of three round wreaths, which denoted his perfection in the three arts. I won't tell you about the order of the

194

Mirabello Cavalori: sketch for a painting, hung in S. Lorenzo for Michelangelo's obsequies, showing the artist seated in the presence of the Grand Duke. The incident, designed to show the respect in which the ruler held the artist, is almost certainly apocryphal. The drawing belonged to Vasari.

music and the solemn Mass with choir and organ, and after that the oration recited in a grave manner, full of eloquence, by Messer Benedetto Varchi. (G.3.141–2.)

He concludes by crediting everything to the honour of the Duke, who was patron of the arts. Perhaps a slightly less ecstatic account is in an anonymous letter in which the writer describes the catafalque and its statues, records the inscriptions, describes the paintings and their inscriptions, and ends:

The oration was recited by Varchi, whom I could not finish hearing because of the great crowd, but I hope to have it to read more comfortably than I heard it there. (W.147.)

He was annoyed that when he returned to the church the next day to copy the poems which had been pinned to the catafalque they had all been taken away.

231   The monument erected in Sta Croce was designed by Vasari, with a tomb chest like those of the Dukes in the Medici Chapel. Bandini, a pupil of Bandinelli, made the figure of *Architecture* (on the right), Valerio Cioli that of *Sculpture* (centre), and Battista di Lorenzo that of *Painting* (left), and he also did the bust, basing himself on the one by Daniele da Volterra. Michelangelo's device of the three rings flanks the bust on either side. Above is a miserable

179   fresco by Naldini, a *Pietà*, with a distant nodding relationship to the Vittoria Colonna drawing. The tomb took until 1578 to finish, and its vicissitudes included proposals to use the four unfinished *Slaves*, but Vasari disliked the idea; he also blocked the proposal to use the *Victory*, since he wanted to put it in the Palazzo della Signoria in the great hall which he had just rebuilt (and

217   where it still is). Then came a proposal to use the *Pietà* with Nicodemus and the Magdalen (which he refers to as being with five figures), which somehow had come into the possession of the sculptor Bandini, but finally this too was discarded. Lionardo Buonarroti had to pay for the monument, and was not very pleased with it.

    Perhaps the last words should be Michelangelo's own:

> *Di giorno in giorno, in sin da' miei primi anni*
> *Signor, soccorso tu me fusti e guida;*
> *Onde l'anima mia ancor si fida*
> *Di doppio aita ne' miei doppi affanni.*

> From day to day, and since my earliest years,
> Lord, you have been my succour and my guide;
> So that my soul still trusts
> In double help in my now double anguish. (MR.287.)

Detail from the *Pietà* which Michelangelo carved between 1547 and 1555, intending it for his tomb. Nicodemus, supporting the body of Christ, is clearly a self-portrait (the only one known apart from the skin of St Bartholomew in the *Last Judgment*). The group remained unfinished because of a flaw in the marble; Michelangelo, in a rage, smashed the left leg of the *Christ* with a hammer. It never occurred to him to add a piece to a defective block or figure; his sculptures are monolithic and self-contained in form. As the Belgian sculptor Victor Rousseau said, 'You could roll them down a mountain and no piece would come off.'

Michelangelo was appointed chief architect of the new St Peter's on 1 January 1547, on the death of Antonio da Sangallo the Younger. He was nearly seventy-two years old, and still half-way through painting the frescoes in the Cappella Paolina. He at once reverted to the centrally planned St Peter's envisaged by his old enemy Bramante in 1506. ('He who departs from Bramante departs from truth,' he said.) The Bramante project survives (far left) in a medal struck by Julius II for the laying of the foundation. Sangallo, as can be seen from the model which took Labacco seven years to make (left, below) proposed adding a virtually free-standing façade structure to accommodate processions and the obligatory benediction loggia. Michelangelo, remarking that Sangallo's elaborate outer galleries would be an invitation to rapists and robbers, scrapped the design and demolished part of Sangallo's outer shell (seen in Vasari's fresco, left, where Paul III and his train of allegorical figures are directing work on site). Like his predecessors, Michelangelo increased the mass of the four piers which were to support the dome. Dupérac's engraving of 1569 (below) shows a section of Michelangelo's design taken west-east, with some vague construction at the east end into which the benediction loggia would have had to be inserted. Neither in the plans nor in any surviving drawing is there a hint of the solution intended by Michelangelo for the east front.

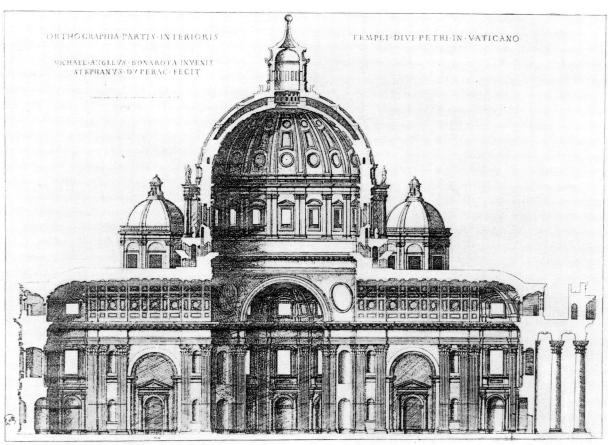

ORTHOGRAPHIA·PARTIS·INTERIORIS   TEMPLI·DIVI·PETRI·IN·VATICANO

MICHAEL·ANGELVS·BONAROTA·INVENIT
STEPHANVS·DVPERAC·FECIT

The dome

When Michelangelo died, early in 1564, the drum of the dome of St Peter's was nearly complete. It was twenty years before a forceful pope, Sixtus V, ventured upon the appallingly difficult task of building the dome itself. Michelangelo had hesitated between a hemispherical and a pointed shape, as his drawings show. The small drawing (left) shows a pointed design; Dupérac's engraving (previous page), based on Michelangelo's final intentions, shows a hemispherical one. The model (below) must accordingly have been changed after Michelangelo's death into the structurally sounder pointed form. The dome itself (far left) was built in 1585–90 by Della Porta and Fontana, appointed on the advice of Tommaso Cavalieri. St Peter's was completed in 1607–23 by Maderno, who added a long nave to Michelangelo's central plan.

Late architecture

The Sforza Chapel in Sta Maria Maggiore was one of Michelangelo's last works. It was completed, after his death and that of his assistant Tiberio Calcagni, by Della Porta. This tiny chapel (left and below left), one of the most sophisticated architectural designs of any age, is based on a circle, stressed by projecting groups of columns. Side apses, altar and entrance all have different vaulting systems.

S. Giovanni dei Fiorentini, the Florentine church in Rome, stood on unstable ground by the Tiber. In 1559 Michelangelo offered to produce a worthy new design, and made three, all of the centrally planned type that tended to be more popular with architects than with their Church patrons. All have the high altar placed, very unusually, in the centre under the dome, and all would have been so large as to require piling of the river bed. Money ran out, and none was built, although one (below) reached the stage of a model.

The Porta Pia (right) was a new gateway in the Aurelian walls, at the end of the old Via Nomentana which Pius IV straightened in 1561. Michelangelo's gateway was not finished in his lifetime, and the upper part in the 1568 engraving (right) does not match that in a commemorative medal (far right, above). Michelangelo's portals and windows are of extraordinary freedom and inventiveness. The upper part was finished in 1853, to a new design.

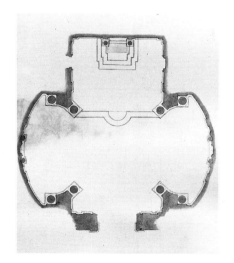

Disegno d'un Modello non messe in Opera fatto per San Gioãni [...] de i Fiorentini in Roma la reduttione del quale e di doi palmi per oncie la longhezza et larghezza è di [...] Pal'9 ¾ et laltezza di Pal'7

Michel'Angelo Bonarota Inuentore

Iacobus Mercier Gallus fecit Romæ Ano 1607

PORTAM·PIAM·A·MICHAELIS·ANGELI
BONAROTI·EXEMPLARI·ACCVRATISSIM
DELINEATAM·ROMÆ·CIↃIↃ·LXVIII

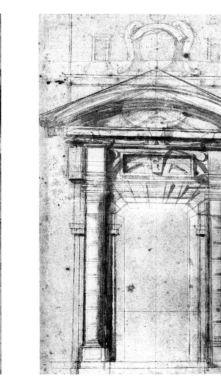

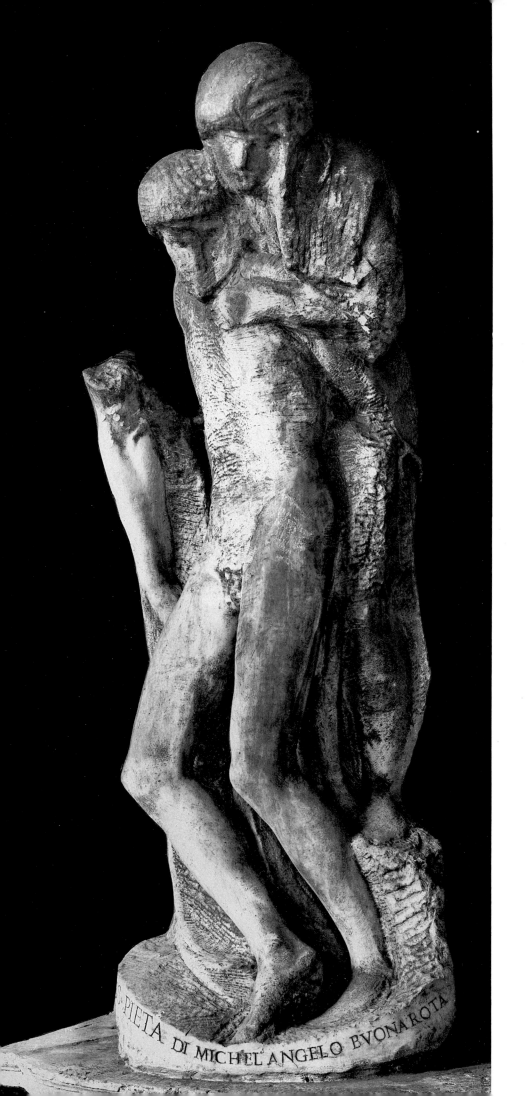

Last works

The *Rondanini Pietà* (left) was Michelangelo's last work in sculpture, and he is recorded as working on it within a few days of his death in 1564. There is a series of small drawings (below and right, below) in which he works out the theme of the dead body of Christ borne between two figures, and also upheld by the Virgin, and these provide the best clues as to what the group was intended to look like. Whether Michelangelo changed his mind about the composition, or whether a serious flaw in the block forced him to cut back the body of Christ until it merges into that of His mother, will never be known; but the violence of the change in intention can be seen from the severed arm, in a fairly advanced state of completion, which still adheres to Christ's side. In its mutilated state the work is a tragic record of the artist's last struggle to express a deeply felt theme.

The huge cartoon of the *Holy Family with Saints*, of about 1553 (below), was probably made for Ascanio Condivi to work from. Unfortunately the pupil was unworthy of his master; according to Vasari he was so poor a painter that Michelangelo sometimes took pity on him and did some of the painting himself (not very often, if we are to judge from Condivi's finished work). The cartoon is mysterious, in that the occasion for the commission is unknown, and several of the figures are ambiguous.

The *Crucifixion* of about 1555 (above) is one of the late religious drawings which increase in quantity after the death of Vittoria Colonna. Their mounting poignancy is matched by the increasingly profound religious expression of his late poems.

Michelangelo's fame

Giorgio Vasari, seen (below) in the self-portrait in which he wears the gold chain given him by Pius V in 1571, included Michelangelo as the only living artist in the first edition (1550) of his *Lives*, in which Michelangelo features as the summit of Florentine artistic achievement. This first edition (but not the second in 1568) was printed by the ducal printer Torrentino. The two *putti* at the foot of the title page (below right), displaying a view of Florence, are evidently derived from the *ignudi* of the Sistine Ceiling.

Soon after his eighty-sixth birthday, in 1561, Michelangelo was presented with two silver and two bronze examples of the portrait medal by Leone Leoni. On the back of the wax medallion (near left) is the inscription 'Portrait of Michelangelo Buonarroti, done from life by Leone Aretino his friend'. The medal (below, detail, and below right) was struck in Milan. According to Vasari the blind man led by a guide dog on the reverse symbolizes Faith, and was Michelangelo's own choice of emblem – as presumably, was the text from Psalm 50 (A.V. 51): 'Then will I teach transgressors thy ways; and sinners shall be converted unto thee.' The portrait drawing by Daniele da Volterra (right) was made about 1550, and is pricked for transfer to a fresco; perhaps, as Ernst Steinmann suggests, one in the Rovere Chapel in SS. Trinità dei Monti. It was, with a death mask, the source of Daniele's posthumous bust (p. 177).

As others saw him

In the bottom right-hand corner of El Greco's *Christ Driving the Money-changers from the Temple* (*c.*1575) is a group of portraits (above) of artists whom El Greco admired: Titian, Michelangelo, Giulio Clovio the miniaturist, who was El Greco's patron in Rome, and Raphael. In Rome about 1550, Jacopino del Conte painted a fresco cycle in the oratory of the Confraternità della Misericordia, whose members accompanied criminals to their execution. In his *Angel Appearing to Zachary* is a striking portrait which surely, despite the nose, is that of Michelangelo (left).

Raphael was Michelangelo's rival, in the service of Julius II, and never became a friend. But in 1511, when Michelangelo uncovered the first instalment of the Sistine Ceiling, Raphael was at work on the frescoes of the Stanza della Segnatura nearby. He filled a gap in the composition (right) with a figure of the misanthropic Heraclitus which is based on the Isaiah of the Sistine Ceiling; it is also said to be a portrait of Michelangelo himself.

Obsequies

Michelangelo's princely funeral took place in S. Lorenzo, Florence, on 14 July 1564. It was organized by Vasari and by Vincenzo Borghini (centre left), Prior of the Hospital of the Innocenti and art adviser to Duke Cosimo I. It featured a huge catafalque, of which the first design is shown here (far left); the construction includes the usual classical *putti* with reversed torches and contains quotations from Michelangelo's works, such as the body on the 'tomb' taken from one of the designs for the Julius Tomb, and the river gods borrowed from the projects of the Medici Chapel. Among the paintings made for the catafalque, and known only through subsequent drawings, was Giovanmaria Butteri's representation of Michelangelo being received (far left, below) by Apollo and the Nine Muses.

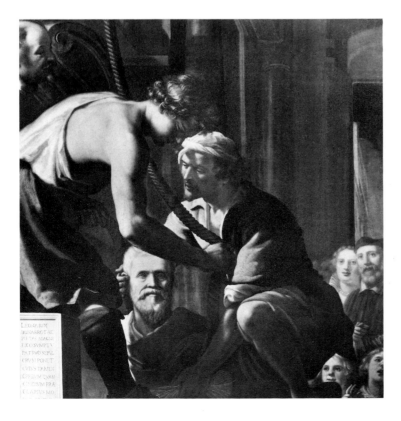

The monument (above left), erected in Sta Croce, the Buonarroti parish church, in 1570, was designed by Vasari. It incorporates a version of the Daniele da Volterra bust, and on either side, transformed into wreaths, are the same interlaced circles that Michelangelo marked for the stonecutters on blocks intended for his use. In Casa Buonarroti (below left) is an allegorical painting by Tiberio Viti of the bust being placed on the tomb by the nephew and heir, Lionardo Buonarroti.

ELIQVIA   REGIO CVLTV
DVCTAE REGIA FRANCISCI
PRINCIPIS PRAESENTIA DECORANT...
MMERITO CVI ENIM OB VIRTVTEM ADSCENSVS IN COELVM PA
...ICET MAXIMA IN TERRIS DEBITO TAMEN MINORA TRIBVNTVR

The funeral in S. Lorenzo, recorded in this painting done for Michelangelo's grand-nephew some fifty years later by Agostino Ciampelli, incorporated a lofty *chapelle ardente*, a pyramid of candles. In his oration, the Florentine scholar Benedetto Varchi is said to have wearied very many of his hearers, and not only the young.

BIBLIOGRAPHY

Abbreviations used for sources in the text

AC.   Ascanio Condivi, *Vita di Michelangelo Buonarroti* (see II, below).

BC.   Benvenuto Cellini, *Autobiography* (see II, below).

C.   *Il carteggio di Michelangelo*, ed. Barocchi and Ristori (see I, below). Letters listed by volume and number, except for vol. 5, published too late to be used in compiling this book, for which references are to Milanesi (see M.).

DM.   R. De Maio, *Michelangelo e la Controriforma* (see IV, below).

EHR.   *The Letters of Michelangelo*, ed. and tr. E.H. Ramsden (see I, below).

G.   G. Gaye, *Carteggio inedito d'artisti . . .* (see III, below).

M.   *Le lettere di Michelangelo Buonarroti . . .* , ed. G. Milanesi (see I, below).

MR.   *Rime di Michelangelo Buonarroti*, ed. E.N. Girardi (see I, below).

P.   L. von Pastor, *The History of the Popes . . .* (see IV, below).

R.   *I ricordi di Michelangelo*, ed. Barocchi and Ristori (see I, below).

S.   L. Steinberg, *Michelangelo's Last Paintings* (see IV, below).

SK.   Ernst Steinmann, *Die sixtinische Kapelle* (see IV, below).

V1.   Giorgio Vasari, *Vite . . .* , 1550 version (see II, below).

V2.   Giorgio Vasari, *Vite . . .* , 1568 version, ed. Milanesi, Florence, 1878–81 (see II, below).

W.   R. and M. Wittkower, *The Divine Michelangelo* (see IV, below).

Since this is a documentary biography of Michelangelo and not an art-historical essay, few books quoted here deal with him exclusively as an artist; on the other hand several books are cited which seem to have little to do with him, but which contain first-hand material of great importance – e.g. Pastor's *History of the Popes* or Gaye's *Carteggio*. No attempt has been made to record the latest critical opinion on his works, but early writings on him have been quoted to give, as far as possible, a picture of the man as he appeared to contemporaries.

The literature on Michelangelo is immense. An enormous bibliography was published in 1927 by Ernst Steinmann and Rudolf Wittkower, listing 2107 items published between 1510 and 1926: in 1974 this bibliography was continued to 1970 by Luitpold Dussler, incorporating several earlier revisions and including more items (2220) in the forty-three years covered than in the four hundred and sixteen years of the earlier volume. It is not difficult to find information on almost every aspect of Michelangelo.

The sources used for this book may be divided into groups. First, there are Michelangelo's own writings – letters, notes and poems, some of which were very probably meant for publication. A project to publish some in his own lifetime, though abandoned, met with no resistance from him. Included in this group are the numerous letters from others to him. Second, there are no less than three full-scale biographies, one by Condivi and two by Vasari. Very few artists before Michelangelo had received any kind of notice from biographers – Jan van Eyck and Pisanello were mentioned briefly by contemporary writers, probably because they were Court artists, but the very short biographical sketches by Paolo Giovio of Leonardo, Michelangelo and Raphael (see p. 6) were novel, although there were precedents in the Anonymous Life of Brunelleschi (late fifteenth century) and in Ghiberti's *Commentarii*. The Lives by Condivi and Vasari are full-scale biographies and also critical interpretations by men who knew him well – indeed, Condivi's book is to some extent an authorized biography. Next comes the group of contemporary documentation, beginning in 1504, with the earliest mention of him, and going on to the elaborate funeral oration given by Benedetto Varchi – this includes the polemical writings on the *Last Judgment* which continued after his death. The final section contains a small selection of recent books and articles which have been used, but it is not a guide to the literature on Michelangelo as an artist.

I. The first great collection of Michelangelo's letters was made by G. Milanesi, *Le lettere di M. B. edite ed inedite, coi ricordi ed i contratti . . .* , Florence, 1875. The *Lettere* formed the basis of the English translation by E.H. Ramsden, *The Letters of Michelangelo*, London and Stanford, 1963. These two volumes contain not only a complete English translation of Michelangelo's letters, in some cases correcting Milanesi's dating and attribution, but also an immense amount of background information in the form of appendices on people, events and things mentioned in the letters. An entirely new edition, including all the known letters to Michelangelo, was begun by G. Poggi and continued by P. Barocchi and R. Ristori, *Il carteggio di Michelangelo*, Florence, 1965–83. About 1400 letters are included in the first four volumes. Uniform with this is Bardeschi Ciulich, L., and Barocchi, P., *I ricordi di Michelangelo*, Florence, 1970. The standard modern Italian edition of Michelangelo's poems is E.N. Girardi, *Rime di Michelangelo Buonarroti*, Bari, 1960. English translations include those by J.A. Symonds (1878 and later eds.), C. Gilbert, New York, 1963, and E. Jennings, 1961.

II. The first version of Vasari's Life was published in his *Vite de piu eccellenti architetti, pittori, et scultori italiani . . .*

Florence, 1550 (quoted in the ed. publ. by Broude, New York, 1980). This was followed by Ascanio Condivi's *Vita di Michelagnolo Buonarroti*, Rome, 1553, and then by Vasari's revised version in *Le vite de più eccellenti Pittori, Scultori...*, Florence, 1568. Both Vasari's Lives appear together in the exemplary edition by P. Barocchi, *Giorgio Vasari, la vita di Michelangelo nelle redazioni del 1550 e del 1568...*, 5 vols., Milan and Naples, 1962. Later eds. of Condivi include that by P. d'Ancona, Milan, 1928. The English versions of Vasari in this book are by the author (for the first ed.) and adapted from G. Bull's translation of Vasari's *Lives* (for the second ed.), published by Penguin, 1965, and as a separate *Life*, 1971; English translations of Condivi are by C. Holroyd, London, 1903, and A.S. and H. Wohl, Oxford, 1976. A recently discovered copy of the Condivi Life with annotations by a contemporary of Michelangelo has been published by U. Procacci in the *Atti del Convegno di Studi Michelangioleschi*, Rome, 1967.

III. Pietro Aretino, *Selected Letters*, ed. and trans. G. Bull, Penguin Classics, London, 1976, for the letter to Corvino (95) on the *Last Judgment*; P. Barocchi (ed.), *Scritti d'arte del Cinquecento*, Milan and Naples, vol. I, 1971, vol II, 1973, contains extracts reprinted from Giovio, Varchi, Lomazzo and other sixteenth-century writers; id., *Trattati d'arte del Cinquecento*, 3 vols., Bari, 1960–62, reprints Varchi, *Due Lezzioni*, Gilio da Fabriano, *Degli errori ... de' pittori ...* and other texts. Cellini, *Autobiography*, written, but not published, 1558–62; English translation by G. Bull, Penguin Classics, London, 1956. Pomponius Gauricus, *De sculptura*, Florence, 1504; French translation ed. A. Chastel and R. Klein, Paris, 1969. G. Gaye, *Carteggio inedito d'artisti dei secoli XIV, XV, XVI...*, Florence, 1839–40 (reprinted Turin, 1961). Gilio da Fabriano, *Due Dialogi ... Nel secondo si ragiona degli errori de' pittori ... sopra il Giuditio di MA...*, Camerino, 1564 (reprinted in Barocchi, *Trattati d' arte del Cinquecento*, II, 1961). P. Giovio, *Michaelis Angeli vita*, written c 1523/7?. Latin text printed in P. Barocchi (ed.), *Scritti d'arte del Cinquecento*, Milan and Naples, 1971 (English trans. in P. Murray, below). G.P. Lomazzo, *Idea del Tempio della Pittura*, Milan, 1590. B. Varchi, *Due lezzioni...*, Florence, 1549, and *Orazione funerale recitata nell'essequie di Michelagniolo Buonarroti*, Florence, 1564. The *Lezzioni* reprinted in P. Barocchi (ed.), *Trattati d' arte...*, 1960. For the funeral oration see P. Murray and R. and M. Wittkower, below.

IV. J. Ackerman, *The Architecture of Michelangelo*, London, 2 vols., 1961, and revised and abridged ed., London, 1970. T.S.R. Boase, *Giorgio Vasari: the Man and the Book*, Princeton, N.J., 1979. R. De Maio, *Michelangelo e la Controriforma*, Rome and Bari, 1978, with extensive quotations from contemporary writers, especially on the controversy over the *Last Judgment*. L.D. Ettlinger, 'The Liturgical Function of Michelangelo's Medici Chapel', in *Mitteilungen des kunsthistorischen Institutes in Florenz*, 1978. F. Hartt, *Michelangelo: The Complete Sculpture*, London, 1969 and *The Drawings of Michelangelo*, New York, 1970 & London, 1971. P. Murray, 'Michelangelo', in *Journal of the Royal Society of Arts*, London, 1976, contains an English translation of Giovio's *Vita* and passages from Varchi's funeral oration and other contemporary eulogies. L. von Pastor, *The History of the Popes*, especially vols. 5–16 (Engl ed., London, 1901–28), contains an immense amount of information on papal patronage of the arts and Michelangelo in particular, as well as the historical and religious background. U. Procacci, *La Casa Buonarroti a Firenze*, Milan, 1967. L. Steinberg, *Michelangelo's Last Paintings*, London, 1975. Ernst Steinmann, *Die sixtinische Kapelle*, Munich, 1901–06. J.A. Symonds, *The Life of Michelangelo Buonarroti*, 3rd ed., London, 1899, the pioneer work in English. C. de Tolnay, *Michelangelo*, Princeton, NJ, 1943–60: I. *The Youth of M.*, 1943 (2nd ed. 1947); II. *The Sistine Ceiling*, 1945 (2nd ed. 1949); III. *The Medici Chapel*, 1948; IV. *The Julius Tomb*, 1954; V. *The Final Period*, 1960. The major monograph of recent times. J. Wilde, *Michelangelo: Six Lectures*, Oxford, 1979. R. and M. Wittkower, *The Divine Michelangelo*, London and new York, 1964, includes facsimile reprint of *Esequie del divino Michelagniolo*, Florence, 1564.

LIST OF ILLUSTRATIONS

Dimensions are given in centimetres and inches, height before width
Photo credits are in italic

2 Giorgio Vasari, *Le Vite*, Florence, 1568. Woodcut portrait of Michelangelo.

7 Giorgio Vasari, *Le Vite*, Florence, 1568. Woodcut portrait of Vasari.

8 Ascanio Condivi, *Vita di Michelagnolo Buonarroti*, Florence, 1553.

12 Martin Schongauer (before 1465–1491). *Temptation of St Antony*, 1470s. Engraving. British Museum, London.

13 Giorgio Vasari, *Le Vite*, Florence, 1568. Woodcut portrait of Domenico Ghirlandaio.

16 Michelangelo. Studies of nude and draped figures, c. 1501–03. Pen, detail of sheet 26.4 × 38.7 (10⅜ × 15¼). Musée Condé, Chantilly (29 recto). *Giraudon.*

17 Michelangelo. *Angel with Candlestick*, 1495. Marble, h. with base 56.5 (22¼). Shrine of St Dominic, S. Domenico Maggiore, Bologna. *Alinari.*

19 Giovanantonio Dosio (fl. 1560–69). *View of the Vatican Obelisk, S. Andrea and Old St Peter's*, 1560–65. Pen and wash, details of sheet 27.3 × 22.5 (10¾ × 8⅞). Uffizi, Florence (2536/A). *Soprintendenza Beni Artistici e Storici di Firenze.*

20 Line drawing after Michelangelo's signature inscribed on the Pietà, 1497–1500 (see p. 37). St Peter's, Rome.

22 Paolo Giovio, *Elogia virorum litteris illustrium*, Basle, 1577. Woodcut portrait of Soderini.

23 Reconstruction of the Hall of the Great Council, Palazzo della Signoria, Florence before 1512, from Johannes Wilde, *Journal of the Warburg and Courtauld Institutes*, VII, 1944, pl. 18.

25 Interior and exterior of Michelangelo's birthplace, Caprese Michelangelo (Arezzo). *Linda Murray.*

26 Cristoforo Landino, *Formulario di lettere*, Florence, 1492.
Francesco Granacci (1477–1543). *Charles VIII entering Florence in 1494* (detail), after 1527. Oil on panel, 76 × 122 (30 × 48). Palazzo Riccardi, Museo Mediceo, Florence. *Alinari.* Stefano Bonsignori. Map of Florence in 1584 (detail). Engraving.

27 Niccolò Fiorentino (1430–1514). Portrait medal of Marsilio Ficino, before 1500. British Museum, London.
Domenico Ghirlandaio (1449–94). Study for the portrait of Agnolo Poliziano in the fresco *The Annunciation to Zacharias* (Sta Maria Novella, Florence), 1490. Chalk drawing. Corcoran Gallery of Art, Washington.
Michelangelo. *Battle of the Centaurs*, (1491–

234

92). Marble relief, 84.5 × 90.5 (33¼ × 35½). Casa Buonarroti, Florence. *Alinari*.

28–29 Florentine School. Bird's eye view of Florence after the 'Catena' woodcut map of *c.* 1500. Painting, 96 × 146 (37¾ × 57½). Private Collection, London.

28 Buonarroti family house, Via Benticordi, Florence. *Linda Murray*.

29 School of Giorgio Vasari, (1511–74). *Jousting in the Piazza Sta Croce, Florence, c.* 1555–59. Fresco. Sala della Guardaroba, Palazzo della Signoria, Florence. *SCALA/Firenze*.

30 Giotto (1266?–1337). *St John the Baptist raising Drusiana*, detail of the spectators, *c.* 1326–36. Fresco. Peruzzi Chapel, Sta Croce, Florence. *Alinari*.
Leonardo da Vinci (1452–1519). *Virgin and Child with St Anne and St John the Baptist*, *c.* mid 1490s. Cartoon, black chalk heightened with white, 141.5 × 104.6 (55¾ × 41⅛). Reproduced by courtesy of the Trustees, The National Gallery, London.
Masaccio (1401–probably 1428). *The Tribute Money*, detail of St Peter, 1425–26. Fresco. Brancacci Chapel, Sta Maria del Carmine, Florence. *Alinari*.

31 Michelangelo. Drawing of two figures after Giotto, *c.* 1489–90. Pen 32 × 19.7 (12⅝ × 7¾). Louvre, Paris (706 recto). *Giraudon*.
Michelangelo. *Virgin and Child with St Anne*, 1501–02. Pen, 25.7 × 17.8 (10⅛ × 7). Ashmolean Museum, Oxford (P. 291 recto).
Michelangelo. Drawing of St Peter, after Masaccio's *Tribute Money*, *c.* 1489–90. Pen with additions in red chalk. 31 × 18.5 (12¼ × 7¼). Graphische Sammlung, Munich (2191).

32 Domenico Ghirlandaio (1449–94). *Confirmation of the Franciscan Rule*, detail with portraits of Agnolo Poliziano and Giuliano de' Medici, *c.* 1483–86. Fresco. Sassetti Chapel, SS. Trinità, Florence. *SCALA/Firenze*.

33 Domenico Ghirlandaio (1449–94). *Confirmation of the Franciscan Rule*, detail with portrait of Lorenzo de' Medici, *c.* 1483–86. Fresco. Sassetti Chapel, SS. Trinità, Florence. *SCALA/Firenze*.
Domenico Ghirlandaio (1449–94). *Confirmation of the Franciscan Rule*, detail with portraits of Giovanni and Piero de' Medici, *c.* 1483–86. Sassetti Chapel, SS. Trinità, Florence. *SCALA/Firenze*.

34 Giovanni delle Corniole (*c.* 1470–p.1516). Intaglio with portrait of Fra Girolamo Savonarola. Cornelian and gold, 4.15 × 3.27 (1⅝ × 1¼). Museo degli Argenti, Florence. *Soprintendenza Beni Artistici e Storici di Firenze*.
Fra Girolamo Savonarola, *Della semplicità della vita cristiana*, Florence, 1496. Woodcut showing Savonarola in his cell in S. Marco, Florence.
Cloister of the monastery of S. Marco, Florence. *Werner Neumeister*.

35 Fra Girolamo Savonarola, *Compendio di rivelazioni*, Florence, 1495. Woodcut showing the author preaching to a segregated audience in the Duomo, Florence.
Portrait medal of Savonarola with a vision of the destruction of Florence (reverse). Bronze, Collection Tom Eden.
Florentine School, 16th century. *Execution of Savonarola and his Companions in the Piazza della Signoria, 25 May 1498*. Oil on panel,

21.2 × 16.5 (8⅜ × 6½). Reproduced by courtesy of the Trustees, The National Gallery, London.

36 Michelangelo. *Madonna of the Stairs, c.* 1491–92. Marble relief. 55.5 × 40 (21⅞ × 15¾). Casa Buonarroti, Florence. *SCALA/Firenze*.

37 Michelangelo. *Pietà*, 1497–1500. Marble, 174 × 195 (68½ × 76¾). St Peter's, Rome. *SCALA/Firenze*.

38 Michelangelo. *Bacchus, c.* 1497–98. Marble, h. with base 202.5 (79¾). Museo Nazionale (Bargello), Florence. *Alinari*.
Façade of the Palazzo della Cancelleria, Rome. *Georgina Masson*.
Raphael (1483–1520). *The Mass of Bolsena*, detail with the portrait of Cardinal Raffaelle Riario, 1511–2. Fresco. Stanza d'Eliodoro, Vatican, Rome. *Alinari*.

39 Marten van Heemskerck (1498–1574). *Garden of Antiquities of Lorenzo Galli, Rome, c.* 1535. Engraving.
Marten van Heemskerck (1498–1574). *View of the Vatican*. Pen drawing from the artist's *Roman Notebook*, 1532–35. Kupferstichkabinett, Staatliche Museen, West Berlin.

40 Andrea Mantegna (1430/31–1506). *Madonna of the Quarries* (detail). Panel, 29 × 21.5 (11⅜ × 8½). Galleria degli Uffizi, Florence. *SCALA/Firenze*.
Michelangelo. *St Matthew* (detail), 1503–06. Marble (unfinished), h. 271 (106¾). Accademia delle Belle Arti, Florence. *SCALA/Firenze*.
The marble quarries at Carrara. *Italian Tourist Board*.

41 Michelangelo. *St Matthew*, 1503–06 Marble (unfinished), h. 271 (106¾). Accademia delle Belle Arti, Florence. *SCALA/Firenze*.

42 Italian School, early 16th century. *Tomb of Pope Pius III*. Grotte Vaticane, Rome. *Alinari*.
Andrea Bregno (1421–1506). Piccolomini Altar, 1481–85. Siena Cathedral. *Alinari-Brogi*.
Michelangelo. Study for a hand, a leg, a male figure seen from behind, *c.* 1498–1500. Pen, 27.6 × 21.6 (10⅞ × 8½). Archivio Buonarroti, Florence (II–III, 3 verso). *Soprintendenza Beni Artistici e Storici di Firenze*.

43 Michelangelo. Study of the *Madonna and Child, c.* 1504. Black chalk and pen over lead-point, detail of sheet, 31.5 × 27.8 (12½ × 11). British Museum, London (w.5 recto).
Michelangelo. *Madonna and Child (Bruges Madonna)*, 1503–04. Marble, h. with base 128 (50⅜). Church of Notre-Dame, Bruges. *Alinari*.

44 Michelangelo. *Madonna and Child with the Infant St John (Pitti Tondo)*, 1504–05. Marble relief (unfinished), diam. 82 (32¼). Museo Nazionale (Bargello), Florence. *SCALA/Firenze*.
Michelangelo. *Madonna and Child with the Infant St John (Taddei Tondo)*, 1504–05. Marble relief (unfinished), diam. 121.5 (47⅞). Royal Academy of Arts, London.

45 Michelangelo. *Holy Family (Doni Tondo)*, 1503–04. Tempera on circular panel, 91 × 80 (35⅞ × 31½). Uffizi, Florence. *SCALA/Firenze*.
Raphael (1483–1520). Portrait of Angelo Doni, *c.* 1505. Panel, 63 × 45 (24¾ × 17¾). Pitti Palace, Florence. *SCALA/Firenze*.

Raphael (1483–1520). Portrait of Maddalena Doni, *c.* 1506. Panel, 63 × 45 (24¾ × 17¾). Pitti Palace, Florence. *SCALA/Firenze*.

46 Michelangelo. Study for the bronze *David, c.* 1501–02. Pen, detail of sheet, 26.7 × 18.7 (10½ × 7⅜). Louvre, Paris (714 recto). *Giraudon*.
Michelangelo. *David*, 1501–04. Marble, h. 410 (161⅜). Accademia delle Belle Arti. Florence. *Alinari*.
Leonardo da Vinci (1452–1516). Cavalcade (study for the right-hand group of *Battle of Anghiari*), *c.* 1503–04. Black chalk, 16 × 19.7 (6¼ × 7¾). Royal Library, Windsor (12339). Reproduced by gracious permission of Her Majesty The Queen.

47 Michelangelo. Study for the *Battle of Cascina, c.* 1504. Black chalk over stylus preparations, heightened with white, 19.5 × 26.5 (7½ × 10⅜). Albertina, Vienna (s.r. 157 verso)
Aristotile (Bastiano) da Sangallo (1481–1551). Copy of part of Michelangelo's cartoon for the *Battle of Cascina, c.* 1542. Grisaille on panel. Holkham Hall, Norfolk, by kind permission of the Earl of Leicester. *Courtauld Institute of Art, London*.

48 Michelangelo. Study of a seated nude man for the *Bathers* cartoon of the *Battle of Cascina, c.* 1504–05. Pen and brush with two coloured inks, heightened with white, 42.1 × 28.7 (16⅝ × 11¼). British Museum, London (w.6 recto).

52 Piero di Cosimo (*c.* 1462–1521?). Portrait of Giuliano da Sangallo, *c.* 1500–04. Panel, 47.5 × 33.5 (18¾ × 13¼). Rijksmuseum, Amsterdam. *Alinari*.

54 Reconstruction of the portal of S. Petronio, Bologna, with the bronze statue of Julius II by Michelangelo, 1508. Drawing by Linda Murray.

55 Baccio Bandinelli (1493–1560). Design for the projected monument to Pope Clement VII. Pen. Louvre, Paris. *Caisse nationale des Monuments historiques*.

56 Attributed to Donato Bramante (1444–1514). Scaffolding and centering for the main arches of St Peter's, Rome. Pen, detail of a sheet. Uffizi, Florence A. 226 *Soprintendenza Beni Artistici e Storici di Firenze*.

57 Reconstruction of the scaffolding erected for Michelangelo for the painting of the Sistine Chapel ceiling. Drawing by Linda Murray.

58 Michelangelo. Sketches for the *Ignudi* of the Sistine Chapel ceiling, 1508(?). Leadpoint and pen, detail of a sheet 18.7 × 24.5 (7⅜ × 9⅝). British Museum, London (w. 8 verso).

64 Giorgio Vasari, *Le Vite*, Florence, 1568. Woodcut portrait of Raphael.

66 Letter from Michelangelo to his father written in Rome, October 1512. British Library, London (Add. ms. 23140 f. 37, Mil. xv).

68 Michelangelo. Detail of a letter to Luigi del Riccio, with crow, 1544. Pen, detail of a sheet 21.6 × 23.2 (8½ × 9⅛). Archivio Buonarroti, Florence (XIII, f. 33).

69 Leonardo Bufalini. Map of Rome, 1551 (detail). Woodcut.

72 Reconstruction of project for the tomb of Julius II, 1516. From Charles de Tolnay, *Michelangelo*, Florence, 1951.

73 Raphael (1485–1520). *The Mass of Bolsena*, detail with the portrait of Pope Julius II, 1511–12. Fresco. Stanza d'Eliodoro,

Vatican, Rome. *SCALA/Firenze.*

74 Reconstruction of the Sistine Chapel, Vatican, Rome, in the early 1500s, before the addition of Michelangelo's ceiling frescoes and *Last Judgment* and Raphael's tapestries. From Ernst Steinmann, *Die sixtinische Kapelle*, Munich, 1901–06. Interior of Sistine Chapel. *Alinari-Anderson.*

75 Michelangelo. Sketch for the Sistine Chapel ceiling; study of left hand and torso, 1508, 1509, 1510. Pen, black chalk, detail of sheet, 25 × 36.2 (9⅞ × 14¼). City of Detroit Purchase, The Detroit Institute of Arts (27.2 recto). Michelangelo. Sketch for the Sistine Chapel ceiling, 1508–09. Pen over leadpoint, black chalk, detail of sheet 27.5 × 39 (10⅞ × 15⅜). British Museum, London (w. 7 recto). Michelangelo. Self-portrait painting the Sistine ceiling, detail from a manuscript page of the poem 'To Giovanni, the One from Pistoia', *c.* 1512. Pen, 28.3 × 18 (11⅛ × 7⅛). Biblioteca Medicea Laurenziana, Florence (XIII, f. III).

76 Michelangelo. Sistine Chapel ceiling, Vatican, Rome, 1508–12. Fresco, *c.* 40 m × 13 m. (*c.* 131 ft × 43 ft). *SCALA/ Firenze.*

77 Michelangelo. Sistine Chapel ceiling lunette, detail with an Ancestor of Christ, 1511–12. Fresco before cleaning. Vatican, Rome. *SCALA/Firenze.* Michelangelo. Sistine Chapel ceiling lunette, detail with an ancestor of Christ, 1511–12. Fresco, after recent cleaning. *Musei Vaticani.*

78 Michelangelo. Studies for the *Execution of Haman*, Sistine Chapel ceiling fresco, 1511. Red chalk, 40.6 × 21 (16 × 8¼). British Museum, London (w. 13 recto). Michelangelo. Sistine Chapel ceiling, detail with the *Execution of Haman*, 1511. Fresco, Vatican, Rome. *Alinari-Anderson.*

79 Michelangelo. Study of the *Libyan Sibyl*, 1511. Red chalk, 28.5 × 20.5 (11¼ × 8⅛). Metropolitan Museum of Art, New York (24.197.2 recto). Purchase, 1924, Joseph Pulitzer Bequest. Michelangelo. Sistine Chapel, ceiling, detail with the *Libyan Sibyl*, 1511. Fresco. Vatican, Rome. *Alinari-Anderson.*

80 Michelangelo. *Entombment*, begun *c.* 1500. Panel, 161 × 149 (63⅔ × 59). Reproduced by courtesy of the Trustees, The National Gallery, London.

81 Michelangelo. *Resurrection*, 1512 (?). Black chalk. 37.5 × 22.2 (14¾ × 8¾). Royal Library, Windsor (12768). Reproduced by Gracious Permission of Her Majesty The Queen. Michelangelo. *Risen Christ (Christ of the Minerva)*, 1519/20. Marble, h. 205 (80¾). Santa Maria sopra Minerva, Rome. *Istituto Centrale per il Catalogo e la Documentazione, Rome.*

82 Michelangelo. *Madonna and Child (The Medici Madonna)*, 1524–33. Marble, h. with base 253 (99½). New Sacristy, S. Lorenzo, Florence. *Alinari-Anderson.* Arch of Septimius Severus AD 203, detail with reclining River God. The Forum, Rome. *Courtauld Institute of Art, London.* Roman copy after Hellenistic original. *Muse.* Marble, h. with base 135 (53). Ashmolean Museum, Oxford.

83 Michelangelo. Sistine chapel ceiling lunette, detail with an Ancestor of Christ, 1511–12. Fresco. *Alinari.*

84 Michelangelo. *Dying Slave*, 1513–16. Marble, h. 229 (90⅛). Louvre, Paris, *Giraudon.* Michelangelo. *Rebellious Slave*, 1513–16. Marble, h. 215 (84⅝). Louvre, Paris, *Giraudon.* Michelangelo. *Young Slave*, *c.* 1530–34. Marble (unfinished), h. 256 (100¾). Accademia delle Belle Arti, Florence. *Alinari.*

85 Bernardo Buontalenti (1536–1608). Grotto in the Boboli Gardens, Florence, which incorporated the *Bearded Slave* and the *Young Slave* by Michelangelo until 1908. *Alinari.* Michelangelo. *Bearded Slave.* Marble (unfinished), h. with base 255.5 (100⅝). Accademia delle Belle Arti, Florence. *Alinari.* Michelangelo. *Atlantean Slave*, *c.* 1530–34. Marble (unfinished), h. 277 (109). Accademia delle Belle Arti, Florence. *Alinari.* Michelangelo. *Crossed-leg Slave*, *c.* 1530–34. Marble (unfinished), h. 267 (105⅛). Accademia delle Belle Arti, Florence. *Alinari-Brogi.*

86 Jacopo Rochetti (16th c.). Drawing after Michelangelo's 1513 project for the tomb of Julius II. Pen and ink, 52.5 × 39 (20⅝ × 15⅜). Staatliche Museen zu Berlin (East) (k.d.z. 15.306). Michelangelo. Sketches of Slaves for the Julius Tomb, 1513. Pen, detail of a sheet 28.5 × 19.5 (11¼ × 7⅝). Ashmolean Museum, Oxford (P. 297 recto).

87 Michelangelo. Tomb of Julius II. Marble, S. Pietro in Vincoli, Rome. *Alinari.* Federico Zuccaro (*c.* 1540/43–1609). *Michelangelo as Moses.* Pen, 41 × 24 (16⅛ × 9½). Louvre, Paris (4588). Michelangelo. Study for the effigy of Pope Julius II, *c.* 1516–17. Pen, 21.3 × 14.3 (8⅜ × 5⅝). Casa Buonarroti, Florence (43 A verso). *Soprintendenza Beni Artistici e Storici di Firenze.*

97 Michelangelo. Sketch for the lower storey of the Tomb of Julius II, 1518, for Lionardo Sellaio. Pen, detail of a sheet 26 × 22.9 (10¼ × 9). British Museum, London (w. 23 recto).

103 Italian School, 19th century. Michelangelo's *Risen Christ* in the niche designed by Federigo Frizzi in Sta Maria sopra Minerva, Rome, *c.* 1830. Pen and wash, detail of sheet. Casa Buonarroti, Florence. *Guido Sansoni.*

106 Section of the Old Sacristy, S. Lorenzo, Florence begun in 1419. From W. and E. Paatz, *Die Kirchen von Florenz*, Frankfurt, 1940–53.

107 Section of the New Sacristy, S. Lorenzo, Florence, begun in 1520. From C. von Stegmann and H. von Geymüller, *Die Architektur der Renaissance in Toskana*, Munich, 1885–1909.

109 Sebastiano del Piombo (Sebastiano Luciani, *c.* 1485–1547). Portrait of Pope Clement VII, 1526. Oil on canvas, 145 × 100 (57⅛ × 39⅜). Galleria Nazionale di Capodimonte, Naples. *Alinari.*

112 Michelangelo. Studies for the ceiling of the Laurentian Library, Florence, 1526. Red and black chalks, 37.5 × 21 (14¾ × 8¼). Casa Buonarroti, Florence (126 A). *Soprintendenza Beni Artistici e Storici di Firenze.*

115 Michelangelo. Notation on the back of a letter to Bernardo Niccolini written 18 March 1518, with sketches for menus. Pen, detail of sheet, 21.3 × 14.6 (8⅜ × 5¾).

Archivio Buonarroti, Florence (X.f. 578 verso). *Soprintendenza Beni Artistici e Storici di Firenze.*

116 Luigi Rossini, *I monumenti più interessanti di Roma*, Rome, 1818. Vestibule and staircase of Michelangelo's house, Rome. Etching.

120 Sigismondo Fanti, *Triomfo di Fortuna*, Venice, 1527. Woodcut with Michelangelo carving a statue.

122 After Marten van Heemskerck (1498–1574). Pope Clement VII in the Castel Sant'Angelo during the Sack of Rome, 1527. Engraving, 1555. Pecci Blunt Collection, Rome. *Josephine Powell.*

126 Michelangelo. Lower half of the statue of Giuliano de'Medici, Duke of Nemours, in the New Sacristy 1529. Charcoal, 115 × 96 (45¼ × 37¾). Mural drawing in the crypt of the New Sacristy, Lorenzo, Florence. *Soprintendenza Beni Artistici e Storici di Firenze.*

127 Giorgio Vasari, *Le vite*, Florence, 1568. Woodcut portrait of Sebastiano del Piombo.

132 Michelangelo. Portrait of Andrea Quaratesi, *c.* 1532. Black chalk, 41.1 × 29.2 (16⅛ × 11½). British Museum, London (w. 59).

135 Michelangelo. Sketches of the 1555 project for the staircase of the Laurentian Library, Florence, in the margin of a letter to Vasari of 28 September 1555. Biblioteca Apostolica Vaticana (Cod. Vat. 3211 f. 87 verso).

137 Aerial view of the buildings of S. Lorenzo, Florence, taken from the Campanile. *Linda Murray.*

138 Michelangelo. Sketch for the façade of S. Lorenzo, Florence, 1517. Red and black chalks, 14 × 18 (5½ × 7⅛). Casa Buonarroti, Florence (47 A). *Alinari-Brogi.* Wooden model for the façade of S. Lorenzo, *c.* 1517, probably executed by Pietro Urbano to Michelangelo's final design. Casa Buonarroti, Florence. *Alinari.*

139 Attributed to Giulio Romano (1492/99–1546). Portrait of Pope Leo X, *c.* 1515. Black chalk, 48 × 29.3 (18⅞ × 11½). Reproduced by permission of the Trustees of the Chatsworth Settlement. *Courtauld Institute of Art, London.* S. Lorenzo, Florence, before the demolition of the buildings around the New Sacristy in 1939–42. *Alinari.*

140 Michelangelo. *Dusk.* Marble, l. 194.9 × d. 80 (l. 76¾ × d. 31½). Tomb of Lorenzo de' Medici, Duke of Urbino (d. 1519), *c.* 1524. New Sacristy, S. Lorenzo, Florence. *SCALA/Firenze.*

140–41 Michelangelo. *Night.* Marble, l. 193 × d. 62.9 (l. 76 × d. 24¾). *Day.* Marble, (unfinished) l. 184.8 × d. 86 (l. 72¾ × d. 33⅞). Tomb of Giuliano de' Medici, Duke of Nemours (d. 1516), *c.* 1531–32. New Sacristy, S. Lorenzo, Florence. *SCALA/Firenze.*

141 Michelangelo. *Dawn.* Marble, l. 205.7 × d. 67.7 (l. 81 × d. 26⅝). Tomb of Lorenzo de' Medici, Duke of Urbino (d. 1519), *c.* 1524. New Sacristy, S. Lorenzo, Florence.

142 Roman school. Portrait medal of Giuliano II de' Medici, Duke of Nemours, 1513–15. National Gallery of Art, Washington D.C., Samuel H. Kress Collection. Michelangelo. Head of Giuliano de' Medici, Duke of Nemours (d. 1516), *c.* 1531–32, from his tomb in the New Sacristy, S. Lorenzo, Florence, Marble, h. 173 (68). *Alinari.*

London (w. 35 recto).

Michelangelo. Modello for *Hercules and Cacus* (*Samson and the Philistine*), c. 1525. Clay, h. 41 (16⅛). Casa Buonarroti, Florence. *Soprintendenza Beni Artistici e Storici di Firenze*.

Michelangelo. Drawing for the stonecutters of blocks of marble with measurements. Pen, detail of sheet 31.4 × 21.8 (12⅜ × 8⅝). Casa Buonarroti, Florence (A B. 1. 82 f. 223). *Soprintendenza Beni Artistici e Storici di Firenze*.

Michelangelo. Model for a *River God* for the new Sacristy, S. Lorenzo, c. 1524. Clay, over tow, wood and wool, l. 180 (70⅞). Casa Buonarroti, Florence. *Soprintendenza Beni Artistici e Storici di Firenze*.

195 Michelangelo. *Victory*, c. 1530/33. Marble, h. 261 (102¾). Palazzo della Signoria, Florence. *Alinari*.

Michelangelo. *Brutus*, c. 1540. Marble, h. without base 74 (29⅛). Museo Nazionale (Bargello), Florence. *Alinari*.

196 Michelangelo. *The Flagellation*, c. 1516. Red chalk, 23.5 × 23.6 (9¼ × 9¼). British Museum, London (w. 15).

Sebastiano del Piombo (c. 1485–1547). *The Flagellation*, 1517–24. Oil mural. S. Pietro in Montorio, Rome. *Alinari-Anderson*.

Michelangelo. Studies possibly for Eve in the *Expulsion* fresco, Sistine Chapel ceiling, 1510, with additions by Sebastiano del Piombo. Red chalk, touches of pen, 27 × 19.1 (10⅝ × 7½). Albertina, Vienna (S R. 155 verso).

Sebastiano del Piombo (c. 1485–1547). *Pietà*, before 1516. Oil on panel, 270 × 225 (106¼ × 88⅝). Museo Civico, Viterbo. *Alinari*.

197 Michelangelo. *The Risen Lazarus Supported by Two Figures*, c. 1516. Red chalk, 25.1 × 14.5 (9⅞ × 5¾). British Museum, London (w. 17).

Sebastiano del Piombo (c. 1485–1547). *Raising of Lazarus*, 1517–19. Wood, transferred to canvas and remounted on board, 381 × 289.6 (150 × 114). Reproduced by courtesy of the Trustees, the National Gallery, London.

Michelangelo. Sketch for *Venus and Cupid*. Panel, 147.3 × 198.1 (58 × 78). Hampton Court Palace. Reproduced by gracious permission of Her Majesty The Queen.

198 Italian School. Drawing of the Capitoline Hill, Rome, c. 1554–60. Louvre, Paris (11028). *Musées Nationaux, Paris*.

Etienne Dupérac (1525–1604). Engraving of Michelangelo's design for the Capitoline Hill, Rome, 1568.

Piazza del Campidoglio with the equestrian statue of Marcus Aurelius, Rome. *Georgina Masson*.

199 Antonio da Sangallo (1483–1546) and Michelangelo. Palazzo Farnese, entrance façade, Rome. *Alinari*.

Antonio Lafreri. Project for the rear wing of the Palazzo Farnese, Rome, by Michelangelo. Engraving, 1560.

Michelangelo. Design for a window of the Palazzo Farnese courtyard, Rome, 1547–49. Black chalk and wash, 42 × 27.8 (16½ × 11). Ashmolean Museum, Oxford (P. 33).

Michelangelo. Window of the second storey of the courtyard of the Palazzo Farnese, Rome. *Alinari-Anderson*.

Michelangelo. *Grotesque Mask*, 1546(?). Red and black chalks 24.8 × 12.1 (9¾ × 4¾).

Royal Library, Windsor (12762 recto). Reproduced by gracious permission of Her Majesty the Queen.

200 Jacopino del Conte (1515–98). Portrait of Michelangelo (detail). Oil on panel, 88.3 × 64.1 (34¾ × 25¼). The Metropolitan Museum of Art, Gift of Clarence Dillon 1977.

203 Giorgio Vasari, *Le Vite*, Florence, 1568. Woodcut portrait of Antonio da Sangallo. Plans for St Peter's, Rome, from James A. Ackerman, *The Architecture of Michelangelo*, London, 1961.

205 Antonio Lafreri (1512–77), *Speculum romanae magnificentiae*, Rome, 1575. Engraving of St Peter's.

206 Attributed to Bartolomeo Ammanati (1511–92). The crossing of St Peter's, Rome, looking west, c. 1559–62. Pen, 43 × 29 (16⅞ × 11⅜). Kunsthalle, Hamburg (21311).

207 Federico Zuccaro (c. 1540–1609). Michelangelo watching Taddeo Zuccaro painting the façade of the Palazzo Mattei, Rome, c. 1560. Pen and wash, detail of a sheet. Albertina, Vienna (575).

208 Giovanantonio Dosio (fl. 1561–69). View of the Campidoglio. Pen, detail of sheet 22.3 × 23 (8¾ × 9). Uffizi, Florence (2560/A). *Soprintendenza Beni Artistici e Storici di Firenze*.

208 Dutch School, 16th c. Three views of the Farnese Palace, Rome, c. 1560. Pen, 21.8 × 33.2 (8½ × 13⅛). Herzog-Anton-Ulrich-Museum, Braunschweig (KK. 183).

209 Giovanantonio Dosio (fl. 1561–69). View of the Baths of Diocletian, later to become Sta Maria degli Angeli, c. 1565. Pen, 17 × 23 (6¾ × 9). Uffizi, Florence (2576/A).

Francisco Bianchini, *De Kalendario*, Rome, 1703. Engraving of Sta Maria degli Angeli, view of the chancel and southeast vestibule.

210 Antonio Lafreri (1512–77), *Speculum romanae magnificentiae*, Rome, 1575. Detail of an engraved map of Rome.

211 Michelangelo. Plan for S. Giovanni dei Fiorentini, Rome, 1559 (second design). Pen and wash, black and red chalks, 42.2 × 29.2 (16⅝ × 11½). Casa Buonarroti, Florence (120 A recto).

213 Title page of the *Esequie del Divino Michelagnolo*, Florence, 1564.

214 Mirabello Cavalori (c. 1520–72). Michelangelo with Duke Cosimo I, 1564. Pen, 21.8 × 32.8 (8⅝ × 12⅞). Museum of Fine Arts, Budapest (1797 recto).

217 Michelangelo. *Pietà* (detail), c. 1547–55. Marble, h. 226 (89) Duomo, Florence. *SCALA/Firenze*.

218 Caradosso (c. 1445–1526/7). Foundation medal for St Peter's Rome (reverse), 1506. Bronze. British Museum, London.

218–19 Giorgio Vasari (1511–74). *Paul III directing the Building Works at St Peter's* (detail), 1546. Fresco from the cycle depicting the history of the life of Pope Paul III, Salone dei Cento Giorni, Palazzo della Cancelleria, Rome. *Alinari*.

218 Antonio da Sangallo the Younger (1483–1546). Wooden model showing the projected completion of St Peter's, Rome, 1539–46. Museo di S. Pietro, Rome. *Alinari-Anderson*.

219 Etienne Dupérac (1525–1604). Side elevation of Michelangelo's project for St Peter's Rome. Engraving, 1568.

220 The dome and exterior of apse of St Peter's,

Rome. *SCALA/Firenze*.

221 Michelangelo and Giacomo della Porta (c. 1537–1602). Wooden model for the dome of St Peter's, begun 1558. Museo di S. Pietro, Rome. *Alinari*.

Michelangelo. Study for the drum and dome of St Peter's, Rome, 1546. Black chalk, pen. 24.3 × 26.6 (9⅝ × 10½). Musée Wicar, Lille (93–94 verso).

222 Michelangelo. Interior of the Sforza Chapel, Sta Maria Maggiore, Rome. *Alinari*.

Michelangelo. Plan of the Sforza Chapel, Sta Maria Maggiore, Rome, c. 1560. Pen and wash. Bibliothèque Nationale, Paris.

Jacques Le Mercier (c. 1585–1654). Final model of S. Giovanni dei Fiorentini, Rome, as designed by Michelangelo. Engraving, 1607.

223 Etienne Dupérac (1525–1604). Porta Pia, Rome, as designed by Michelangelo. Engraving, 1568.

Roman School. Portrait medal of Pope Pius V with the Porta Pia, Rome (reverse). Bronze. Photo by courtesy of Sotheby Parke Bernet, London (Sale 27 May 1974, Lot 240).

Roman School. Portrait medal of Pope Pius V. Bronze. Photo by courtesy of Sotheby Parke Bernet, London (Sale 27 May 1974, Lot 240).

Upper blind windows of the Porta Pia, Rome. *Linda Murray*.

Michelangelo. Study for the window frames of the Porta Pia, Rome, 1561. Black chalk, pen, wash and white pigment, 43.5 × 28.3 (17⅛ × 11⅛). Casa Buonarroti, Florence (106 A recto). *Soprintendenza Beni Artistici e Storici di Firenze*.

Michelangelo. Study for the window frames of the Porta Pia, Rome, 1561. Black chalk, pen and wash, 47 × 27.9 (18½ × 11). Casa Buonarroti, Florence (102 A). *Soprintendenza Beni Artistici e Storici di Firenze*.

Lower blind window of the Porta Pia, Rome. *Linda Murray*.

224 Michelangelo. *Rondanini Pietà*, 1555–64. Marble (unfinished), h. 195 (76¾). Castello Sforzesco, Milan. *Alinari*.

224–25 Michelangelo. Sketches for the *Rondanini Pietà*, c. 1555. Black chalk, 11 × 28 (4⅜ × 11). Ashmolean Museum, Oxford (P. 339).

Michelangelo. *Crucifixion with the Virgin and St John*, c. 1555. Black chalk, retouched in white pigment and grey wash, 41.5 × 28.5 (16⅜ × 11¼). British Museum, London (w. 81).

Michelangelo. *Holy Family with Saints*, c. 1553. Cartoon, black chalk, 233 × 166 (91¾ × 65⅜). British Museum, London (w. 75).

226 Leone Leoni (1509–90). Portrait of Michelangelo made in preparation for the medal of c. 1561. Wax relief, 4.2 × 3.6 (1⅝ × 1⅜). British Museum, London.

Giorgio Vasari (1511–74). Self-portrait, after 1571. Oil on canvas, 137.5 × 81.4 (54⅛ × 32). Galleria degli Uffizi, Florence. *Alinari*.

Giorgio Vasari, *Vite*, Florence, 1550. Title page. National Library of Scotland, Edinburgh.

227 Leone Leoni (1509–90). Portrait medal of Michelangelo, c. 1561. Bronze. National Gallery of Art, Washington D.C. Samuel H. Kress Collection.

Daniele da Volterra (1509–66). Portrait of